Exploring the Entrepreneurial Society

Exploring the Entrepreneurial Society

Institutions, Behaviors and Outcomes

Edited by

Jean Bonnet

University of Caen Normandy, France

Marcus Dejardin

University of Namur and Université catholique de Louvain, Belgium

Domingo García-Pérez-de-Lema

Universidad Politécnica de Cartagena, Spain

 Edward Elgar
PUBLISHING

Cheltenham, UK • Northampton, MA, USA

Published by
Edward Elgar Publishing Limited
The Lypiatts
15 Lansdown Road
Cheltenham
Glos GL50 2JA
UK

Edward Elgar Publishing, Inc.
William Pratt House
9 Dewey Court
Northampton
Massachusetts 01060
USA

A catalogue record for this book
is available from the British Library

Library of Congress Control Number: 2017931752

This book is available electronically in the **Elgar**online
Business subject collection
DOI 10.4337/9781783472666

ISBN 978 1 78347 265 9 (cased)
ISBN 978 1 78347 266 6 (eBook)

Typeset by Servis Filmsetting Ltd, Stockport, Cheshire
Printed and bound in Great Britain by TJ International Ltd, Padstow

Contents

Contributors

Elisa Akola, School of Economics, University of Turku, Finland

Serge Allegrezza, STATEC, Luxembourg

Leila Ben Aoun-Peltier, STATEC, Luxembourg

Antonio Aragón Sánchez, University of Murcia, Spain

Joern H. Block, Chair in Management, Universität Trier, Germany

Dieter Bögenhold, University of Klagenfurt, Austria

Jean Bonnet, CREM, University of Caen Normandy, France

Denis Carré, EconomiX, CNRS-University of Paris Ouest, France

Gerrit de Wit, Panteia-EIM Business and Policy Research, the Netherlands

Marcus Dejardin, CERPE, University of Namur and Université catholique de Louvain, Belgium

Anne Dubrocard, STATEC, Luxembourg

Nuria Esteban-Lloret, University of Murcia, Spain

François Facchini, University of Paris-Sud, France

Uwe Fachinger, University of Vechta, Germany

Anna Frankus, FFC Consulting, Germany

Domingo García-Pérez-de-Lema, Universidad Politécnica de Cartagena, Spain

Paolo E. Giordani, LUISS "Guido Carli" University, Italy

Gonzalo Maldonado Guzman, Autonomous University of Aguascalientes, Mexico

Jarna Heinonen, School of Economics, University of Turku, Finland

Ginés Hernández-Cánovas, Universidad Politécnica de Cartagena, Spain

Amélie Jacquemin, Louvain School of Management, Université catholique de Louvain, Belgium

Frank Janssen, Louvain School of Management, Université catholique de Louvain, Belgium

Solène Larue, GOPA Luxembourg s.à r.l., Luxembourg

Nicolas Le Pape, CREM, University of Caen Normandy, France

Nadine Levratto, EconomiX, CNRS-University of Paris Ouest and Kedge Business School, France

Xiaoni Li, Entrepreneurship and Business Creation Chair, Universitat Rovira i Virgili, Spain

Maria del Carmen Martinez Serna, Autonomous University of Aguascalientes, Mexico

Hiroyuki Okamuro, Graduate School of Economics, Hitotsubashi University, Japan

Eleni Papaoikonomou, Entrepreneurship and Business Creation Chair, Universitat Rovira i Virgili, Spain

Mª Camino Ramón-Llorens, Universidad Politécnica de Cartagena, Spain

Anne Risselada, Urban and Regional Research Centre Utrecht, Utrecht University, the Netherlands

Ugo Rizzo, University of Ferrara, Italy

Alicia Rubio Bañon, University of Murcia, Spain

Veronique Schutjens, Urban and Regional Research Centre Utrecht, Utrecht University, the Netherlands

Pere Segarra, Entrepreneurship and Business Creation Chair, Universitat Rovira i Virgili, Spain

Subandono, Centre d'Economie de la Sorbonne, Université de Paris 1, France

Mercedes Teruel, Universitat Rovira i Virgili, Spain

Luc Tessier, ERUDITE, University of Paris Est, France

André van Stel, Trinity College Dublin, Ireland and Kozminski University, Warsaw, Poland

Ingrid Verheul, Rotterdam School of Management, Erasmus University Rotterdam, the Netherlands

Ngo Vi Dung, Hanoi School of Business and Management (HSB), Vietnam National University (VNU), Vietnam

Sascha G. Walter, Management School, Lancaster University, United Kingdom

A journey into the entrepreneurial society

Jean Bonnet, Marcus Dejardin and Domingo García-Pérez-de-Lema

In most countries, entrepreneurship is nowadays celebrated for its contribution to economic development (Acs and Amoros, 2008). Entrepreneurship draws global attention: attention of the policy maker, the business milieu, the citizen, the union, the bureaucrat—and not to mention the research community. Its contribution might be emphasized by citing several statements from various origins, and several studies. Nevertheless, one may notice that some differences regarding the entrepreneurial process and its outcome still may be at work. Regarding the potentiality for growth (Wong et al., 2005; van Stel et al., 2005), it is for example noteworthy that, if the involvement of young people (18–24 years old) in entrepreneurial activity is important for growth in developed countries, it is the older entrepreneurs (45–64) who would bring the stronger contribution to growth in developing countries (Verheul and van Stel, 2010). Older entrepreneurs may compensate for their low level of education by life experience and probably by successful experience in business. Regarding regional development, ongoing research suggests that the effects of entrepreneurship (measured by new business formation) differ according to entrepreneurial motives, the type of startups and the regional environment (Aubry et al., 2015; Dejardin and Fritsch, 2011).

Entrepreneurship appears essential for structural change (Naudé, 2010). It contributes to the transformation of agricultural economies into knowledge and services economies. The weight of the primary sector and the functioning of the informal economy explain the high rates of entrepreneurial activity in developing countries. With economic development and the increase in interesting wage opportunities, one may observe a diminution of entrepreneurial activity. That being the case, the revival of entrepreneurship is also regularly mentioned in some of the most economically developed countries, characterized by *innovation-driven* development (GEM, 2009, p. 9). The observations, collected by the Global

Entrepreneurship Monitor consortium, submitted for interpretation, have been translated into the well-known U-shape curve linking countries' GDP per capita and rate of entrepreneurial activity (Carree et al., 2007). But is it a U or a mirrored J? The latter appears more correct. In any case:

> As an economy matures and its wealth increases, the emphasis of industrial activity shifts towards an expanding services sector . . . The industrial sector evolves and experiences improvements in variety and sophistication. Such a development would be typically associated with increasing research and development and knowledge intensity, as knowledge-generating institutions in the economy gain momentum. This change opens the way for development of entrepreneurial activity with high aspirations. (Szerb et al., 2012, p. 22; GEM, 2009)

When this happens, innovation accounts for 30 per cent of economic activity, and very often small and innovative entrepreneurial firms operate as 'agents of creative destruction' (Szerb et al., 2012).

Considering the situation in developed countries, Wennekers et al. (2010) point to the reemergence of what they call independent entrepreneurship. The content of this reemergence would correspond at least to two underlying phenomena: development of solo self-employment, which is important for societal and flexibility reasons (Bögenhold and Fachinger, 2008; Chapters 17 and 19, this volume), and the ambitious and/or innovative entrepreneurs (van Stel and Carree, 2004; Audretsch, 2007; Hermans et al., 2015). It is then stimulating—though also highly reductive—to conceptualize the entrepreneurial choice to start a new venture with the well-known *refugee/entrepreneurial* or *Schumpeter* effects (Thurik et al., 2008; Abdesselam et al., 2014). According to the refugee effect, unemployment may induce new firms startups. Increasing unemployment reduces the opportunity cost of entrepreneurship, and consequently stimulates entrepreneurship. The refugee effect is sometimes called the *shopkeeper* effect. Contrastingly, the Schumpeter effect refers to the argument that new startups, launched for opportunity motives, may contribute to the reduction of unemployment (Thurik et al., 2008; Koellinger and Thurik, 2012). So, different motives linked to the startup of firms are bringing different potentiality in terms of growth and employment creation.

Furthermore, taking into account that institutions may differ from one jurisdiction to another and that they shape economies in major ways leads to distinguishing several types of development characterized by more or less, and different, entrepreneurial economies. Acs et al. (2014) highlight that venture creation and outcomes are themselves regulated by country-specific institutional characteristics. Relevant variables that take into account differences in entrepreneurial motives must be extended. It appears particularly essential to consider formal and informal institutions affecting the functioning of the labor market that may be specific to each country. Legislation concerning labor market relations, fiscal rules, social security systems, bankruptcy laws as well as the development and the functioning of the financial system—not to mention the administrative burden—all may have an effect upon the new firms' formation and the presence of entrepreneurial firms (Bonnet et al., 2011). Ultimately, this way of addressing the entrepreneurial phenomenon leads to a systemic approach of entrepreneurship.

In brief, entrepreneurship is the engine of economic development; but economic development, in return, impacts entrepreneurship as well. The economic development of a country—of which an assessment would include the quality of institutions overall—is an important factor for entrepreneurial behavior and activity to flourish. It is important because entrepreneurial projects are bound by the wealth of the population and potential demand; by public infrastructures that are essential for the functioning of the private sector (Estache and Iimi, 2011); by the quality of overall regulation and law enforcement (Puppim de Oliveira, 2008); and generally by endowments of individuals in general education and managerial competencies. Even if opportunities exist in developing countries (there is so much to do in a catch-up process), there are probably not so many high-quality projects because the conditions are not conducive.

To develop a lively entrepreneurial society requires attention to several interacting factors. Accordingly, the policy for an entrepreneurial society is not the kind that is focused on one singular, isolated aspect of public affairs and that is handled by one dedicated administration. The policy for an entrepreneurial society is a transversal policy provided by ministries and administrations as a whole (Audretsch, 2008).

The book that we introduce here explores various aspects of primary importance regarding the entrepreneurial society. It collects original works from renowned scholars regularly involved in entrepreneurship research, with theoretical and empirical contributions mainly anchored in economics, management and sociology. The main themes examined may be located at the forefront of scholars' research interests. Contributions have been structured in five parts:

1. entrepreneurship and formal and informal institutions
2. entrepreneurial choice, orientation and success
3. entrepreneurial behaviors
4. entrepreneurial finance, growth and economic crises
5. entrepreneurship, social dimensions and outcomes.

The book is a continuation of *The Entrepreneurial Society: How to Fill the Gap between Knowledge and Innovation* (Bonnet et al., 2010) and *The Shift to the Entrepreneurial Society: A Built Economy in Education, Sustainability and Regulation* (Bonnet et al., 2012). In the first chapter of this volume—"Understanding the drivers of an 'entrepreneurial' economy: lessons from Japan and the Netherlands"—Hiroyuki Okamuro, André van Stel and Ingrid Verheul investigate the differences in entrepreneurial activity between the two countries. While the Netherlands may be recognized as a well-developed entrepreneurial economy, Japan appears more in a process of transition from a managed to an entrepreneurial economy. The authors attempt to identify the factors that facilitate or hinder the transformation from a managed to an entrepreneurial economy. The individual contribution of explanatory variables is interpreted according to a benchmark that makes it easy to recommend specific policies for stimulating entrepreneurial activity.

In the second chapter, "Hofstede's cultural dimensions and modes of entry into entrepreneurship", Joern Block and Sascha Walter explore the effect of national culture on the mode of entry—that is, starting versus taking over a business. Adopting an aggregate trait approach, they hypothesize that individualism and masculinity favor starting a business, whereas uncertainty avoidance and power distance (acceptance of hierarchy) favor taking over a business. Unexpectedly, their results suggest that people in countries with a relatively high power distance are less willing to opt for business takeovers than for starting new ventures. An explanation could be sought in the reaction to an "un-entrepreneurial" culture.

The third chapter, by Amélie Jacquemin and Frank Janssen, is entitled "Entrepreneurs using regulation as a source of opportunity: a study combining quantitative and qualitative approaches". The authors investigate to what extent the legal environment might have a positive impact on entrepreneurship. Using a research design combining quantitative and qualitative approaches, their study aims at understanding who the entrepreneurs are who positively use regulation as a source of business opportunity and how they succeed in this. Not all entrepreneurs use regulation as a source of opportunity, and those who do use two different approaches, which the authors call the "Kirznerian" and "Schumpterian" approaches.

Within the fourth chapter—"Determinants of high-growth firms: why do some countries have more high-growth firms than others?"—Mercedes Teruel and Gerrit de Wit present the first empirical analysis of high-growth firms at the country level. They find indicative empirical evidence for three driving forces of high growth: entrepreneurship, institutional settings and opportunities for growth. They investigate three specific channels of influence toward high-growth firms: enrolment in tertiary education; entrepreneurial motives associated with growth-oriented ambitions; and the promotion of entrepreneurship as a desirable career choice. They also consider the possible impact of institutions and whether fast-growing firms are more likely in dynamic economic environments offering greater business opportunities.

In the fifth chapter, "Institutions, entrepreneurship, and regional growth in Indonesia (1994–2010)", François Facchini and Subandono contribute to the modern Austrian theory of economic development by elaborating an original theory of institutional flexibility. An institutional system is flexible when it constructs an order that is neither contingent nor determinist. Private property rights, contracts and money organize human behavior without determining it. By protecting economic freedom, these institutions give people good reason to believe that they can act to change the future to their advantage. Exploiting Indonesian provincial panel data for the period 1994–2010, the authors collect evidence supporting the theoretical framework that they propose.

The sixth chapter—entitled "Sub-national market-supporting institutions and export behaviors", by Ngo Vi Dung and Frank Janssen—examines whether the market-supporting institutions at the sub-national level influence the export behaviors of firms in the context of an emerging economy, namely Vietnam. Analyzing a dataset of 7818 Vietnamese firms, including 719 exporting firms, the authors find that export propensity is mainly and negatively influenced by provincial financial conditions. Provincial attitudes, bureaucracy, legal and informal charges positively drive the firm's export intensity. The predictability of domestic laws and regulations negatively influences a firm's export intensity. In addition, institutions do matter more for smaller, younger and private firms. Nevertheless, the influence of sub-national market-supporting institutions on export mode choice is ambiguous.

The next three chapters make up the second part of the book around the theme *Entrepreneurial Choice, Orientation and Success*. The seventh chapter, by Nadine Levratto, Denis Carré and Luc Tessier—"Are French industrial establishments equally sensitive to the local atmosphere? An analysis resting upon a panel of manufacturing plants over the period 2003–2010"—examines whether local aspects (workforce qualification, importance of the manufacturing industry, factors impacting the business climate, among others) influence employment changes at the establishment level. Exploiting data for a panel of French establishments operating in the manufacturing industry between 2003 and 2010 and various measurements regarding the local context, the authors are able to distinguish whether local factors exert a positive or negative effect on establishments' growth. Their results suggest that more attention should be paid to locally defined policy tools and objectives.

In the eighth chapter, "The labor market and successful entrepreneurship", Jean Bonnet and Nicolas Le Pape examine empirically the link between successful post-entry strategies of new entrepreneurs and their previous occupation in the labor market. They find that being a *pull* entrepreneur (an individual drawn to entrepreneurship by positive motives such as an economic opportunity to be seized) is related to the implementation of successful post-entry strategies containing a higher intensity of entrepreneurial behavior compared to *push* entrepreneurs—individuals who are driven to entrepreneurship mainly because they suffer from a poor position in the labor market.

The contribution by Gonzalo Maldonado Guzman, Maria del Carmen Martinez Serna and Domingo García-Pérez-de-Lema—"The relationship between knowledge management and innovation level in Mexican SMEs: empirical evidence"—constitutes the ninth chapter, and ends the second part of this book. The authors investigate the transformation of current society from an industry-based economy to a knowledge management and innovation-based economy. They show that it changes the design and implementation of business strategies and the nature of the competition among the organizations which are mainly small and medium-size enterprises (SMEs). Using data from a sample of 125 Mexican manufacturing SMEs, the authors find that knowledge management has a positive impact in products, process and management systems innovation.

The third part of the book comprises three chapters examining highly contrasted topics. The tenth chapter, "Entrepreneurial opportunity recognition and exploitation in academic spin-offs" by Ugo Rizzo, considers the differences between businesses created to market research results within the academic environment. The author examines how opportunities are recognized and exploited, and how they can be linked to the process of creation and development of academic spin-off firms. Analyzing empirical material collected through interviews with academic spin-offs of the University of Manchester (UK) leads to the conclusion that commercial and non-commercial academic spin-offs cannot be compounded. Even more heterogeneity can be suspected. This may have important implications and definitely calls for further research.

In the eleventh chapter—"Firm location choice in the New Economy: exploring the role of entrepreneurial work-lifestyles of neighborhood entrepreneurs in the business location decision"—Anne Risselada and Veronique Schutjens investigate to what extent the choice to run a business from home is linked to the entrepreneur's work-lifestyle. This question has been largely neglected in studies on firm location processes, although it appears that a growing number of firms that are active in developing sectors such as the knowledge, personal services and consumer sectors that contribute to feed the new economy are home-based businesses. The authors use information collected from 370 entrepreneurs operating in 41 residential neighborhoods in five Dutch cities. Their results show that work-lifestyle factors matter to whether neighborhood firms are home based: the likelihood of being home based increases with caring for family needs or when the business does not provide the primary household income. It decreases with the growth ambition of the entrepreneur.

The twelfth chapter, "How to explain gender differences in self-employment ratios: towards a socioeconomic approach" by Dieter Bögenhold and Uwe Fachinger, ends the third part. Business ownership and self-employment are increasing dramatically among women, raising the question of motives behind this development. Is it driven by necessity or does it reflect new modes of labor market integration and a strategy for women to achieve a better work–life balance? Combining conceptual thoughts with German Microcensus data over the period 1989–2009, the authors explore the possible influence of personal, household and labor market characteristics in a family context on the probability of being self-employed. The labor market integration of women through self-employment appears highly contextual with the occurrence of multiple factors related to the family life.

The fourth part of the book is devoted to *Entrepreneurial Finance, Growth and Economic Crises*. In the thirteenth chapter, "Entrepreneurship and Schumpeterian growth", Paolo E. Giordani extends Schumpeterian economic growth models by introducing a role for Knightian uncertainty. His modeling is driven by the idea that producing innovation is an intrinsically uncertain economic activity and, accordingly, that agents can be uncertain about the probability of any innovation occurrence. The proposed model echoes the micro-evidence that suggests a relationship between an individual's occupational choice, including being an entrepreneur, and attitude to uncertainty. With respect to economic growth, it supports the idea that the agent's attitude to uncertainty enters an explanation of entrepreneurial innovation and, therefore, of the economic performance of the whole economy.

In the fourteenth chapter, "Venture capital contracts and the institutional theory: differences between public and private Spanish venture capital firms", Mª Camino Ramón-Llorens and Ginés Hernández-Cánovas show, through analysis of a survey dataset of 41 Spanish venture capital firms (VCFs), that most Spanish venture capital contracts are standard. However, when they study the VCFs according to the public or private origin of resources, they find some heterogeneity in the design of the contracts due to government coercion on public entities, with the private sector remaining the stronger in the application of standard terms. Their results contribute to shed light on the design of financial contracts between entrepreneurial firms and their VC investors, to the benefit of the policy maker, the firm, and the venture capitalist.

The contribution by Eleni Papaoikonomou, Xiaoni Li and Pere Segarra, the fifteenth chapter of the book, entitled "Exploring SMEs' strategic response to the financial and economic crisis: empirical evidence from Catalonia", examines the perception among firms of the crisis that started in 2007 and how it might affect their strategic decision making. The authors use a dataset based on a survey conducted in 2011 of managers of Catalan SMEs. Applying a non-hierarchical typological analysis, they identify three clusters of firms characterized by the degree of perceived difficulties, which they then put in relation to different strategic actions. The firms that perceive the crisis more negatively are also those that more often take strategic action. Perceptions appear to play an important role, and this is quite challenging for managers and policy makers. Overall, cost-reduction measures are the most widely used, and this leads to the question of their appropriateness.

The sixteenth chapter, "Does the financial crisis make SMEs reluctant to ask for finance in Luxembourg?" by Serge Allegrezza, Leila Ben Aoun-Peltier, Anne Dubrocard and Solène Larue, analyzes the determinants of finance seeking by Luxembourgish independent SMEs during and after the 2007–2009 financial crisis. The study is conducted for different types of funding (loans, equity and other sources), and regressions estimate how individual characteristics, past behavior and business environment perceptions affect decisions about seeking or not seeking external finance.

Three further chapters form the fifth and final part of the book: *Entrepreneurship, Social Dimensions and Outcomes*. In the seventeenth chapter—"Self-employment and independent professionals: labor market transitions and myths of entrepreneurship"—Dieter Bögenhold, Jarna Heinonen and Elisa Akola are interested in the overlapping areas of entrepreneurship, self-employment and professions. Their study presents empirical findings from a unique Finnish survey including freelance journalists, translators, interpreters and artists at the blurred boundaries between waged work and entrepreneurship. The manifestations of entrepreneurship vary, reflecting the work and the labor market situation within the professions. Many different socioeconomic situations can be found "in between", which are driven by different social logics. In such circumstances, the term "entrepreneurship" can be misused when it is used indiscriminately and, therefore, can easily generate myths and stereotypes, which are challenged by the study.

The eighteenth chapter, "How distinct is social entrepreneurship from commercial entrepreneurship?"—by Alicia Rubio Bañon, Nuria Esteban-Lloret and Antonio Aragón Sánchez—reports the results of an original comparative analysis. While it has been documented that social companies share the pursuit of revenue generation with commercial firms, but look as well to achieve social goals such as positive social and environmental impact, little is yet known about the specificities (if any) regarding the characteristics and motivations of social entrepreneurs. Using data from the 2009 Spanish GEM survey, the authors find key differences that significantly distinguish commercial entrepreneurs from social entrepreneurs. Three individual factors particularly emerge: opportunity perception, entrepreneurial self-efficacy perception and risk perception.

The contribution by Uwe Fachinger and Anna Frankus—"Self-employed people and pension: is old age poverty the inevitable dark side of an entrepreneurial society?"—is the nineteenth and final chapter of this book. The development of self-employment may be interpreted as being the result of structural reform policy aimed at labor market flexibility and economic prosperity. Contrastingly, it may also correspond to the outcome of a poor economic situation, with people becoming self-employed out of the need to earn a living. What then will be their situation in retirement as they depend highly on private provisions? With a focus on solo self-employment, the authors use data from the German Microcensus for 1989–2009 to study the ability and willingness of people to save money for old-age provision. Their results lead us to emphasize what would be a growing poverty risk, calling for overall attention and policy response.

We hope that the reader will appreciate the journey into the entrepreneurial society as much as we enjoy it. Much remains to be discovered for those interested.

REFERENCES

Abdesselam, R., Bonnet, J., Renou-Maissant, P. (2014). "Typology of the French regional development: revealing the refugee versus Schumpeter effects in new-firm start-ups", *Applied Economics*, **46** (28), 3437–3451.

Acs, Z.J., Amoros, J.E. (2008). "Introduction: the startup process", *Estudios de Economía*, **35** (2), 121–132.

Acs, Z.J., Autio, E., Szerb, L. (2014). "National systems of entrepreneurship: measurement issues and policy implications", *Research Policy*, **43** (3), 476–494.

Aubry, M., Bonnet, J., Renou-Maissant, P. (2015). "Entrepreneurship and the business cycle: the 'Schumpeter' effect versus the 'refugee' effect. A French appraisal based on regional data", *Annals of Regional Science*, **54** (1), 23–55.

Audretsch, D.B. (2007). "Entrepreneurship capital and economic growth", *Oxford Review of Economic Policy*, **23** (1), 63–78.

Audretsch, D.B. (2008). "Creating the entrepreneurial society", Conferencia Magistral, Fundación Rafael del Pino, April 23.

Bögenhold, D., Fachinger, U. (2008). "Do service sector trends stimulate entrepreneurship? A socio-economic labour market perspective", *International Journal of Services, Economics and Management*, **1** (2), 117–134.

Bonnet, J., Brau, T., Cussy, P. (2011). "Entrepreneurial decision-making", in Léo-Paul Dana, ed., *World Encyclopedia of Entrepreneurship*, Cheltenham, UK and Northampton, MA, USA: Edward Elgar Publishing, 65–79.

Bonnet, J., Dejardin, M., Madrid-Guijarro, A., eds (2012). *The Shift to the Entrepreneurial Society: A Built Economy in Education, Sustainability and Regulation*, Cheltenham, UK and Northampton, MA, USA: Edward Elgar Publishing.

Bonnet, J., García-Pérez-de-Lema, D., Van Auken, H., eds (2010). *The Entrepreneurial Society: How to Fill the Gap between Knowledge and Innovation*, Cheltenham, UK and Northampton, MA, USA: Edward Elgar Publishing.

Carree, M., van Stel, A., Thurik, R., Wennekers, S. (2007). "The relationship between economic development and business ownership revisited", *Entrepreneurship and Regional Development*, **19** (3), 281–291.

Dejardin, M., Fritsch, M. (2011). "Entrepreneurial dynamics and regional growth", *Small Business Economics*, **36** (4), 377–382.

Estache, A., Iimi, A. (2011). *The Economics of Public Infrastructure Procurement in Developing Countries: Theory and Evidence*, London: Centre for Economic Policy Research.

Global Entrepreneurship Monitor (2009). *Executive Report*, Babson Park, MA: Babson College.

Hermans, J., Vanderstraeten, J., Van Witteloostuijn, A., Dejardin, M., Ramdani, D., Stam, E. (2015). "Ambitious entrepreneurship: a review of growth aspirations, intentions, and expectations", *Advances in Entrepreneurship, Firm Emergence, and Growth*, **17**, 127–160.

Koellinger, P.D., Thurik, A.R. (2012). "Entrepreneurship and the business cycle", *Review of Economics and Statistics*, **94** (4), 1143–1156.

Naudé, W. (2010). "Entrepreneurship, developing countries, and development economics: new approaches and insights", *Small Business Economics*, **34** (1), 1–12.

Puppim de Oliveira, J.A., ed. (2008). *Upgrading Clusters and Small Enterprises in Developing Countries: Environmental, Labour, Innovation and Social Issues*. Aldershot: Ashgate.

Szerb L., Aidis R., Acs, Z.J. (2012). "A comparative analysis of Hungary's entrepreneurial performance in the 2006–2010 time period based on the Global Entrepreneurship Monitor and the Global Index methodologies", Carbocomp Ltd, Pecs, Hungary.

Thurik, R., Carree, M., van Stel, A., Audretsch, D.B. (2008). "Does self-employment reduce unemployment?", *Journal of Business Venturing*, **23** (6), 673–686.

van Stel, A., Carree, M.A. (2004). "Business ownership and sectoral growth; an empirical analysis of 21 OECD countries", *International Small Business Journal*, **22** (4), 389–419.

van Stel, A., Carree, M.A., Thurik, A.R. (2005). "The effect of entrepreneurial activity on national economic growth", *Small Business Economics*, **24** (3), 311–321.

Verheul, I., van Stel, A. (2010). "Entrepreneurial diversity and economic growth", in J. Bonnet, D. García-Pérez-de-Lema, H. Van Auken, eds, *The Entrepreneurial Society: How to Fill the Gap between Knowledge and Innovation*. Cheltenham, UK and Northampton, MA, USA: Edward Elgar Publishing, 17–36.

Wennekers, S., van Stel, A., Carree, M., Thurik R. (2010). "The relationship between entrepreneurship and economic development: is it U-shaped?", *Foundations and Trends in Entrepreneurship*, **6** (3), 167–237.

Wong, P.K., Ho, Y.P., Autio, E. (2005). "Entrepreneurship, innovation and economic growth: evidence from GEM data", *Small Business Economics*, **24** (3), 335–350.

PART I

Entrepreneurship and formal and informal institutions

1. Understanding the drivers of an 'entrepreneurial' economy: lessons from Japan and the Netherlands*

Hiroyuki Okamuro, André van Stel and Ingrid Verheul

1. INTRODUCTION

Many developed economies have now experienced a transition from a more *managed* to a more *entrepreneurial* economy (Thurik et al., 2013). An entrepreneurial-type economy is characterized by a high importance of entrepreneurship in terms of small and, in particular, new ventures for creating innovative activity and boosting macro-economic performance. Anglo-Saxon countries, including the United States, Canada and Australia, were the first to show such a 'regime' switch. Already in the 1970s these countries experienced a considerable increase in the share of entrepreneurs (self-employed) in the labor force. Other developed countries in Western Europe later followed their example. In the Netherlands the rate of entrepreneurship has been increasing relatively fast since the mid-1980s.

At the same time, the Japanese economy appears to have switched from an entrepreneurial economy to a more managed economy. The business ownership rate has been decreasing since the 1980s (see Figure 1.1). Hence, the Japanese economy shows a trend contrary to other developed economies. During 'the lost decades' starting with the collapse of the *bubble economy* at the beginning of the 1990s, various public policy measures have been introduced to maintain and reactivate the entrepreneurial economy, so far without remarkable effects (according to official statistics). However, there are recent signals from other sources that these efforts have paid off: the number of new entrepreneurs in Japan as measured by the Global Entrepreneurship Monitor (GEM's) Total Early-Stage Entrepreneurial Activity (TEA) rate is now at a structurally higher level as compared to the beginning of the twenty-first century (see Figure 1.2).

In the present chapter we aim to create more insight into the underlying factors of both the current level and the historical development of entrepreneurial activity in two developed but otherwise dissimilar countries. Whereas the Netherlands is seen as an example of a more entrepreneurial economy, Japan can be regarded as a more managed economy that could be on the verge of a regime switch. Indeed, there are some interesting contradictions in terms of entrepreneurial activity in the two countries that demand further investigation, such as the contradictory developments of the business ownership rate. Besides examining the factors that explain the differences in entrepreneurial activity between the two countries, we also attempt to derive some specific policy recommendations for the two countries under study.

We base our analysis on a comprehensive study by Hartog et al. (2010), who investigate a wide range of factors determining entrepreneurship at different stages—namely nascent entrepreneurship, young business (YB) entrepreneurship, established entrepreneurship—for twenty developed countries. Building on their empirical analysis, we apply a decomposition analysis to better understand the country differences in entrepreneurial activity. On the basis of regression outcomes and the underlying data of the study by Hartog et al. we analyze the fitted values for Japan and the Netherlands to find out which factors are most important for explaining the lower entrepreneurial activity rates witnessed in Japan and the higher entrepreneurship rates witnessed in the Netherlands in the period 2002–2006. In our analysis we benchmark the results for Japan and the Netherlands against the results for the group of twenty developed countries used in Hartog et al.

A more general contribution of our analysis lies in the identification of factors that facilitate or hinder the transformation process from a managed to an entrepreneurial economy. This is helpful for decision makers designing and implementing government policies aimed at stimulating entrepreneurial activity. Moreover, since contributions of individual variables are expressed relative to a benchmark (i.e., the average for twenty developed countries), we can easily assess whether specific targets in terms of required changes in determining factors are realistic. For instance, when a factor contributes negatively to entrepreneurship in a country *relative to other countries*, it should be feasible to improve the performance of this factor since other countries apparently are able to do so as well.

The remainder of this chapter is structured as follows. In the next section we will illustrate the level and developments in entrepreneurial activity in Japan and the Netherlands. Subsequently, we discuss five groups of determinants of entrepreneurship as used in this study, based on Verheul et al. (2002). In Section 4 we explain the decomposition method and provide a description of the variables included in the model of Hartog et al. (2010). We present and discuss the results in Section 5, and conclude with Section 6.

2. HISTORICAL DEVELOPMENT AND CURRENT STATE OF ENTREPRENEURSHIP: A COMPARISON OF JAPAN AND THE NETHERLANDS

In this section we give a brief overview of the developments over time for two main entrepreneurship indicators at the aggregate level: the business ownership rate and GEM's TEA rate. Figure 1.1 shows the development in *established* entrepreneurial activity, as measured by the non-agricultural business ownership rate, for the period 1972–2012. Here we see clear differences between Japan and the Netherlands. Whereas in Japan the business ownership rate has been constantly decreasing since the beginning of the 1980s, business ownership in the Netherlands shows a U-shaped development, with the lowest point in the mid-1980s. There are several reasons for the re-emergence of self-employment in the Netherlands (and several other developed economies), including:

the rapidly growing services sector with its smaller scale and lower entry barriers, an increasing differentiation of consumer preferences, declining transactions

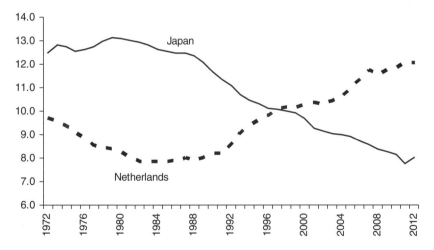

Note: The non-agricultural business ownership rate is defined as the number of owner-managers of unincorporated and incorporated businesses (excluding businesses in agriculture, hunting, forestry and fishing), expressed as a percentage of the total labor force.

Source: COMPENDIA database, version 2011.1.

Figure 1.1 Business ownership rate (non-agriculture) in Japan and the Netherlands, 1972–2012

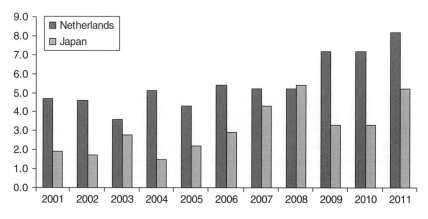

Source: GEM Adult Population Surveys.

Figure 1.2 TEA rates in Japan and the Netherlands, 2001–2011

> costs, and a trend in occupational preferences toward more autonomy and self-realization. Additionally, globalization in concert with the spread of ICT (information and communication technologies) enables solo entrepreneurs and small firms to reap the fruits of scale economies through loosely organized networks. And last but not least new technologies create opportunities for new technology-based business start-ups. (Wennekers et al., 2010, p. 169)

One of the main reasons for the declining self-employment rate in Japan in the 1990s is the decline in real income of self-employed workers relative to employees, especially in the segment of workers older than 35 years (Genda and Kambayashi, 2002).

Figure 1.2 presents the TEA rate, GEM's most well-known measure. It is a measure of *new* entrepreneurial activity, expressing the percentage of people in the adult population who are actively taking steps to start a new business or are owner-managers of YBs (< 3.5 years). At the beginning of the twenty-first century new-firm activity in Japan was relatively low. However, between 2004 and 2008, Japan's TEA rate has been catching up fast, corresponding with a period of high economic growth rates. The crisis seems to have caused a temporary setback of TEA rates, but in 2011 Japan's rate was back at the level of 2008. Hence, new entrepreneurship activity in Japan seems to lie at a structurally higher level compared to the beginning of the century. The Netherlands traditionally has an average level of start-up activity, but since 2009 it has been among the top industrialized countries in terms of early-stage entrepreneurial activity.

To be able to draw conclusions about factors that inhibit or promote entrepreneurial activity in Japan and the Netherlands, it is essential to develop a better understanding of the current state and the historical development of entrepreneurship in these two countries. Besides the entrepreneurship indicators above, we have also compared Japan and the Netherlands (with the United States as a benchmark country) on a wide range of indicators representing entrepreneurial activity at different stages (future and nascent entrepreneurial and intrapreneurial activity, entry of firms, YB activity, established business owners, business growth, and exit activity); specific types of entrepreneurship (female versus male, opportunity versus necessity, ambitious versus non-ambitious entrepreneurship); and entrepreneurial climate indicators (opportunity perception, fear of failure, entrepreneurial self-efficacy, role models and informal investor rates). For these comparisons we refer to Okamuro et al. (2011). In summary, the Netherlands scores higher than Japan on most of the indicators considered, suggesting that the Dutch economy is closer to 'entrepreneurial economy' on the 'managed economy/entrepreneurial economy' spectrum. In the empirical analysis of this chapter we will investigate the causes of these differences.

3.　DETERMINANTS OF ENTREPRENEURSHIP

A broad range of factors have been proposed to explain levels of entrepreneurship, including economic and social factors. Moreover, it is generally accepted that policy measures can influence the level of entrepreneurship in a country or region (Storey, 1994, 1999). Several models have been developed to create insight into the origin of entrepreneurship and its consequences. Examples of such models include the GEM conceptual model by Reynolds et al. (1999, 2000); the framework of entrepreneurship policy measures and policy typology as proposed by Stevenson and Lundström (2007); the country institutional profiles by Busenitz et al. (2000); and the eclectic framework as proposed by Verheul et al. (2002). Despite substantial differences, these models have in common that they integrate factors from different disciplines to create a more complete understanding of the origin of the complex phenomenon of entrepreneurship. Indeed, the study of entrepreneurship cannot be confined to one discipline:

- Psychology studies have focused on motives and character traits of (potential) entrepreneurs.
- Sociological studies have focused on the (collective) background of entrepreneurs (margination theory).
- Economic studies have focused on the interaction of entrepreneurship

  with the economic climate, including scarcity and opportunity costs,
  and technological development.
- The demographic perspective focuses largely on the impact of the
  demographic composition on entrepreneurship.
- Finally, from a policy perspective, governments can influence entrepreneurship through direct assistance and through reducing imped-
  iments to entrepreneurship, such as the administrative burden
  (Dennis, 2004).

To investigate the determinants of entrepreneurial activity in the Netherlands
and Japan we will use five groups of factors as derived from the eclectic
framework (Verheul et al., 2002). These include macro-economic conditions, technological factors, socio-demographics, the institutional environment, and cultural factors. In the eclectic framework these factors are
captured by the demand side of entrepreneurship (creating opportunities for
entrepreneurship), the supply side (generating potential individuals from the
population who can perceive of and seize these opportunities), and government policies, respectively. For a detailed discussion of how each of these
factors influence entrepreneurship, we refer to Okamuro et al. (2011). The
focus is on the factors included in the study by Hartog et al. (2010).

4.   METHODOLOGY

We build on the empirical analysis by Hartog et al. who, on the basis of
data for twenty developed countries over the period 2002–2006, investigate a range of determining factors of entrepreneurship at three different
stages: nascent, YB and established entrepreneurship.[1] Their estimation
results can be found in Appendix 1.1. We apply a decomposition analysis
to better understand the differences in entrepreneurial activity between
Japan and the Netherlands. More specifically, the fitted (predicted) values
of the levels of nascent, YB, and established entrepreneurship of the two
countries (averaged over 2002–2006) are decomposed into individual contributions of explanatory variables by multiplying the estimated coefficient
by the country value of the variable. Furthermore, by grouping similar
explanatory variables, we are able to assess the contribution to entrepreneurial activity of five groups of explanatory factors: macro-economic
conditions, technological factors, socio-demographics, institutional environment, and cultural factors.

  In our decomposition analysis we compute the contribution of each
explanatory variable in deviation from the variable's overall sample
average. In this way we can identify which variables contribute positively

and negatively to entrepreneurship levels in Japan and the Netherlands. The twenty countries in the data set of Hartog et al. serve as a benchmark for assessing entrepreneurship determinants in Japan and the Netherlands. As a second benchmark, we also compare the results of the two countries with those of the United States.

Table 1.1 describes both the dependent and independent variables in this study, based on Hartog et al. (2010). Data on nascent and YB entrepreneurship are taken from GEM, while data on established entrepreneurship (non-agricultural business ownership) are taken from the COMPENDIA database (Van Stel, 2005; Van Stel et al., 2010). Information on macro-economic, technological, socio-demographic and institutional factors is derived from several Organisation for Economic Co-operation and Development (OECD) and World Bank sources, whereas the cultural indicators are taken from Hofstede (2001). Table 1.2 describes the dependent and independent variables for Japan, the Netherlands and the United States. Okamuro et al. (2011) also presents the entrepreneurship rates for the three countries in comparison with the other 17 countries included in Hartog et al. (2010).

Table 1.3 presents the results of the decomposition analysis for YB entrepreneurship. Due to space limitations we are not able to include the corresponding results for nascent and established entrepreneurship, but we refer the reader to Okamuro et al. (2011) for results relating to these indicators. Though we include only data for YB entrepreneurship in the present chapter, the results relating to all three entrepreneurship indicators are still discussed below. The first data column in Table 1.3 shows the average contribution of the determining factor to entrepreneurship (the coefficient times the value of the variable), averaged over all sample observations (all countries and years in the Hartog et al. sample). The second column provides the contribution for Japan (average 2002–2006). For instance, we can see that, for the all-country sample, the contribution of the female labor share to the YB entrepreneurship rate is 2.29. For Japan this contribution is 2.11, i.e. lower than average. The third column indicates the deviation (2.11−2.29 = −0.18), expressed as a percentage of the overall sample average of the YB rate (2.97). Hence, the deviation is −0.18/2.97 = −6.30 percent.[2] In this way, the deviation of the Japanese YB rate from the overall country average can be decomposed into contributions per variable. So, as can be seen from the last row of the table, the YB rate for Japan (averaged over 2002–2006) is 1.14, while the overall country average is 2.97. Hence, the YB rate for Japan is 61.53 percent lower than the overall average YB rate. The 61.53 percent difference is composed of 57.66 percent for the explanatory variables in Hartog et al.'s model and 3.86 percent for the residual (the unexplained part). In turn, the 57.66 percent can be

Table 1.1 Measurement of dependent and independent variables in Hartog et al. (2010)

Variable	Measure	Source
Nascent entrepreneurship rate	Percentage of the adult population (18–64 years of age) actively involved in setting up a business	GEM (Reynolds et al., 2005)
YB entrepreneurship rate	Percentage of adult population (18–64) currently owning and managing a business that is less than 42 months old	GEM (Reynolds et al., 2005)
Business ownership rate	Total number of unincorporated and incorporated self-employed (excluding agriculture) as a share of the total labor force	Compendia (Van Stel, 2005)
Share service sector	Share of service sector in total (non-agricultural) employment	OECD Labour Force Statistics
Unemployment rate	Number of unemployed as % of total labor force	OECD Main Economic Indicators
Per capita income	GDP p.c. in thousands of ppp per US$ at 1990 prices	OECD National Accounts, OECD LFS
R&D expenditures	R&D expenditures as % of GDP	OECD Science and Technology (R&D)
		OECD Economic Outlook (GDP)
Enrollment secondary education	Gross enrollment rate in secondary education	World Bank EdStats
Enrollment tertiary education	Gross enrollment rate in tertiary education	World Bank EdStats
Age composition	Population aged 25–39 years as share of population aged 25–64	OECD Demographic and Labour Force database, US Census Bureau International database, and UNStats
Female labor share	Female labor force as a share of the total labor force	OECD LFS
Social security	Unemployment gross replacement rate	OECD Benefits and Wages stats
Taxes	Total tax revenue as % of GDP	OECD Revenue stats
Corporate tax rate	Tax rate of corporate and capital income	OECD Tax database
Employment protection	Strictness of employment protection (Nickell, 2006)	CEP-OECD Institutions data set
'Rule of Law'	'Perceptions of the extent to which agents have confidence in and abide by the rules of society' (Kaufmann et al., 2009, p.6)	World Bank Worldwide Governance Indicators
Power distance index	Power distance index (PDI) (Hofstede, 2001, p.98)	Hofstede's cultural dimensions
Individualism	Individualism (IDV) – versus collectivism (Hofstede, 2001, p.225)	
Masculinity	Masculinity (MAS) – versus femininity (Hofstede, 2001, p.297)	
Uncertainty avoidance index	Uncertainty avoidance index (UAI) (Hofstede, 2001, p.161)	

Table 1.2   Descriptive statistics, average values 2002–2006

	All-country average	Japan	Netherlands	United States
Entrepreneurship variables				
Nascent entrepreneurship rate	3.91	0.99	2.68	7.78
YB entrepreneurship rate	2.97	1.14	2.00	4.55
Business ownership rate	10.85	9.03	10.80	10.02
Macro-economic conditions				
Share service sector	56.27	60.45	67.17	78.53
Unemployment rate	6.37	4.65	3.98	5.40
Per capita income	21.22	20.85	20.82	28.16
Technological factors				
R&D expenditure (% of GDP)	2.12	3.27	1.74	2.62
Socio-demographics				
Enrollment secondary education	113.62	101.76	119.78	94.43
Enrollment tertiary education	67.31	54.22	59.48	82.86
Age composition	40.25	38.28	39.80	40.70
Female labor share	44.86	41.20	44.16	46.16
Institutional environment				
Social security	29.73	7.78	43.50	13.64
Taxes (% of GDP)	37.75	26.83	38.08	26.77
Corporate tax rate	31.60	39.87	32.92	39.30
Employment protection	1.94	2.44	3.05	0.17
'Rule of Law'	1.61	1.35	1.73	1.54
Cultural factors				
Power distance	39.77	54.00	38.00	40.00
Individualism	72.40	46.00	80.00	91.00
Masculinity	47.69	95.00	14.00	62.00
Uncertainty avoidance	57.81	92.00	53.00	46.00

decomposed into contributions of individual variables and contributions of groups of variables. For instance we can see that, as a group, the cultural factors in Japan contribute particularly negatively to YB entrepreneurship: out of a 61.53 percent lower YB rate (compared to the all-country average), the cultural factors are responsible for 46.56 percent.

While Table 1.3 focuses on the contributions of individual variables for three specific countries, Okamuro et al. (2011) also show the contributions of the five groups of explanatory factors for all countries in Hartog et al.'s database, in deviation from the overall average of the entrepreneurship variable under consideration. For example, here it can be seen that

Table 1.3 Contribution of individual determinants to explanation of YB entrepreneurial activity rate, average values 2002–2006

	All-country average contribution	Japan Contribution	Japan % Deviation (relative to YB rate)	Netherlands Contribution	Netherlands % Deviation (relative to YB rate)	United States Contribution	United States % Deviation (relative to YB rate)
Share service sector	-1.09	-1.17	-2.71	-1.30	-7.09	-1.52	-14.47
Unemployment rate	-1.31	-0.96	11.88	-0.82	16.52	-1.11	6.69
Per capita income	-4.03	-3.96	2.35	-3.96	2.53	-5.35	-44.38
Macro-economic conditions	**-6.43**	**-6.09**	**11.52**	**-6.07**	**11.96**	**-7.98**	**-52.17**
R&D expenditure (% of GDP)	-1.00	-1.54	-18.28	-0.82	5.98	-1.24	-7.99
Technological factors	**-1.00**	**-1.54**	**-18.28**	**-0.82**	**5.98**	**-1.24**	**-7.99**
Enrollment secondary education	0.58	0.52	-2.03	0.61	1.05	0.48	-3.28
Enrollment tertiary education	2.68	2.16	-17.55	2.37	-10.49	3.30	20.83
Age composition	9.83	9.35	-16.27	9.72	-3.74	9.94	3.66
Female labor share	2.29	2.11	-6.30	2.26	-1.21	2.36	2.23
Socio-demographics	**15.39**	**14.13**	**-42.15**	**14.96**	**-14.38**	**16.08**	**23.45**
Social security	-1.34	-0.35	33.22	-1.96	-20.84	-0.61	24.35
Taxes (% of GDP)	-2.64	-1.87	25.68	-2.66	-0.77	-1.87	25.82
Corporate tax rate	-0.46	-0.58	-4.01	-0.47	-0.64	-0.57	-3.74
Employment protection	-1.40	-1.76	-12.19	-2.20	-27.02	-0.12	42.99

'Rule of Law'	1.49	1.24	-8.31	1.60	3.71	1.42	-2.30
Institutional environment	**-4.34**	**-3.32**	**34.39**	**-5.70**	**-45.55**	**-1.75**	**87.12**
Power distance	-1.84	-2.50	-22.19	-1.76	2.76	-1.85	-0.35
Individualism	2.86	1.82	-35.10	3.16	10.11	3.60	24.74
Masculinity	-0.80	-1.59	-26.57	-0.23	18.93	-1.04	-8.04
Uncertainty avoidance	1.87	2.98	37.31	1.72	-5.24	1.49	-12.88
Cultural factors	**2.10**	**0.71**	**-46.56**	**2.89**	**26.56**	**2.20**	**3.46**
Constant term plus year dummies	**-2.74**	**-2.64**	**3.42**	**-2.75**	**-0.29**	**-2.75**	**-0.29**
Fitted value	**2.97**	**1.26**	**-57.66**	**2.50**	**-15.73**	**4.56**	**53.58**
Residual	**0.00**	**-0.11**	**-3.86**	**-0.51**	**-17.00**	**-0.01**	**-0.34**
YB entr. act. rate	**2.97**	**1.14**	**-61.53**	**2.00**	**-32.73**	**4.55**	**53.24**

Note: The contributions of the individual variables (including the constant term and the year dummies) add up to the fitted value. The fitted value and the residual add up to the dependent variable (i.e., the YB entrepreneurial activity rate).

the 46.56 percent negative deviation for the cultural variables for Japan is indeed extreme: for this group of explanatory variables, Japan has the lowest contribution to the YB entrepreneurship rate of all countries.

5.   RESULTS

In this section we describe the results of the decomposition analysis, as shown in Table 1.3 for the YB rate and in Okamuro et al. (2011) for the nascent rate and business ownership rate. It is important to mention that we will analyze the contributions of certain variables to entrepreneurship levels in the three countries *relative* to the sample averages of the 20 countries in the Hartog et al. study, which thus serve as a benchmark. This means, for instance, that we will sometimes speak of a positive contribution for a certain variable for a certain country, even if the sign in the estimation, as shown in Appendix 1.1, is negative. A positive contribution then means that the negative effect is smaller than average, so that, *compared to the all-country average*, the contribution to entrepreneurship is positive.

5.1   Macro-Economic Conditions

The decomposition results show that, as a whole, the macro-economic climate does not have a large effect on the three types of entrepreneurship (nascent, YB and established entrepreneurial activity), either in Japan or the Netherlands.

5.2   Technology

We find that the high R&D intensity in Japan (see Table 1.2) contributes relatively strongly to lower rates of nascent and YB entrepreneurship rates in Japan. *Ceteris paribus*, the high R&D intensity in Japan explains 19.36 and 18.28 percentage points of the total gap between the Japanese entrepreneurship rates and the overall sample averages. This negative association reflects that formal R&D investments are dominated by large firms. Indeed, according to the OECD (2008), the share of business R&D expenditure of SMEs is only 8 percent in Japan (27 percent in the Netherlands and 14 percent in the United States).

5.3   Socio-Demographics

From the decomposition analysis we can derive that socio-demographics in both Japan and the Netherlands negatively contribute to nascent and

YB activity (relative to the all-country average), where the contribution for Japan is even extremely low (again, relative to the benchmark). For nascent entrepreneurship this can mainly be attributed to the relatively low female labor share in Japan over the period 2002–2006 (as compared to other countries). In fact, with a relatively low share of women in the labor force, there are effectively fewer people to undertake steps to start a company and pursue an entrepreneurial career. Nevertheless, according to the Employment Status Survey by the Ministry of Internal Affairs and Communications (MIC), the labor participation ratio of Japanese women increased between 1997 and 2007, especially for the 25–34 age group on which the burden of childcare falls.

Furthermore, both in Japan and the Netherlands, the relatively low enrollment rates in tertiary education (which is lower than the US rate and the country average) seem to contribute to lower nascent and young entrepreneurial activity rates. In fact, new entrepreneurship energy often comes from young and highly educated people.[3]

5.4   Institutional Environment

The decomposition analysis shows that, whereas for Japan (and the United States) the institutional environment positively affects entrepreneurship compared to the all-country average (the overall negative effects are relatively weak for these countries), for the Netherlands institutions are particularly harmful, especially for YB and established entrepreneurial activity. It appears that the largest part of the relatively strong negative effect for the Netherlands can be ascribed to the high levels of social security entitlements and employment protection that find their origin in the Dutch Polder Model which represents the consensus model in the Netherlands, introduced after the economic recessions of the 1970s and early 1980s. Obviously, high levels of social security discourage people from leaving secure waged jobs to start their own entrepreneurial career. Furthermore, stringent employment protection complicates hiring and firing, which could discourage potential entrepreneurs from starting new businesses. Although the Netherlands has recently reduced employment protection (for regular employment), it is still among the highest of all OECD countries (Ochel and Rohwer, 2009).[4] In addition, social contributions still account for a large part of Dutch government revenues (Auer, 2000).

The relative weakness of the negative effect (positive deviation) for Japan can be ascribed to a relatively low level of social security combined with relatively low taxes. In fact, in terms of taxes Japan seems to be on a par with the United States, a country that traditionally is characterized by low tax rates (see Table 1.2). Note that, as opposed to tax as a percentage of GDP, the corporate tax rate in Japan is relatively high, which has a nega-tive contribution to the business ownership rate (see Okamuro et al., 2011).

5.5 Culture

Investigating the decomposition results for the cultural factors, we see again a striking difference for our two countries under investigation. Whereas cultural factors have overall positive effects on young and estab-lished entrepreneurial activity, these effects are considerably weaker in Japan than in the Netherlands. More specifically, we find that in Japan the high scores on Hofstede's (2001) power distance and masculinity indices, and the low score on the individualism index, strongly contribute to lower rates of young and established entrepreneurial activity in Japan, compared to the all-country average rates. Similar to Hofstede, Kashima et al. (1995) find that Japanese people scored higher on collectivism than Americans and Australians. The traditional collectivistic nature of Japanese people is not in line with the essentially individualistic nature of entrepreneurial activity, which explains the negative deviation.

6. CONCLUSIONS

Globalization and an increasing importance of knowledge in the produc-tion process have caused many developed countries to move from a more 'managed' to a more 'entrepreneurial' economy in recent decades. In the former type of economy, large and incumbent firms play a dominant role, exploiting economies of scale in a relatively certain economic environment. In the latter type, small and new firms play an increasingly important role, introducing new products and services in highly uncertain economic environments while quickly adapting to rapidly changing consumer prefer-ences. The speed of adjustment in this transition process from a managed to an entrepreneurial economy varies by country. In this chapter we inves-tigated the differences between a more 'managed' economy, Japan, char-acterized by relatively low levels of entrepreneurial activity, and a more 'entrepreneurial' economy, the Netherlands.

Building on earlier work by Hartog et al. (2010), who explain cross-country differences in three measures of entrepreneurial activity using five broad groups of explanatory variables, we applied a decomposition analysis to better understand the differences in entrepreneurial activity between Japan and the Netherlands. Our analysis offers a large array of interesting results. First, the contribution of individual explanatory factors varies across nascent, YB, and established entrepreneurship. This suggests that entrepreneurship in different stages of the entrepreneurial process is stimulated by different factors.

Second, we find that, in spite of higher levels of YB entrepreneurial activity and business ownership in the Netherlands, the country's institutional framework (in particular high levels of social security and employment protection) is considerably *less* favorable to entrepreneurship compared to Japan. On the other hand, cultural differences between the Netherlands and Japan explain a substantial part of the difference in entrepreneurship rates between the two countries.

Third, in terms of socio-demographics we have found that in Japan, the relatively low female labor force participation rate negatively contributes to the level of nascent entrepreneurial activity (relative to the all-country average). The low participation by women implies that the supply of potential (female) entrepreneurs is smaller than in other countries, resulting in fewer female entrepreneurs.

Our findings have implications for policy in the two selected countries. To the extent that governments want to (further) increase rates of entrepreneurship, policy in the Netherlands could consider altering incentive structures for labor market participants in favor of self-employment (relative to wage-employment), while Japan could consider stimulating an enterprising culture focusing more on, for example, rewarding individual achievement. Furthermore, encouraging more women to enter the labor force may also increase (nascent) entrepreneurship rates in Japan (Okamuro and Ikeuchi, 2017). Although our empirical analysis provides guidance on how to raise national entrepreneurship rates, policy makers should understand that more entrepreneurs is not always better from an economic perspective. Just promoting new and small firms may be too simplistic a policy response (Thurik et al., 2013). Our analysis did not take into consideration the quality (skills and education level) of these entrepreneurs (Shane, 2009; Van Praag and Van Stel, 2013). Although focusing on the quality of entrepreneurship is naturally desirable for any economy, it may be particularly appropriate for the Netherlands, given the current high rates of entrepreneurship (see Figures 1.1 and 1.2). Thus, it is reassuring that altering incentive structures in favor of self-employment (in particular, lowering employment protection) is likely to stimulate particularly high-aspiration entrepreneurs and opportunity entrepreneurs (Autio, 2011; Van Stel et al., 2007).

In terms of research implications, the method applied in this chapter can also easily be applied to investigate and compare the entrepreneurial climate in other countries. Furthermore, it can also be used to study the conditions for particular types of entrepreneurship, such as high-growth, female and minority entrepreneurship.

NOTES

* This chapter is an updated version of EIM Research Report H201102. It has been written in the framework of the research program SCALES, carried out by Panteia/EIM and financed by the Dutch Ministry of Economic Affairs. The chapter benefited from a research visit by André van Stel and Ingrid Verheul to Hitotsubashi University in January and February 2010. We would like to thank Niels Bosma, Martin Carree, Kenta Ikeuchi, Yuji Honjo, Viktoriya Kan, Masatoshi Kato, Junichi Nishimura, and Ryuichiro Tsuchiya for providing us with helpful comments and suggestions.

1. The 20 countries are: Austria, Belgium, Denmark, Finland, France, Germany, Ireland, Italy, the Netherlands, Portugal, Spain, Sweden, the United Kingdom, Norway, Switzerland, the USA, Japan, Canada, Australia, and New Zealand.
2. Actually, $-0.18/2.97 = -6.06$ percent. However, the number in the table (-6.30 percent) is computed based on more decimals for the contribution variables, and the overall average of YB entrepreneurial activity.
3. For Japan this is not straightforward, however, as highly educated individuals tend to opt less often for self-employment, possibly because of higher risk and opportunity costs (Okamuro, 2008).
4. Note that employment protection for temporary workers in the Netherlands is less strict as compared to other OECD countries.

REFERENCES

Auer, P., 2000, *Employment Revival in Europe: Labour Market Success in Austria, Denmark, Ireland and the Netherlands*, Geneva: International Labour Office.

Autio, E., 2011, High-aspiration entrepreneurship, in: M. Minniti (ed.), *The Dynamics of Entrepreneurship: Evidence from the Global Entrepreneurship Monitor Data*, Oxford: Oxford University Press, 251–276.

Busenitz, L.W., Gomez, C. and J.W. Spencer, 2000, Country institutional profiles: Unlocking entrepreneurial phenomena, *Academy of Management Journal* **43** (5), 994–1003.

Dennis, W.J., Jr., 2004, Creating and sustaining a viable small business sector, Paper presented at School of Continuing Education, University of Oklahoma, 27 October 2004.

Genda, Y. and Kambayashi, R., 2002, Declining self-employment in Japan, *Journal of the Japanese and International Economies* **16** (1), 73–91.

Hartog, C., Van Stel, A.J. and D.J. Storey, 2010, Institutions and entrepreneurship: The role of the rule of law, EIM Scales paper H201003, Zoetermeer: Panteia/EIM.

Hofstede, G., 2001 [1980], *Culture's Consequences: Comparing Values, Behaviors, Institutions and Organizations across Nations*, Thousand Oaks, CA: Sage.

Kashima, Y., Yamaguchi, S., Kim, U., Choi, S.C., Gelfand, M. and M. Yuki, 1995, Culture, gender, and self: A perspective from individualism-collectivism research, *Journal of Personality and Social Psychology* **69** (5), 925–937.

Ochel, W. and A. Rohwer, 2009, Reduction of employment protection in Europe: A comparative fuzzy-set analysis, CESifo working paper No. 2828, Munich: CESifo.

OECD, 2008, *Science, Technology and Industry Scoreboard 2007*, Paris: Organisation for Economic Co-operation and Development.

Okamuro, H., 2008, How different are the regional factors of high-tech and low-tech start-ups? Evidence from Japan, *International Entrepreneurship and Management Journal* **4**, 199–215.

Okamuro, H., Van Stel, A.J. and I. Verheul, 2011, Understanding the drivers of an 'entrepreneurial' economy: Lessons from Japan and the Netherlands, EIM Research Report H201102, Zoetermeer: Panteia/EIM.

Okamuro, H. and K. Ikeuchi, 2017, Work-life balance and gender differences in self-employment income during the start-up stage in Japan, *International Review of Entrepreneurship* **15** (1), 107–130.

Reynolds, P.D., Hay, M. and S.M. Camp, 1999, *Global Entrepreneurship Monitor 1999 Executive Report*, Babson Park, MA: Babson College and London Business School.

Reynolds, P.D., Hay, M., Bygrave, W.D., Camp, S.M. and E. Autio, 2000, *Global Entrepreneurship Monitor 2000 Executive Report*, Babson College, Kauffman Center for Entrepreneurial Leadership and London Business School.

Reynolds, P.D., Bosma, N., Autio, E., Hunt, S., De Bono, N., Servais, I., Lopez-Garcia, P. and N. Chin, 2005, Global Entrepreneurship Monitor: Data collection design and implementation 1998–2003, *Small Business Economics*, **24** (3), 205–231.

Shane, S., 2009, Why encouraging more people to become entrepreneurs is bad public policy, *Small Business Economics* **33** (2), 141–149.

Stevenson, L. and A. Lundström, 2007, Dressing the emperor: the fabric of entrepreneurship policy, in: D.B. Audretsch, I. Grilo and A.R. Thurik (eds.), *Handbook of Research on Entrepreneurship Policy*, Cheltenham, UK and Northampton, MA, USA: Edward Elgar Publishing, 94–129.

Storey, D.J., 1994, *Understanding the Small Business Sector*, London/New York: Routledge.

Storey, D.J., 1999, Six steps to heaven: Evaluating the impact of public policies to support small business in developed economies, in: D.L. Sexton and H. Landström (eds.), *Handbook of Entrepreneurship*, Oxford: Blackwell, 176–194.

Thurik, A.R., E. Stam and D.B. Audretsch, 2013, The rise of the entrepreneurial economy and the future of dynamic capitalism, *Technovation* **33**, 302–310.

Van Praag, C.M. and A.J. Van Stel, 2013, The more business owners, the merrier? The role of tertiary education, *Small Business Economics* **41** (2), 335–357.

Van Stel, A.J., 2005, COMPENDIA: Harmonizing business ownership data across countries and over time, *International Entrepreneurship and Management Journal* **1** (1), 105–123.

Van Stel, A.J., J. Cieslik and C.M. Hartog, 2010, Measuring business ownership across countries and over time: Extending the COMPENDIA data base, EIM Research Report H201019, Zoetermeer: Panteia/EIM.

Van Stel, A.J., D.J. Storey and A.R. Thurik, 2007, The effect of business regulations on nascent and young business entrepreneurship, *Small Business Economics* **28** (2–3), 171–186.

Verheul, I., Wennekers, S., Audretsch, D. and R. Thurik, 2002, An eclectic theory of entrepreneurship: Policies, institutions and culture, in: D.B. Audretsch, A.R. Thurik, I. Verheul and A.R.M. Wennekers (eds.), *Entrepreneurship: Determinants and Policy in a European–US Comparison*, Boston/Dordrecht: Kluwer Academic Publishers, 11–81.

Wennekers, A.R.M., Van Stel, A.J., Carree, M.A. and A.R. Thurik, 2010, The relationship between entrepreneurship and economic development: Is it U-shaped?, *Foundations and Trends in Entrepreneurship* **6** (3), 167–237.

APPENDIX

Table 1A.1 presents the estimation results of the Hartog et al. (2010) study which forms the basis of our empirical analysis.

Table 1A.1 *Explaining entrepreneurial activity across countries*

	Nascent entrepreneurship rate		YB entrepreneurship rate		Business ownership rate	
Constant	−28.122***	(−3.75)	−2.609	(−0.49)	44.796***	(6.55)
Demography						
Enrollment in secondary education	0.0050	(0.51)	0.0051	(0.73)	0.032***	(3.61)
Enrollment in tertiary education	0.041**	(2.20)	0.040***	(3.02)	0.011	(0.67)
Age composition	0.187**	(2.06)	0.244***	(3.82)	−0.204**	(−2.46)
Female labor share	0.461***	(4.32)	0.051	(0.68)	−0.247**	(−2.54)
Macro-economic conditions						
Service share	0.041	(1.32)	−0.019	(−0.88)	0.078***	(2.73)
Unemployment rate	0.157	(1.41)	−0.206***	(−2.62)	0.313***	(3.07)
Per capita income	0.066	(0.88)	−0.190***	(−3.59)	−0.390***	(−5.68)
Institutions						
Social security	0.020	(0.77)	−0.045**	(−2.44)	−0.119***	(−4.97)
Taxes as % GDP	−0.100**	(−2.34)	−0.070**	(−2.31)	−0.014	(−0.36)
Corporate tax rate	0.025	(0.79)	−0.014	(−0.65)	−0.187***	(−6.47)
Employment protection	−0.325	(−0.96)	−0.722***	(−3.03)	−0.091	(−0.29)
'Rule of Law'	−0.549	(−0.65)	0.923	(1.54)	−8.162***	(−10.53)

Attitudes/culture						
Power distance index	−0.087***	(−3.03)	−0.046**	(−2.30)	−0.184***	(−7.04)
Individualism	0.024	(0.79)	0.040*	(1.87)	0.144***	(5.28)
Masculinity	0.0048	(0.29)	−0.017	(−1.41)	−0.051***	(−3.33)
Uncertainty avoidance index	0.046**	(2.04)	0.032**	(2.05)	0.116***	(5.68)
Innovation						
R&D	−0.659**	(−2.34)	−0.473**	(−2.39)	−0.564**	(−2.20)
Log-likelihood	−128.260		−97.426		−120.189	
R^2	0.752		0.806		0.925	
Adjusted R^2	0.674		0.744		0.901	
Periods included	5 (2002–2006)		5 (2002–2006)		5 (2002–2006)	
Countries included	20		20		20	
N	88		88		88	

Notes: * Significant at 10% level; ** significant at 5% level; *** significant at 1% level; t-values in brackets; year dummies included but not reported. Results obtained through seemingly unrelated regression (SUR) estimation.

2. Hofstede's cultural dimensions and modes of entry into entrepreneurship

Joern H. Block and Sascha G. Walter

1. INTRODUCTION

Prior research has analyzed the effects of national culture on entrepreneurship. This study extends this line of research and investigates the effects of national culture on the *modes of entry* into entrepreneurship. There are at least two distinct ways to become an entrepreneur: starting a new firm (new venture start) or taking over an existing firm (business takeover) (Bastié et al., 2013; Block et al., 2013; Cooper and Dunkelberg, 1986; Parker and Van Praag, 2012).

We use an aggregate trait perspective to develop hypotheses about the effects of different cultural dimensions on business takeover versus new venture start as mode of entry into entrepreneurship. This perspective argues that societies with a higher prevalence of people having traits that are conducive to entrepreneurship (e.g., individualists, risk takers) increase the supply of potential entrepreneurs, which then leads to higher entrepreneurship rates (Davidsson and Wiklund, 1997; Hayton et al., 2002). We argue that becoming an entrepreneur by means of new venture start-up is associated with higher levels of uncertainty and potential for self-actualization than is the case with business takeover. Both uncertainty and self-actualization are core elements of entrepreneurship, thus making new venture start the more 'entrepreneurial' option than takeover. Thus, we hypothesize that countries with more individualistic and masculine values have a larger supply of people preferring new venture start, whereas countries with high levels of uncertainty avoidance and power distance have a larger supply of people preferring takeover. Drawing on Hofstede's (1980) cultural dimensions and data from 3,498 individuals in 34 countries, our hierarchical logistic regressions show that people in individualistic and power-distant countries favor new venture starts, whereas people in uncertainty-avoiding countries favor business takeovers.

The study extends prior work by Block et al. (2013) and the scant literature on entry modes in general (e.g., Bastié et al., 2013; Parker and Van Praag, 2012) by showing that, in addition to individual influences, specific aspects of national culture determine an individual's path to entrepreneurship. We also add to the literature about national culture as a determinant of national levels of entrepreneurship (e.g., Adam-Müller et al., 2015; Davidsson, 1995; Hayton et al., 2002; Linán and Chen, 2009; Thomas and Mueller, 2000; Stephan and Uhlaner, 2010). Past research has revealed that entrepreneurship is associated with high levels of individualism and low levels of uncertainty avoidance and power distance (Busenitz and Lau, 1996; McGrath et al., 1992; Shane, 1993; Taylor and Wilson, 2012). Our results suggest that national culture influences not only entrepreneurship activity per se, but also the modes of entry into entrepreneurship.

2. BACKGROUND AND THEORY

2.1 Business Takeovers versus New Venture Starts

Any individual who is willing to embark on an entrepreneurial career path faces the critical question of whether to create a completely new venture or to buy an existing and established firm (Parker and Van Praag, 2012). However, the choice of one option over the other may not be straightforward, because these options differ along at least two dimensions: uncertainty and potential for self-actualization. Starting a new venture is associated with higher *uncertainty* than taking over an already established firm. Hiring employees and creating a new organization are uncertain endeavors by nature. Moreover, new ventures suffer from the liabilities of newness and smallness. They also receive fewer benefits from scale economies compared to established firms. The empirical research pertaining to industrial organization and organizational ecology has shown that the probability of failure is highest in the early start-up phase. Also the potential for *self-actualization* should be higher for new ventures than for business takeovers. Extant research has shown that entrepreneurs value the non-monetary aspects of entrepreneurship, particularly the opportunity to work independently and be creative. When starting a new venture, entrepreneurs can strongly influence an organization's structure and products and define their own roles within that organization. The influence of entrepreneurs over these aspects is lower when taking over an existing business, in which the organizational routines and products already exist.

Past research has typically sought explanations for either starting a new venture or taking over an existing firm. More recently, scholars have begun to examine why individuals prefer one option over the other, but have focused on individual-level influences. For instance, Parker and Van Praag find that individuals who are more educated or perceive lower income risks tend to opt for new venture starts. Other research has shown country differences in preferred entry modes. Block et al. (2013) report that more than 50 percent of potential entrepreneurs in Japan prefer business takeovers, whereas, for example, in Romania this figure is only 17 percent. In extending Block et al.'s work, we suggest that cultural values may provide an explanation for the cross-country variance. Thus culture, the "collective programming of the mind which distinguishes the members of one human group from another" (Hofstede 1980, p. 25), provides a context shaping a general proclivity for one mode of entry.

2.2   The Effect of National Culture on Mode of Entry into Entrepreneurship

Hofstede has suggested that cultural differences between societies can be captured by quantifiable dimensions, including power distance, individualism, uncertainty avoidance, and masculinity. We argue that, after controlling for socio-economic and other important differences between individuals, the preferred mode of entry into entrepreneurship relates to these cultural dimensions.

2.2.1   Power distance
Power distance refers to the extent to which less powerful individuals in a country accept inequality in organizations and institutions. Countries with high power distance (e.g., China) are characterized by high levels of hierarchy, vertical communication patterns, and centralization of power. Supervisors have a high degree of control over subordinates, and there is strong resistance to change in the distribution of power. In contrast, countries with low power distance show low levels of hierarchy, horizontal communication, and decentralized power. People in more power-distant countries should be more likely than people in other countries to prefer business takeover to start-up. Established firms are typically characterized by a formal or informal power structure that has evolved over time and is accepted by most members of the organization. Changes in the structure and hierarchy of an organization may be difficult or impossible in the short term, may disturb the social and power equilibrium, and can lead to (short-term) performance losses of a firm. Therefore, the decision to take over a firm requires a willingness to accept a given hierarchy and pursue changes carefully and slowly. Individuals who are willing to accept these conditions are more likely to be found in countries with a high power distance.

Hypothesis 1: People in more power-distant countries will be more likely to enter entrepreneurship through business takeovers rather than new venture starts compared with people in low power-distant countries.

2.2.2   Individualism

Individualism describes the degree to which individuals are integrated into groups. In individualistic countries, such as the United States, the ties between individuals are loose, and people are expected to be concerned with themselves and their immediate families. By contrast, in collectivistic countries people are integrated into strong, cohesive groups (e.g., their employers and their families). Individualism should increase the preference of starting a business as opposed to takeover. In more individualistic societies, people are more likely to pursue their personal goals, focus on externalities, and aim to achieve high levels of self-actualization. As discussed above, the process of starting a new venture involves more possibilities of achieving a high level of self-actualization than the process of taking over an existing business. By starting a new venture, an entrepreneur has the opportunity to create his/her own organization, whereas an entrepreneur taking over a business must accept many facets of the organization and business as given. Moreover, entrepreneurs who opt for new venture starts have greater influence on product design and firm strategy. In particular, by becoming inventors, entrepreneurs can achieve high levels of self-actualization.

Hypothesis 2: People in collectivistic countries will be more likely to enter entrepreneurship through business takeovers rather than new venture starts compared with people in individualistic countries.

2.2.3   Uncertainty avoidance

Uncertainty avoidance refers to a country's tolerance for uncertainty and ambiguity. A country's level of uncertainty avoidance indicates the extent to which its people feel either uncomfortable or comfortable in unstructured situations. Unstructured situations are novel, unknown, surprising, and different from usual situations. People in uncertainty-avoiding countries aim to minimize the possibility of unstructured situations through the use of strict laws, rules, and bureaucracy. Moreover, people in uncertainty-avoiding countries attempt to avoid unstructured situations through detailed planning, and tend to prefer order and certainty. They should tend towards takeover of an existing business rather than starting a business from scratch. Business takeover is associated with lower levels of uncertainty versus the process of starting a new firm. Through takeover, an entrepreneur can build on existing products, market access, and an established organization, whereas new venture starts must develop such assets over time, and significant uncertainty exists regarding whether an entrepreneur will be successful. Moreover, the business opportunity has already proven to be successful in business takeover situations, whereas with new venture starts these opportunities are not yet clear. In summary, in many business aspects, the novelty and thus uncertainty intrinsic to entrepreneurial actions is higher with new venture starts than with business takeovers. Individuals from uncertainty-avoiding societies will attempt to avoid such uncertainty and thus prefer business takeovers over new venture starts.

Hypothesis 3: People in more uncertainty-avoiding countries will be more likely to enter entrepreneurship through business takeovers rather than new venture starts compared with people in less uncertainty-avoiding countries.

2.2.4 Masculinity

Masculinity captures the extent to which the dominant values in a country are masculine and emphasize assertiveness, the acquisition of money and possessions, and lack of concern for others, quality of life, or people. In more masculine societies, people value challenges and recognition and strive for advancement and earnings. A "live to work" mentality prevails and people tend to be more ego-oriented. In more feminine societies, cooperation at work and employment security play important roles. People follow a "work to live" spirit and are more relationship-oriented. Masculinity should lead individuals to create rather than take over a business. In striving for recognition and reputation, people may favor the entry mode in which organizational performance is more directly attributable to individual actions. Starting a new venture offers more possibilities for becoming a reputable and recognized entrepreneur compared with the process of taking over an existing business. Success and failure are closely linked to the founders' decisions, whereas in already existing firms, formal or informal decision-making authority is often distributed among the members of the management team, leading to shared or team leadership. Moreover, start-ups tend to show higher growth rates, at least in the early years, than established firms, signaling higher performance. Finally, creating a firm is often perceived as more challenging than continuing the established business model of an existing firm. These differences should shape a preference for start-up rather than takeover in more masculine societies.

Hypothesis 4: People in feminine countries will be more likely to enter entrepreneurship through business takeovers rather than new venture starts compared with people in masculine countries.

3. MATERIAL AND METHODS

3.1   Data Sources and Sample

Our data source is the Flash Eurobarometer Survey No. 283 on Entrepreneurship (see Gallup, 2010 for a detailed description). The survey covers 36 countries, including the 27 European Union (EU) member states, five other European countries (Croatia, Iceland, Norway, Switzerland, and Turkey), the US, and three Asian countries (China, Japan, and South Korea). The data set is representative of the national population aged 15 years and older. A total of 26,168 randomly selected respondents were interviewed via telephone or during face-to-face meetings conducted between December 10, 2009 and January 16, 2010. The target sample size for each country amounts to either 500 or 1,000 respondents. We limited our sample to individuals of working age (16–65 years) who, at the time of the survey: (1) had thought about establishing a business; (2) had actively taken steps to start a business (nascent entrepreneurs); or (3) had already started or taken over a business. Moreover, we excluded two countries, Cyprus and Iceland, due to missing data pertaining to national culture, and obtained a final sample of 3,489 individuals in 34 countries.

3.2   Measures

3.2.1   Business takeover versus new venture start
The dependent variable was measured in the Flash EB survey with the following question: "If you currently had the means to start your own business, including sufficient funding, would you rather establish a new business or take over an existing business?" The variable takes a value of 1 if "take over an existing business" is answered and a value of 0 if "establish a new business" is given as a response.

3.2.2   National culture
We used Hofstede's (1980) measures for power distance, individualism, uncertainty avoidance, and masculinity to measure cultural differences between countries. Hofstede collected data from more than 50 subsidiaries of IBM, and controlled for biases from different occupational positions and organizational practices. A factor analysis of 32 value statements showed that national cultures vary substantially along the above-mentioned dimensions.

3.2.3 Control variables

At the country level, we control for venture capital which helps start-ups overcome financial barriers. We adopt a measure for the *availability of venture capital* from the Global Competiveness Report (GCR) provided by the World Economic Forum (2010). A total of 13,607 business executives in 139 countries were asked the following question: "In your country, how easy is it for entrepreneurs with innovative but risky projects to find venture capital?" (1 = "very difficult", 7 = "very easy"). The average of their responses constitutes the final measure for each country. Moreover, we consider *national wealth* in terms of GDP per capita in purchasing power standards in millions of international dollars. The data were obtained from the World Economic Outlook database provided by the International Monetary Fund (2010). In poorer countries, economic necessity may drive more individuals to create new ventures.

At the individual level, we used Flash EB survey data to control for several confounding influences. Various barriers and obstacles can hinder the process of starting a company. We control for *perceived start-up barriers* with an index that consists of three items referring to lack of financial support, complex administrative procedures, and lack of available information (four-point Likert scales: 1 = "strongly disagree", 4 = "strongly agree"). The knowledge and skills acquired through *full-time education* can increase the benefits of starting one's own business vis-à-vis taking over an existing business. It was measured with the survey variable "age when completed full-time education" minus six years, the typical age to enter primary school. A *self-employed father* can serve as a credible role model for a start-up or present an opportunity to succeed in a family business. Information regarding the father's occupation was given in the survey. Compared with starting a business, taking over an existing business requires less *risk tolerance* because the business model is already established in the market. The variable was measured with one item on the above four-point Likert scale, as were the following measures. Individuals with high *inventiveness* ("I am an inventive person who has ideas") are more likely to identify opportunities to be exploited through venture creation than opportunities associated with business takeovers. Individuals with a high *desire for competition* ("I like situations in which I compete with others") may prefer starting a venture because this option provides more direct feedback regarding individual performance than continuing the work of someone else.

New ventures often grow faster in their early years than established firms in the same time, and may thus be preferred by individuals with high *growth aspirations* for their businesses. This variable was measured with the question: "Imagine that a friend of yours started a business. What advice would you prefer to give him or her?" (0 = "try to expand your business quickly", 1 = "ensure that your business grows slowly, if at all"). *Age* (measured in years) is another important control variable. A desire for adventure and a lack of financial resources may lead younger individuals to start a venture, whereas a desire for more security and sufficient financial resources may motivate older individuals to take over a business. Moreover, prior research reveals that men are more likely than women to start a business. Thus, we control for *gender* (0 = female, 1 = male). Finally, we control for being an *actual entrepreneur* (0 = planning to become an entrepreneur, 1 = running a business) to examine potential differences between actual and potential entrepreneurs.

4. RESULTS

4.1 Effects of National Culture on Modes of Entry into Entrepreneurship

Table 2.1 reports the results of our hierarchical logistic regression. Models 1 and 2 show the effects of control variables at the individual and country level, respectively. In Model 3, cultural influences are added. To estimate the explained variance, we calculated the deviance differences for the null model containing no predictors. The differences are significant in all models.

We argued in Hypothesis 1 that individuals in countries with a high power distance prefer taking over a business. Our results however show the opposite to be true: a country's level of power distance is negatively related to business takeovers. We further argued that individuals in more individualistic countries are more likely to start a business from scratch (Hypothesis 2). In line with our argument, the relationship between individualism and business takeovers was significant and negative. The literature has reported high correlations between power distance and individualism. Both dimensions are also highly correlated in our study ($r = -0.60$, $p < 0.001$). To confirm the robustness of our results, we reran the regressions excluding individualism. The results for the remaining variables are consistent with the full model (Model 3). We also proposed that countries with high uncertainty avoidance prefer the option of taking over a business (Hypothesis 3). This argument was weakly supported; uncertainty avoidance and business takeover were positively related. Hypothesis 4, that more masculine societies prefer start-up, was not supported.

Table 2.1   Hierarchical logistic regressions regarding mode of entry into entrepreneurship

Variables	Model 1		Model 2		Model 3	
	b	s.e.	b	s.e.	b	s.e.
Country-level hypotheses						
Power distance					−0.02**	0.00
Individualism					−0.01*	0.00
Uncertainty avoidance					0.01^t	0.00
Masculinity					0.00	0.00
Country-level controls						
Availability of venture capital			−0.09	0.15	0.16	0.18
National wealth (GDP per capita, × 10,000)			−0.01	0.06	−0.12^t	0.06
Individual-level controls						
Perceived start-up barriers	0.04^t	0.02	0.04^t	0.02	0.04^t	0.02
Full-time education	−0.03**	0.01	−0.03**	0.01	−0.03**	0.01
Self-employed father	0.14	0.09	0.15	0.09	0.14	0.09
Risk tolerance	−0.13*	0.06	−0.13*	0.06	−0.13*	0.06
Desire for competition	−0.25***	0.06	−0.25***	0.06	−0.25***	0.06
Inventiveness	0.05	0.04	0.05	0.04	0.05	0.05
Growth aspiration	−0.02	0.07	−0.02	0.07	−0.04	0.07
Age	0.01^t	0.00	0.01^t	0.00	0.01^t	0.00
Gender	0.04	0.07	0.04	0.07	0.04	0.07
Actual entrepreneur	0.51***	0.08	0.52***	0.08	0.51***	0.08
Deviance (−2 log likelihood)	10445.18		10444.74		10435.60	
Deviance difference	97.95***		98.39***		107.54***	
Pseudo-R^2	8.04%		8.12%		8.47%	

Notes: Dependent variables: 0 = preference for new venture start; 1 = preference for business takeover.
Level 1 n = 3,489; level 2 n = 34; unstandardized coefficients are reported.
^{t}p < .10.
*p < .05, ** p < .01, *** p < .001 (two-tailed test).

4.2   Robustness Checks

We performed additional analyses to confirm the stability of our results. First, we confirmed that controlling for significant influences in the Block et al. (2013) study—which we extend—did not alter our findings. Second, we added long-term orientation, the fifth Hofstede dimension of culture, to our main models. While the variable was positively significant, the findings for the other four Hofstede dimensions of culture remained virtually unchanged. Third, the availability of informal financing might play an important role for many entrepreneurs. We included two distinct controls for informal finance: the availability of bank loans at the country level (GCR, "How easy is it to obtain a bank loan in your country with only a good business plan and no collateral?"—1 = "very difficult", 7 = "very easy"); and financial support at the individual level (Flash EB; captures how important receiving the necessary funding was for taking steps to start a new venture or take over one—1 = "not important at all", 4 = "very important"). Overall, our results were robust to adding both control variables.

5. DISCUSSION

5.1 Theoretical Implications

A review of the previous research reveals several individual-level determinants regarding business takeovers versus new venture starts as modes of entry into entrepreneurship. Building on a sample of Dutch entrepreneurs, Parker and Van Praag (2012) find that human capital (measured in the number of years of education and management experience) influences preferences regarding modes of entry. In addition, they find that individuals with family business backgrounds are more likely to take over existing businesses (but not necessary the family businesses). Block et al. (2013) show that an individual's risk attitude and inventiveness influence the decision regarding whether to start a new venture or take over an existing firm. Using a sample of French entrepreneurs, Bastié et al. (2013) show that the social and financial capital of entrepreneurs has an important role regarding their entry modes. Finally, previous research also indicates that large differences between countries exist with regard to modes of entry into entrepreneurship (Block et al., 2013). However, no attempt has been made to explain these country-level differences.

Our study contributes to this literature by showing that national culture influences modes of entry into entrepreneurship when individual socioeconomic characteristics and motives for starting a venture are controlled for. Our multilevel regressions show that people in countries with low levels of individualism and power distance and high levels of uncertainty avoidance favor business takeovers rather than new venture starts. Thus, in addition to individual-level factors, there exist factors relating to national culture that influence *how* individuals become entrepreneurs. Thus, aspects of national culture, such as individualism and uncertainty avoidance, determine the path to entrepreneurship.

Surprisingly, we find that people in countries with a high power distance are *less* willing than people in other countries to choose business takeovers versus new venture starts; this result is the opposite of what we expected. This finding can be explained by the view that entrepreneurship can be a reaction to an 'un-entrepreneurial' culture (Hofstede et al., 2004). Organizations in countries with a high power distance are characterized by a centralization of power, vertical communication, and large hierarchies. Individuals who feel uncomfortable with this situation feel compelled to start their own ventures. This argument would be in line with research describing entrepreneurs as self-confident, autonomy-seeking, and less likely to accept power and authority.

5.2   Practical Implications

The study's results hold practical implications for entrepreneurs and potential firm successors. The lack of suitable firm successors is a common reason that firms cease to exist – even in countries with a high number of potential entrepreneurs. Entrepreneurs nearing retirement and seeking venture exit should consider their national culture when considering the exit channel. Selling to competitors or financial investors rather than looking for an individual to become firm successor is favored in those countries where culture is biased against business takeover (i.e., individualistic, uncertainty-tolerant, and short-term oriented societies). Our results suggest opportunities for potential entrepreneurs. The average quality of firms seeking successors should be particularly high in countries in which cultural values influence the inclination of entrepreneurs towards business takeover as a mode of entry (e.g., countries with high levels of individualism and uncertainty acceptance). Our study has implications for venture capital and private equity investors. Venture capital or private equity firms may seek to finance and operate those ventures that are lacking a successor. Our results suggest that more attractive investment opportunities should exist in those countries where the culture is biased against business takeovers.

REFERENCES

Adam-Müller, A., Andres, R., Block, J., and Fisch, C. (2015). Socialist heritage and the opinion on entrepreneurs: micro-level evidence from Europe. *Business Administration Review*, **75**(4), 211–232.

Bastié F., Cieply, S., and Cussy, P. (2013). The entrepreneur's mode of entry: The effect of social and financial capital. *Small Business Economics*, **40**(4), 865–877.

Block, J., Thurik, R., van der Zwan, P., and Walter, S. (2013), Business takeover or new venture? Individual and environmental determinants from a cross-country study. *Entrepreneurship Theory and Practice*, **37**(5), 1099–1121.

Busenitz, L.W., and Lau, C.M. (1996). A cross-cultural cognitive model of new venture creation. *Entrepreneurship Theory and Practice*, **20**(4), 25–39.

Cooper, A.C., and Dunkelberg, W.C. (1986). Entrepreneurship and paths to business ownership. *Strategic Management Journal*, **7**(1), 53–68.

Davidsson, P. (1995). Culture, structure and regional levels of entrepreneurship. *Entrepreneurship and Regional Development*, **7**(1), 41–62.

Davidsson, P., and Wiklund, J. (1997). Values, beliefs and regional variations in new firm formation rates. *Journal of Economic Psychology*, **18**(2–3), 179–199.

Gallup (2010). *Entrepreneurship in the EU and Beyond: A Survey in the EU, EFTA Countries, Croatia, Turkey, the US, Japan, South Korea and China*. Hungary: Gallup Organization.

Hayton, J.C., George, G., and Zahra, S.A. (2002). National culture and entrepreneurship: A review of behavioral research. *Entrepreneurship: Theory and Practice*, **26**(4), 33–52.

Hofstede, G.H. (1980). *Culture's Consequences: International Differences in Work-Related Values*. Beverly Hills, CA: Sage.

Hofstede, G.H., Noorderhaven, N., Thurik, A.R., Uhlaner, L.M., Wennekers, A.R.M., and Wildeman, R.E. (2004). Culture's role in entrepreneurship: Self-employment out of dissatisfaction. In: Brown, T.E. and Ulijn, J.M. (eds.). *Innovation, Entrepreneurship and Culture*. Cheltenham, UK and Northampton, MA, USA: Edward Elgar Publishing.

International Monetary Fund (2010). *World Economic Outlook Database*. Washington, DC: IMF.

Linán, F., and Chen, Y.-W. (2009). Development and cross cultural application of a specific instrument to measure entrepreneurial intentions. *Entrepreneurship: Theory and Practice*, **33**(3), 593–617.

McGrath, R.G., MacMillan, I.C., and Scheinberg, S. (1992). Elitists, risk-takers, and rugged individualists: An exploratory analysis of cultural differences between entrepreneurs and non-entrepreneurs. *Journal of Business Venturing*, **7**(2), 115–135.

Parker, S.C., and Van Praag, M. (2012). The entrepreneur's mode of entry: Business takeover or new venture start? *Journal of Business Venturing*, **27**(1), 31–46.

Shane, S. (1993). Cultural influences on national rates of innovation. *Journal of Business Venturing*, **8**(1), 59–73.

Stephan, U., and Uhlaner, L. (2010). Performance-based vs. socially supportive culture: A cross-national study of descriptive norms and entrepreneurship. *Journal of International Business Studies*, **41**(8), 1347–1364.

Taylor, M.Z., and Wilson, S. (2012). Does culture still matter? The effects of individualism on national innovation rates. *Journal of Business Venturing*, **27**(2), 234–247.

Thomas, A.S., and Mueller, S.L. (2000). A case for comparative entrepreneurship: Assessing the relevance of culture. *Journal of International Business Studies*, **31**(2), 287–301.

World Economic Forum (2010). *The Global Competitiveness Report 2010–2011.*

3. Entrepreneurs using regulation as a source of opportunity: a study combining quantitative and qualitative approaches

Amélie Jacquemin and Frank Janssen

INTRODUCTION

Ever since the 1970s, entrepreneurship researchers have been studying the impact of the legal environment on entrepreneurs (Dana, 1987, 1990; Kent, 1984; Kilby, 1971), and a significant body of literature has been developed on this subject since the late 1990s (e.g. Blackburn and Hart, 2003; Grilo and Irigoyen, 2006; Hart et al., 2008). Most authors have focused on the negative impact of regulation on entrepreneurship (e.g. Djankov et al., 2002; Klapper et al., 2006; van Stel et al., 2007). However, some have approached the question from a more open standpoint (e.g. Arrowsmith et al., 2003; Blackburn and Hart, 2003; Edwards et al., 2004), attempting to break open the regulatory "black box" by considering the positive and neutral impacts of regulation, as well as its negative impacts. However, many questions still remain unanswered. For example, which regulations are used as a source of opportunity? Which entrepreneurs do this? How do they do it? Our study was designed more specifically to understand who the entrepreneurs are that use regulation as a source of business opportunity and how they succeed in this.

This chapter is divided into five sections. The first presents the literature review, our research questions and the theoretical framework used for our qualitative analyses. In the second section, we describe the research methodology, the empirical material collected and the analyses made, as well as the results of our quantitative study. The third section presents the same issues for our qualitative study. The fourth section discusses the results of the two approaches. The fifth section concludes.

REGULATION, ENTREPRENEURSHIP AND BUSINESS OPPORTUNITIES

Impact of Regulation on Entrepreneurship

Since the late 1990s, a large body of literature has gradually been developed on the impact of regulation on entrepreneurship and small and medium-sized enterprises (SMEs) (e.g. Djankov et al., 2002; Grilo and Irigoyen, 2006; Klapper et al., 2006; van Stel et al., 2007). The main aim of these studies was to measure the costs borne by firms to comply with regulations. Very few authors have focused on other impacts that regulations may have for entrepreneurship.

Our review of the literature led us to identify a small group of approximately 20 researchers, mostly from four English universities, who had examined this aspect (e.g. Arrowsmith et al., 2003; Blackburn and Hart, 2003; Edwards et al., 2004). They used qualitative research methodologies, including semi-structured interviews. In addition to the negative aspects of regulation for entrepreneurship (costs, requirements, constraints), these authors were also able to identify cases where regulation had had no effect on entrepreneurship (neutral impact), and others in which regulation had actually supported entrepreneurship (positive impact). While these authors were able to identify the potentially positive impact of regulation on entrepreneurship, they did not study the phenomenon in any depth. It would therefore be appropriate to look in more detail at the regulatory black box (Mayer-Schönberger, 2010; Parker, 2007).

Regulation and Business Opportunity Theory

All the above elements led us to the conclusion that we know very little about the regulations that provide opportunities for entrepreneurial activity creation or development. Our study is therefore designed to see whether regulation can in fact be regarded as a source of opportunity. This is why we speak of "regulatory opportunities". We use the business opportunity theory (Ardichvili et al., 2003; Casson and Wadeson, 2007; Casson, 1982; Eckhardt and Shane, 2003; Ibrahim and Smith, 2008; Shane and Venkataraman, 2000; Shane, 2003; Short et al., 2010). This is one of the main paradigms for doing research on entrepreneurship (Verstraete and Fayolle, 2005).

We will structure our analyses around two main research questions concerning business opportunities as classically defined by Shane and Venkataraman (2000):

- The emergence of regulatory opportunities: Which regulations create opportunities? (level of analysis: the regulation).
- The localized nature of regulatory opportunities: Who discovers these regulations? Why are some entrepreneurs able to discover them while others are not? (level of analysis: the entrepreneur).

To study these questions, we used the two paradigms from the theory of business opportunity (e.g. Alvarez and Barney, 2007, 2010; Vaghely and Julien, 2010). The first is the so-called "opportunity discovery" paradigm, also known as the Kirznerian approach. It postulates that objective business opportunities exist in the environment, and need only to be discovered by entrepreneurs. They are created by exogenous shocks, such as social, demographic or regulatory changes. Key factors in the discovery process include the entrepreneur's cognitive capacity to be alert and search systematically for information on the environment, and his or her prior knowledge of information on the environment. The second paradigm is the "opportunity creation" paradigm, also known as the Schumpeterian approach (1934). Here, opportunities do not exist of themselves, but are created by entrepreneurs through a process of "enactment". The key element in such a process is learning: entrepreneurs try to understand their environment and seize the signals sent by the market regarding their beliefs about its dynamism.

Based on these two paradigms, we expect to empirically find two main situations about regulatory opportunities. First, the lawmaker adopts regulations or policies designed on purpose to support entrepreneurship (e.g. export subsidies, R&D tax deductions). Second, the lawmaker may also adopt regulations not specifically designed to support entrepreneurship, but which some entrepreneurs are able to use to create opportunities.

THE QUANTITATIVE PART OF THE STUDY

Our research field was Belgium. Research is carried out every two years in Belgium to study the costs borne by entrepreneurs to comply with regulations (e.g. Kegels, 2008, 2010), but so far no work has been done to study the opportunities created by regulations.

Methodology and Material

We began by asking several Belgian business federations for help with our research. Two of them agreed and sent their members a letter inviting them to complete a questionnaire that we developed, containing three series of questions on three fairly well-known regulations in Belgium that were applicable to all businesses. The regulations selected were those governing investment tax deductions, business working hours and joint offers.

We collected 354 questionnaires, but unfortunately many were not properly completed. We therefore used only those questionnaires (152 in all) where the respondents had answered all the questions for at least one of the three regulations studied. The characteristics of our sample are described in Table 3.1, which also indicates the characteristics of the entrepreneurs interviewed in the qualitative part of the study.

Table 3.1   The study sample of entrepreneurs

	Questionnaire (N = 152)	Case studies (N = 8)
Gender	Male: 87.5% Female: 12.5%	Male: 100%
Age	25–35: 10.1% 36–45: 24.3% 46–55: 36.5% 56 or over: 29.1%	25–35: 12.50% 36–45: 25% 46–55: 62.50%
Education	First level: 9.3% Second level: 55.6% Third level: 35.1%	First level: 12.50% Second level: 50% Third level: 37.50%
Does the entrepreneur have any legal background?	Yes: 50% No: 50%	Yes: 100%
Size of the firm	Under 10 employees: 33.7% 10–50: 33.7% 50–250: 32.6%	Under 10 employees: 25% 10–50: 75%
Age of the firm	Under 5: 11.3% 5–10: 15.5% 11–15: 14.4% 16–20: 6.2% 21–25: 8.2% 26–30: 11.3% 31 or over: 33%	Under 5: 25% 5–10: 25% 11–15: 25% 21–25: 12.50% 26–30: 12.50%
Sector	Primary: 4% Secondary: 48% Tertiary: 48%	Secondary: 25% Tertiary: 75%

Note: Education: first level = primary and/or secondary school; second level = bachelor and/or master's degree; third level = PhD.

Table 3.2   Correlation matrix between knowledge level of regulations and detection of regulatory opportunities

Knowledge of regulations	Detection of regulatory opportunities
** = p ≤ 0.01; * = p ≤ 0.05.	0.312**

Analyses and Results

All our analyses were conducted using SPSS 19.0 software. The dependent variable in the analyses was the detection of regulatory opportunities. For this variable, we asked the entrepreneurs to assess their agreement level with ten opportunity-detection statements. We made a sum of the answers for the ten statements, to end up with a binary variable for the detection of a regulatory opportunity. Only 19.1 per cent of the sample (29 respondents) reported having identified regulatory opportunities.

Our very first analysis was a correlation test between the control variables used in our questionnaire – the entrepreneur's gender, age, education and legal background; the size of the firm and its sector – and our dependent variable (the detection of regulatory opportunities). This test was not conclusive, since we found no significant correlation.

We then turned to the analysis of the influence of our independent variables. Our questionnaire asked the entrepreneurs about their knowledge of the three regulations studied. In this regard, we found a significant positive correlation between the knowledge level about regulations and the detection of regulatory opportunities (Table 3.2).

This result shows that there is a positive association between the level of knowledge that an entrepreneur has about the existing regulations within the legal environment and the detection of business opportunities associated with regulations.

We made a further analysis to better understand how entrepreneurs develop their knowledge about regulations. First, we checked whether the use of certain sources of information may be associated with the detection of regulatory opportunities, but we found no significant results. Second, we tested whether experience of regulations could be associated with the detection of regulatory opportunities. Our questionnaire was based on the literature that distinguishes between experience of regulation in the framework of entrepreneurial activities and experience of regulations through contact with public authorities (e.g. Baldock et al., 2006; Chittenden and Derregia, 2010). We found that experience of regulations in the framework of entrepreneurial activities and contacts with public authorities and inspection services is positively associated with the detection of regulatory opportunities (Table 3.3).

Table 3.3   Correlation matrix between experience of regulations and detection of regulatory opportunities

	Detection of regulatory opportunities
Experience of regulations through disputes	−0.079
Experience of regulations through entrepreneurial activities and contact with public authorities	0.226*

Note: ** = p ≤ 0.01, * = p ≤ 0.05.

THE QUALITATIVE PART OF THE STUDY

Methodology, Material and Analyses

In the second phase of the research, we contacted the 29 respondents (19.1 per cent of the sample) who reported having identified business opportunities in the regulations, in order to carry out in-depth case studies (Hamel et al., 1993; Yin, 2003). In all, eight case studies were carried out to achieve theoretical saturation of results (Glaser and Strauss, 1967; Neergaard, 2007). We conducted semi-structured interviews with these entrepreneurs and gathered documentation on their companies and on the regulations they mentioned during the interviews.

Results

Most of the entrepreneurs we questioned worked in highly technical sectors requiring technological expertise:

- cellular therapy (THERAPY)
- human diagnosis tests (DIAGNOSISHU)
- animal diagnosis tests (DIAGNOSISAN)
- industrial machinery manufacturing (MACHINERY)
- energy production through bio-methanization (BIOMETH)
- energy certification of buildings (ENERGY).

Of the other two entrepreneurs, one worked in communications and advertising (COMMUNIC), a field that requires a great deal of creativity and techniques to produce packaging and visual identifiers for client companies (logos, advertising spots, etc.). The other managed a large grocery store (GROCERY), a field that requires very little creativity or technological expertise, but which is extremely competitive, where companies must stand out if they are to survive, especially in times of economic recession.

The entrepreneurs identified no fewer than nine regulations that had created business opportunities for the creation or the development of their activities (available from the authors on request). As expected, these regulations fall within two regulatory approaches. A first group of regulations objectively create business opportunities. They include export support measures, investment support measures, pre-activity grants and venture capital tax deduction. A second group of regulations were not adopted with the specific initial goal of supporting entrepreneurship. They include the building energy certification regulation, food product packaging rules and European Commission (EC) branding, all of which were used by some of our entrepreneurs to subjectively create business opportunities. This distinction between these two approaches will be used in the remainder of the chapter to address our results analysis and discussion.

ANALYSIS AND DISCUSSION

Emergence of Regulatory Opportunities

The interviews revealed the existence of a group of regulations containing measures that objectively support entrepreneurship, in the form of grants and subsidies or tax exemptions and reductions. An in-depth analysis of these measures revealed that they were somewhat cumbersome to implement. Firms wishing to benefit from them had to complete application forms, submit an application file containing a large amount of information, and complete an attestation to justify their use of the measure. Several entrepreneurs mentioned these constraints during the interviews. Clearly, this aspect partly explains why some entrepreneurs do not take advantage of the measures; they are put off by the administrative formalities, while others are not.

Three entrepreneurs responded somewhat surprisingly, citing as examples of "positive" regulation certain measures that had not originally been intended to create business opportunities. Although these measures introduced constraints for firms, they had also created new business opportunities for the entrepreneurs concerned. One such measure was the regulation requiring all owners of buildings in Belgium to obtain energy certification from a qualified agent. This regulation led an entrepreneur to create his own business. In another case, the entrepreneurs had developed a competitive advantage over competitors in the same sector due to their specific expertise with EC branding and food packaging regulations. In all cases, the texts were highly complex and subject to frequent change. According to the entrepreneurs we interviewed, the administrative authorities did a remarkable job of informing and supporting businesses. We also observed that the authorities' websites were full of practical information presented in clear and easy to understand formats.

The Localized Nature of Regulatory Opportunities

The group of entrepreneurs who used regulations aimed at supporting entrepreneurship shared a number of characteristics. First, they all had a legal background, either from university or from prior legal training; and they all engaged in search activities. Our interviews also showed that these entrepreneurs either carried out and/or supervised systematic search activities within their firms. This was done by searching for legislative information relevant to the firms' activities. The entrepreneurs used publications (professional journals, legislative newsletters and public authority websites) and their own professional networks (business federations or associations). Their research allowed them to calculate the costs and benefits of using support regulations.

The group of entrepreneurs who identified opportunities in regulations not originally intended to support entrepreneurship also had good legal backgrounds, obtained mainly at university, and also carried out extensive search activities. However, they appeared to have moved beyond the legal information search phase (legislative alertness) begun when the business started. In this case, alertness to legal information had given way to a learning process of legal issues, and public authorities played an important role in that learning. The entrepreneur who worked in the energy certification sector (ENERGY) said he had learned a great deal from his contacts with the authorities through advisory services and requests for clarification of legislative measures, and from his discussions with other entrepreneurs on a certification forum set up by the Walloon Region. As for EC branding, the European Commission's website offers training for entrepreneurs, organized by the different member states.

Here, opportunity is created through the development of knowledge and experience of a complex legislative measure. In the case of food packaging and EC branding regulations, the entrepreneur did not have a deliberate strategy to develop legal expertise in order to stand out from other companies in the sector. In both cases, the firm's customers said they were using its services rather than those of another firm because of the entrepreneur's mastery of the legal measures. These entrepreneurs did not objectively calculate the costs and benefits of regulations, but engaged in an iterative process that led them to perceive a source of dynamism and desirable gain in the regulatory environment.

CONCLUSIONS

The research described in this chapter emerged from an observation that, although the negative impacts of regulations on entrepreneurship had been studied extensively, very little attention had been paid to their potentially positive impacts. The goal of our study was therefore to better understand who the entrepreneurs are that positively use regulations as a source of business opportunity, and how do they succeed in this. Our findings confirm that not all entrepreneurs use regulations as a source of opportunity. This is explained by a number of factors: prior knowledge of regulation, entrepreneurial alertness, experience of regulation, characteristics of the regulation itself, the legal background of the entrepreneur and, finally, the sector in which the entrepreneur is active. We show that entrepreneurs who use regulation as a source of business opportunity use two different approaches, which we have called the Kirznerian and Schumpeterian approaches.

REFERENCES

Alvarez, S.A., Barney, J.B. (2010), "Entrepreneurship and epistemology: the philosophical underpinnings of the study of entrepreneurial opportunities", *Academy of Management Annals*, **4** (1), 557–583.

Alvarez, S.A., Barney, J.B. (2007), "Discovery and creation: alternative theories of entrepreneurial action", *Strategic Entrepreneurship Journal*, **1**, 11–26.

Ardichvili, A., Cardozo, R., Ray, S. (2003), "A theory of entrepreneurial opportunity identification and development", *Journal of Business Venturing*, **18** (1), 105–123.

Arrowsmith, J., Gilman, M., Edwards, P., Ram, M. (2003), "The impact of the national minimum wage in small firms", *British Journal of Industrial Relations*, **41** (3), 435–456.

Baldock, R., James, Ph., Smallbone, D., Vickers, I. (2006), "Influences on small-firm compliance-related behaviour: the case of workplace health and safety", *Environment and Planning C: Government and Policy*, **24** (6), 827–846.

Blackburn, R., Hart, M. (2003), "Employment rights in small firms: some new evidence, explanations and implications", *Industrial Law Journal*, **32** (1), 60–67.

Casson, M. (1982), *The Entrepreneur: An Economic Theory*, Oxford: Martin Robertson.

Casson, M., Wadeson, N. (2007), "The discovery of opportunities: extending the economic theory of the entrepreneur", *Small Business Economics*, **28** (4), 285–300.

Chittenden, F., Derregia, M. (2010), "The role of tax incentives in capital investment and R&D decisions", *Environment and Planning C: Government and Policy*, **28** (2) 241–256.

Dana, L.P. (1990), "Saint Martin/Sint Maarten: a case study of the effects of culture on economic development", *Journal of Small Business Management*, **25** (4), 91–98.

Dana, L.P. (1987), "Entrepreneurship and venture creation: an international comparison of five commonwealth nations", in Churchill, N.C., Homaday, J.A., Kirchhoff, B.A., Krasner, O.J., Vesper, K.H. (eds), *Frontiers of Entrepreneurship Research*, Wellesley, MA: Babson College, 573–583.

Djankov, S., La Porta, R., Lopez-de-Silanes, F., Shleifer, A. (2002), "The regulation of entry", *Quarterly Journal of Economics*, **117** (1), 1–37.

Eckhardt, J., Shane, S. (2003), "Opportunities and entrepreneurship", *Journal of Management*, **29** (3), 333–349.

Edwards, P., Ram, M., Black, J. (2004), "Why does employment legislation not damage small firms?", *Journal of Law and Society*, **31** (2), 245–265.

Glaser, B., Strauss, A. (1967), *The Discovery of Grounded Theory: Strategies for Qualitative Research*, New York: de Gruyter.

Grilo, I., Irigoyen, J.M. (2006), "Entrepreneurship in the EU: to wish and not to be", *Small Business Economics*, **26** (4), 305–318.

Hamel, J., Dufour, S., Fortin, D. (1993), *Case Study Methods*, Newbury Park, CA: Sage.

Hart, M., Athayde, R., Blackburn, R., Kitching, J., Smallbone, D., Wilson, N. (2008), "The impact of regulation on small business performance". Stage 1 Report. London: Small Business Service, DTI.

Ibrahim, D., Smith, G. (2008), "Entrepreneurs on horseback: reflections on the organization of law", *Arizona Law Review*, **50**, 71–89.

Kegels, Ch. (2010), "Les charges administratives en Belgique pour l'année 2008", Bureau Fédéral du Plan. Analyses et prévisions économiques, Planning Paper 108.

Kegels, Ch. (2008), "Les charges administratives en Belgique pour l'année 2006", Bureau Fédéral du Plan. Analyses et prévisions économiques, Planning Paper 103.

Kent, C.A., ed. (1984), *The Environment for Entrepreneurship*, Lexington, MA: D.C. Heath.

Kilby, P. (1971), *Entrepreneurship and Economic Development*, New York: Free Press.

Klapper, L., Laeven, L., Rajan, R. (2006), "Entry regulation as a barrier to entrepreneurship", *Journal of Financial Economics*, **82** (3), 591–629.

Mayer-Schönberger, V. (2010), "The law as stimulus: the role of law in fostering innovative entrepreneurship", *I/S: A Journal of Law and Policy*, **6** (2), 153–188.

Neergaard, H. (2007), "Sampling in entrepreneurial settings", in Neergaard, H., Ulhoi, J.P. (eds), *Handbook of Qualitative Research Methods in Entrepreneurship*, Cheltenham, UK and Northampton, MA, USA: Edward Elgar Publishing, 253–278.

Parker, S. (2007), "Law and the economics of entrepreneurship", *Comparative Labor Law and Policy Journal*, **28** (4), 695–817.

Schumpeter, J.A. (1934), *The Theory of Economic Development*, Cambridge, MA: Harvard University Press.

Shane, S. (2003), *A General Theory of Entrepreneurship: The Individual–Opportunity Nexus*, Cheltenham, UK and Northampton, MA, USA: Edward Elgar Publishing.

Shane, S., Venkataraman, S. (2000), "The promise of entrepreneurship as a field of research", *Academy of Management Review,* **25** (1), 217–226.

Short, J., Ketchen, D., Shook, C., Ireland, R. (2010), "The concept of 'opportunity' in entrepreneurship research: past accomplishments and future challenges", *Journal of Management,* **36** (1), 40–65.

Vaghely, I., Julien, P.-A. (2010), "Are opportunities recognized or constructed? An information perspective on entrepreneurial opportunity identification", *Journal of Business Venturing,* **25** (1), 73–86.

Van Stel, A., Storey, D., Thurik, R. (2007), "The effect of business regulations on nascent and young business entrepreneurship", *Small Business Economics,* **28** (2–3), 171–186.

Verstraete, Th., Fayolle, A. (2005), "Paradigmes et entrepreneuriat", *Revue de l'Entrepreneuriat,* **4** (1), 33–52.

Yin, R.K. (2003), *Case Study Research: Design and Methods* (3rd edn), Thousand Oaks, CA: Sage.

4. Determinants of high-growth firms: why do some countries have more high-growth firms than others?*

Mercedes Teruel and Gerrit de Wit

1. INTRODUCTION

Because of the importance of high-growth firms for the economy, these firms have drawn growing attention from policy makers as well as academics. Research in the field of fast-growing firms has expanded rapidly since the mid-1990s (Storey, 1994; Birch et al., 1997; Schreyer, 2000; Audretsch, 2002; Delmar et al., 2003; Autio, 2007; Acs et al., 2008; Henrekson and Johansson, 2009, 2010; Hölzl, 2009; Coad and Rao, 2008). However, knowledge about such firms is still scattered, and little is available regarding differences over countries. According to Henrekson and Johansson (2010, p. 230) the number of studies analysing fast-growing firms is still surprisingly small.

Previous evidence points out that fast-growing firms are found in all industries and in all regions of countries (e.g. Hölzl, 2009). However, Schreyer (2000, p. 29) highlights the importance of "appropriate institutional, legal and administrative framework conditions". Hence, one critical point is to shed light on these framework conditions which may erode the entrepreneur's motivation to grow. This will be done – to a certain extent – in this chapter.

Adopting an eclectic approach, we will try to determine why some countries have more high-growth firms than others. Hence, the purpose of this chapter is to analyse the determinants of the percentage of high-growth firms at the country level. Our database contains 17 countries over a period of seven years (1999–2005) with information from the Amadeus data set, the Global Entrepreneurship Monitor (GEM), and others.

The first remarkable feature of this contribution is that it is the first empirical analysis of high-growth firms at the country level. Second, we find indicative empirical evidence for three driving forces of high growth: entrepreneurship, institutional settings, and opportunities for growth. Third, the contribution gives a tentative explanation of the differences in the average percentage of high-growth firms between countries. Finally, it gives some clues for policy makers on how to promote high-growth firms.

The chapter is structured as follows. Section 2 is on theory: what sort of determinants are proposed in the literature? Subsequently, Section 3 describes the database and presents the model. In Section 4, the empirical results are presented. Finally, we sum up and discuss the policy relevance of our results.

2.   THEORY

2.1   Entrepreneurial Environment

A starting point for our empirical model is that the entrepreneurial environment may affect the percentage of high-growth firms in a country because entrepreneurship exerts a positive impact on competitiveness and growth by creating knowledge spillover, and increasing diversity and competition (Audretsch and Thurik, 2004). Moreover, the link between entrepreneurial abilities and the growth of firms is obvious. Hence, the level of entrepreneurship in a country may in some way or other influence the percentage of high-growth firms. In this study we investigate three different channels in which the entrepreneurial environment may be of influence.

First, we consider the level of education in a country, because it is thought to affect positively entrepreneurs' motivations and firm performance (Hessels et al., 2008). Education generates higher levels of (expected) entrepreneurial ability that, in turn, increases the levels of entrepreneurial performance (Lucas, 1978; Van Praag and Cramer, 2001). Empirical evidence shows a positive relationship between level of education and high-growth entrepreneurs because more-educated entrepreneurs may be better prepared to identify market opportunities (Davidsson, 1991) and have more growth-oriented aspirations (Cassar, 2006, 2007; Stam et al., 2009) given that they will pursue higher returns for their investment (Levie and Autio, 2008; Autio, 2009). Furthermore, van Stel et al. (2011) have shown that a higher level of education has a positive impact on the performance of the average entrepreneur because: (i) it will modify the demand function and the entrepreneur's output; (ii) it will affect positively the productivity of the firm; and (iii) it may be a signal of the presence of universities, which may generate knowledge spillover to nearby firms.

Second, the psychological research shows that entrepreneurs with higher growth-oriented ambitions may allocate more effort to pursue higher returns for their investment, and thereby realize higher growth (Orser and Hogarth-Scott, 2002; Wiklund and Shepherd, 2003).[1] But what kind of motivation is important for firm growth? On the one hand, income motivation may affect entrepreneurial growth preferences (Cassar, 2007; Hessels et al., 2008). On the other hand, another reason to opt for entrepreneurship is greater independence. We argue that entrepreneurs who created a firm in order to achieve a higher level of independence may be less motivated to undertake risky projects in order to expand their firm.

Third, if entrepreneurship is thought to be a desirable career choice in a country, we expect a relatively high percentage of high-growth firms in that country. The idea is that in such a country more people will try entrepreneurship, eventually leading to better entrepreneurs and more high-growth firms (Tominc and Rebernik, 2007).

2.2   Institutional Obstacles

We argue that institutions may have an impact on firm growth. The more obstacles government impose on firms, the less attractive and the more difficult running a business becomes.

First, high employment protection represents an extra advantage for working as an employee. Furthermore, high-growth firms need easy access to the labour market in order to fuel their growth (Henrekson, 2007). Falkenhall and Junkka (2009) argue that, in order to promote fast-growing firms, countries should ensure competitive markets and low barriers to entry. Hence, we expect that employment protection negatively affects high-growth firms.

Second, a higher administrative burden will diminish entrepreneurial activity and firm growth (Djankov et al., 2002). However, Capelleras et al. (2005) find no significant differences in the subsequent growth of new enterprises in two different regulated countries, England and Spain. Nevertheless, we expect that administrative burden influences high-growth firms negatively.

2.3   Opportunities for Growth

Limitation of growth opportunities may moderate the impact of growth aspirations on actual growth (Wiklund and Shepherd, 2003). First, exporting to other countries presents extra difficulties that not all firms are able to face. In line with Davidsson (1991, p. 412), we expect countries with a large domestic market to have a higher percentage of high-growth firms.

Second, dynamic economies may enhance the opportunities for firms to grow fast. Bosma et al. (2009) and Bowen and De Clercq (2008) indicate that higher-income countries offer more opportunities for growth and higher availability of necessary resources for growth entrepreneurship.

Hence, we expect a positive relationship between real GDP growth and the presence of high-growth firms.

Third, distance from the technological frontier may influence the growth opportunities in a country. The further a country is from this technological frontier, the more growth opportunities will exist in such a country and the more high-growth firms it will have. Stenholm et al. (2010) find that growth expectations are higher in so-called transit economies compared to Western European countries. Hölzl (2010) shows that R&D plays a more important role for high-growth firms in countries close to technological frontiers. Also there is evidence that high-growth firms are able to obtain higher returns from innovation and invest more in R&D (Coad and Rao, 2008, 2010).

Fourth, the perception of good business opportunities may affect the existence of high-growth firms. First, it may be the case that this perception is actually true, so that there are indeed more and better business opportunities and more firms will actually manage to grow fast. Second, the general perception of profitability opportunities in the market, as seen by the people of the country themselves, may affect firm growth in itself (Reitan, 1997). This very perception may encourage the creation of new firms and their performance (Davidsson, 1991; Tominc and Rebernik, 2007). Consequently, our hypothesis is that the percentage of people who think there are good business opportunities in their country has a positive relation with the percentage of high-growth firms.

Finally, we expect that the growth expectations of the entrepreneurs themselves will be positively related to the percentage of high-growth firms in a country. Again there are two mechanisms: (i) the growth expectations can be based on really better prospects; and (ii) they can act as self-fulfilling prophesies.

3. DATA AND ECONOMETRIC MODEL

3.1 Data

This study uses a wide variety of data sources: first, the Amadeus database to obtain information on high-growth firms; second, the Adult Population Survey (APS) data collected in the GEM study. It also uses the World Bank statistical and Doing Business databases, the IMF World Economic Outlook database, the CEP-OECD Institutions data set, and Eurostat. We consider 17 countries (Austria, Belgium, the Czech Republic, Denmark, Finland, France, Germany, Hungary, Ireland, Italy, Japan, the Netherlands, Poland, Spain, Sweden, the United Kingdom and the United States) for the period 1999–2005. We have 112 observations.[2]

3.1.1   Dependent variable

High growth is the percentage of firms with 50–1000 employees that have realized an average turnover growth of 20 per cent per year over the last three years (Snel et al., 2010; Timmermans et al., 2009).[3]

3.1.2   Variables characterizing the entrepreneurial environment

- *Tertiary education*: percentage of students in tertiary education over the population in the 18–23 age group.
- *Income motive*: percentage of early-stage entrepreneurs declaring that their motive to become an entrepreneur was to increase their personal income. The value corresponds to the year 2005.
- *Independence motive*: percentage of early-stage entrepreneurs declaring that their motive to become an entrepreneur was to obtain greater independence. The value corresponds to the year 2005.
- *Desirable career choice*: percentage of inhabitants of a country who think that most people in their country consider starting a new business a desirable career choice. The value corresponds to the year 2006.

3.1.3   Variables indicating institutional obstacles

- *Employment protection*: index that measures the strictness of employment protection legislation, where higher values correspond to higher employment protection.
- *Start-up procedures*: number of procedures that a start-up has to comply with in order to obtain a legal status. The value corresponds to 2005.

3.1.4   Variables indicating opportunities for growth

- *Population size*: log number of inhabitants (with base 2).
- *GDP growth*: percentage of the annual change of GDP at constant prices.
- *Technological development*: ratio of overall productivity (added value per worker at constant prices and expressed in US$) of the USA and the country under consideration.
- *Business opportunities*: percentage of inhabitants who think that in the next six months there will be good opportunities for starting a business in the area where they live.
- *Growth expectation*: percentage of early-stage entrepreneurs who expect to have over 19 employees in five years.

3.2   Model

Our model uses the following expression:

$$HG_{i,t} = \alpha + \beta_1 X_{1i,t} + \beta_2 X_{2i} + u_{i,t}$$

where $HG_{i,t}$ denotes the percentage of high-growth observations of a country (i) in a year (t), $X_{1i,t}$ the time-dependent variables, X_{2i} the time-invariant variables, and $u_{i,t}$ the error term. Since the dependent variable is a fractional response form, Papke and Wooldridge (1996) propose the Fractional Logit Regression Model (FLRM) using Quasi-Maximum Likelihood Estimation (QMLE), which maximizes the Bernoulli log-likelihood function:

$$Max \ln L = \sum \ln L_{i,t} = \sum [HG_{it} \ln G(\beta_1 X_{1i,t}, \beta_2 X_{2i}) + (1-HG_{it}) \ln(1-G(\beta_1 X_{1i,t}, \beta_2 X_{2i}))]$$

Because high growth is a phenomenon over a three-year period, one could argue that there is an inherent dependence between consecutive observations because of the two overlapping years. For instance, the percentages of high-growth firms in the periods 2002–2004 and 2003–2005 might be correlated because they share two overlapping years (2003 and 2004). However, most of the high-growth firms in one period are no longer high growth in the consecutive period. Indeed, in practice high growth appears to be a highly volatile phenomenon at the individual firm level.[4]

4.   RESULTS

Table 4.1 shows our results. Model (1) includes our five independent variables for which we have information for the whole period. The influence of all variables appears to be significant with the expected sign and with a low level of dispersion.[5]

The quality of entrepreneurship in a country seems to matter. Hence, higher enrolment in tertiary education can be associated with better potential for entrepreneurship country, which may give rise to more high growth.

We find also evidence that institutional obstacles may play a negative role with respect to the percentage of high-growth firms. In Section 2 we explained why a larger domestic market may lead to more high growth. Indeed, we find that if population size – our proxy for the size of the domestic market – doubles, this is associated with approximately 0.7 percentage points more high-growth firms.[6] We have argued that high GDP

Table 4.1 Explaining the percentage of high-growth firms: marginal effects of FLRMs

	Model (1)	Model (2)	Model (3)	Model (4)	Model (5)
Entrepreneurship					
Tertiary education	0.22***	0.23***	0.22***	0.18***	0.23***
	(0.04)	(0.05)	(0.04)	(0.05)	(0.04)
Income motive		0.23***			
		(0.06)			
Independence motive			−0.30***		
			(0.06)		
Desirable career choice		0.17***			
		(0.05)			
Institutional obstacles					
Employment protection	−3.27***	−2.28***	−2.23***	−3.02***	−2.37***
	(0.70)	(0.74)	(0.65)	(0.69)	(0.85)
Start-up procedures		−0.38*			
		(0.26)			
Opportunities for growth					
Population size	0.67**	0.59*	0.37	1.01***	0.65**
	(0.31)	(0.36)	(0.30)	(0.32)	(0.32)
GDP growth	2.06***	1.62***	1.96***	1.98***	1.98***
	(0.30)	(0.28)	(0.28)	(0.29)	(0.31)
Technological development	2.31***	2.26***	2.18***	2.53***	2.43***
	(0.42)	(0.40)	(0.36)	(0.41)	(0.40)
Business opportunities				0.10**	
				(0.05)	
Growth expectation					2.48
					(0.00)
Pearson χ^2	0.0179	0.0139	0.0152	0.0176	0.0179
AIC	0.7883	0.8369	0.8029	0.8055	0.8058
BIC	−49814	−484.54	−493.79	−493.50	−493.46
Number of observations 112					

Notes: AIC, Akaike information criterion; BIC, Bayesian information criterion.
Standard errors in parentheses.
*** p < 0.01, ** p < 0.05, * p < 0.1.

growth is associated with more high-growth firms. This is a two-way relationship: higher GDP growth leads to more growth opportunities for firms and, vice versa, more high-growth firms may lead to higher GDP growth. Hence, the positive relationship that we find for GDP growth and high-growth firms should not be interpreted as causal. Therefore, GDP growth is a control variable.[7] Finally, countries far from the technological frontier show more opportunities for high growth.

Model (2) incorporates as many independent variables as possible, while taking care to avoid multicollinearity.[8]

Results of model (1) remain robust in model (2). Additionally, the Pearson χ^2 test and the BIC obtain the lowest value in model (2), but the AIC shows a slightly higher value than model (1). Hence, in spite of the increase in AIC it seems that model (2) is the best specified.

The ambition of entrepreneurs in a country seems to influence high growth. If more early-stage entrepreneurs declare that their motive to become an entrepreneur was to increase their personal income, this is associated with more high growth. Furthermore, the status of entrepreneurship seems to matter also. Finally, we find that a higher administrative burden leads to fewer high-growth firms.

Because of multicollinearity we had to leave out three of our independent variables in model (2). In models (3)–(5) of Table 4.1 we inserted these variables separately one by one in model (1). Again model (1) appears robust.

We find that if many entrepreneurs in a country are motivated towards entrepreneurship in this way, we would expect relatively few high-growth firms, as explained in Section 2. Finally, if people in a country see more business opportunities or early-stage entrepreneurs expect more growth, then we would expect more high-growth firms in that country. Models (4) and (5) confirm these expectations.

With the above models it is possible to give a tentative explanation of the differences in the average percentage of high-growth firms between countries. We will do such a tentative exercise on the basis of model (2).

Figure 4.1 shows the percentage points that are explained by each explanatory variable. We may highlight the following results:

- For most countries model (2) explains the average percentage of high-growth firms quite well, except for the Czech Republic, Hungary, Italy and Spain.
- The United States has on average the highest percentage of high-growth firms. The most important determinants are: (i) high enrolment in tertiary education; (ii) many entrepreneurs wishing to obtain a higher income; (iii) a low degree of employment protection; (iv) a large domestic market.

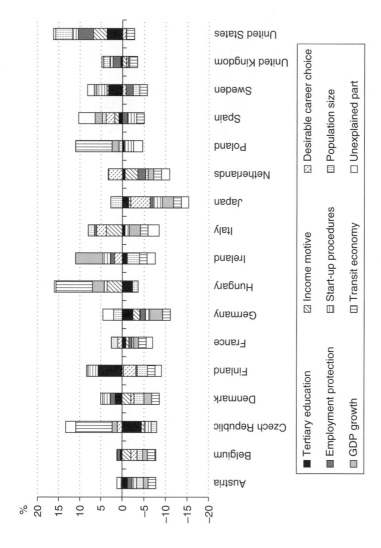

Figure 4.1   Explaining the average percentage of high-growth firms between countries on the basis of model (2) from Table 4.1

- Japan has the lowest percentage of high-growth firms. Nearly all distinguished variables contribute to this. The two most important determinants are: (i) few Japanese think that entrepreneurship is a desirable career choice and (ii) low GDP growth in the period of investigation.

5. SUMMARY

This study gives some insights into the driving forces for the number of high-growth firms in a country. The first contribution is that– as far as we know – it is the first empirical analysis of high growth at the country level on the basis of actual measured growth. The second contribution is that we find indicative empirical evidence for three driving forces of high growth – namely entrepreneurship, institutional settings and opportunities for growth – all in accordance with theory and empirical findings in related fields of research. Third, on the basis of the findings of this study it is possible to give a tentative explanation of the differences in the average percentage of high-growth firms between countries.

For those policy makers seeking to stimulate high growth in their country, the contribution has a number of suggestions. First of all, results suggest that entrepreneurship has a positive influence on high growth. Three specific channels appear to stimulate entrepreneurship:

- enrolment in tertiary education, which may lead to a higher quality of entrepreneurship;
- the ambition of entrepreneurs (as measured by their motive for becoming an entrepreneur);
- promoting the notion that entrepreneurship is a desirable career choice.

Second, results suggest that institutional obstacles play a negative role. The study provides tentative evidence that the following two strategies might be fruitful in this context:

- lowering the degree of employment protection legislation, thereby (i) making the choice for entrepreneurship more attractive and (ii) lowering the risks when attracting employees to the high-growth firm;
- lowering the administrative burden for firms.

Finally, the size of the domestic market has a positive influence on high-growth firms. This suggests that the creation of common markets with other countries may be a good strategy.

NOTES

*   This research was financed by SCALES, SCientific Analysis of Entrepreneurship
    and SMEs (www.entrepreneurship-sme.eu), the Spanish Ministry of Economics and
    Competitiveness and European funds from FEDER in the project ECO2015-68061-R
    and the Consolidated Group of Research 2014–SGR–1395.
1. Even though ambition does not guarantee growth, absence of ambition almost certainly
    guarantees absence of growth (Autio, 2009).
2. There are no observations for the dependent variable in 2002 for Austria, the Czech
    Republic, Poland, Spain and Sweden; for Hungary, there are no observations for 2002
    and 2003.
3. Actually, we investigated the influence of some more independent variables, including
    enrolment in secondary education, development of the financial system and level of
    export barriers, among others. Because these variables did not appear to have significant
    influence, we do not describe them here and do not include them in the final regression
    models in Section 5.
4. We perform several checks on the robustness of the standard errors reported. One of the
    main econometric problems in our estimation procedure may be caused by the fact that
    the observations of our variables within a country are highly correlated. First, we correct
    the standard errors by using the so-called Moulton factor (Moulton, 1986). Second, we
    make such a correction by repeating the main analysis while clustering the standard errors
    by country. Third, we correct the standard errors by bootstrapping the distribution of the
    empirical data with clustered data at the country level. Results are available in Teruel and
    Wit (2011).
5. The Pearson χ^2 test is equal to 0.0179, which indicates that the level of dispersion is low.
6. This holds true because population size is measured by the logarithm with base 2.
7. One way of disentangling this two-way causal relationship would be to introduce various
    lagged GDP growth rates into our model. We refrain from such an exercise here because:
    (i) this is not the primary aim of the study; (ii) because of the sample size, we want to
    restrict ourselves to a minimum number of independent variables. Nevertheless, we have
    experimented with it. The results are available upon request.
8. In this approach, we first tried all 11 independent variables at once. Subsequently, we
    dropped the least significant variable successively until all remaining variables were
    significant.

REFERENCES

Acs, Z.J., Parsons, W. and Tracy, S. (2008): "High-impact firms: gazelles revisited".
    SBA reports. Washington, DC: SBA Office of Advocacy.
Audretsch, D.B. (2002): "The dynamic role of small firms: evidence from the U.S.",
    Small Business Economics, **18**: 13–40.
Audretsch, D.B. and Thurik, R. (2004): "A model of the entrepreneurial economy",
    International Journal of Entrepreneurship Education, **2**: 143–166.
Autio, E. (2007): "GEM 2007 report on high-growth entrepreneurship", GEM
    Global Reports. London: GERA.
Autio, E. (2009): "The Finnish paradox: the curious absence of high-growth entre-
    preneurship in Finland", Research Institute of the Finnish Economy, discussion
    papers no. 1197.
Birch, D., Haggerty, A. and Parsons, W. (1997): *Who's Creating Jobs?*, Cambridge,
    MA: Cognetics.

Bosma, N., Acs, Z.J., Autio, E., Coduras, A. and Levie, J. (2009): "Global Entrepreneurship Monitor 2008", Executive report: Babson College and Universidad del Desarrollo. http://gemconsortium.org/default.aspx.

Bowen, H.P. and De Clercq, D. (2008): "Institutional context and the allocation of entrepreneurial effort", *Journal of International Business Studies*, **39**: 747–767.

Capelleras, J., Mole, K., Greene, F.J. and Storey, D.J. (2005): "Do more heavily regulated economies have poorer performing new ventures? Evidence from Britain and Spain", CSME working paper series no. 86, University of Warwick.

Cassar, G. (2006): "Entrepreneur opportunity costs and intended venture growth", *Journal of Business Venturing*, **21**: 610–632.

Cassar, G. (2007): "Money, money, money? A longitudinal investigation of entrepreneur career reasons, growth preferences and achieved growth", *Entrepreneurship and Regional Development*, **19**: 89–107.

Coad, A. and Rao, R. (2008): "Innovation and firm growth in high-tech sectors: A quantile regression approach", *Research Policy*, **37**: 633–648.

Coad, A. and Rao, R. (2010): "Firm growth and R&D expenditure", *Economics of Innovation and New Technology*, **19**(2): 127–145.

Davidsson, P. (1991): "Continued entrepreneurship: ability, need, and opportunity as determinants of small firm growth", *Journal of Business Venturing*, **6**: 405–429.

Delmar, F.F., Davidsson, P. and Gartner, W.B. (2003): "Arriving at the high-growth firm", *Journal of Business Venturing*, **18**: 189–216.

Djankov, S., La Porta, R., Lopez-de-Silanes, F. and Shleifer, A. (2002): "The regulation of entry", *Quarterly Journal of Economics*, **117**: 1–37.

Falkenhall, B. and Junkka, F. (2009): "High-growth firms in Sweden 1997–2007", Swedish Agency for Growth Policy Analysis.

Henrekson, M. (2007): "Entrepreneurship and institutions", *Comparative Labour Law and Policy Journal*, **28**: 717–742.

Henrekson, M. and Johansson, D. (2009): "Competencies and institutions fostering high-growth firms", *Foundations and Trends in Entrepreneurship*, **5**: 1–80.

Henrekson, M. and Johansson, D. (2010): "Gazelles as job creators: a survey and interpretation of the evidence", *Small Business Economics*, **35**: 227–244.

Hessels, J., van Gelderen, M. and Thurik, R. (2008): "Entrepreneurial aspirations, motivations, and their drivers", *Small Business Economics*, **31**: 323–339.

Hölzl, W. (2009): "Is the R&D behaviour of fast-growing SMEs different? Evidence from CIS III data for 16 countries", *Small Business Economics*, **33**: 59–75.

Hölzl, W. (2010): "High-growth firms, innovation and the distance to the frontier", *Economics Bulletin*, **30**(2): 1016–1024.

Levie, J. and Autio, E. (2008): "A theoretical grounding and test of the GEM model", *Small Business Economics*, **31**: 235–263.

Lucas, Jr, R.E. (1978): "On the size distribution of business firms", *Bell Journal of Economics*, **9**: 508–523.

Moulton, B.R. (1986), "Random group effects and the precision of regression estimates", *Journal of Econometrics*, **32**: 385–397.

Orser, B. and Hogarth-Scott, S. (2002): "Opting for growth: gender dimensions of choosing enterprise development", *Canadian Journal of Administrative Sciences*, 19: 284–300.

Papke, L. and Wooldridge, J. (1996): "Econometric methods for fractional response variables with an application to 401(K) plan participation rates", *Journal of Applied Econometrics*, **11**(6): 619–632.

Reitan, B. (1997): "Where do we learn that entrepreneurship is feasible, desirable and/or profitable", ICSB World Conference.

Schreyer, P. (2000): "High-growth firms and employment", OECD Science, Technology and Industry working papers, 2000/3. doi: 10.1787/861275538813.

Snel, D., Bakker, K., Verhoeven, W.H.J., in't Hout, R. and Timmermans, N.G.L. (2010): "Internationale benchmark ondernemerschap 2010", EIM report A201006, available at www.ondernemerschap.nl.

Stam, E., Suddle, K., Hessels, J. and van Stel, A. (2009): "Public policies for fostering entrepreneurship", *International Studies in Entrepreneurship*, **22**: 91–110.

Stenholm, P., Autio, E. and Acs, Z.J. (2010): "Institutional approach on growth-oriented entrepreneurship", mimeo.

Storey, D.J. (1994): *Understanding the Small Business Sector*. London: Routledge.

Teruel, M. and de Wit, G. (2011): "Determinants of high-growth firms: why do some countries have more high-growth firms than others?, URV working paper no. 33-2011.

Timmermans, N.G.L., Verhoeven, W.H.J. and in't Hout, R. (2009): "Internationale Benchmark 2009 Extra Landen", EIM report M200907, available at www.ondernemerschap.nl.

Tominc, P. and Rebernik, M. (2007): "Growth aspirations and cultural support for entrepreneurship: a comparison of post-socialist countries", *Small Business Economics*, **28**: 239–255.

Van Praag, C.M. and Cramer, J. S. (2001): "The roots of entrepreneurship and labour demand: individual ability and low risk aversion", *Economica*, **68**: 45–62.

Van Stel, A., van Praag, M., Millan, J.M., Congregado, E. and Roman, C. (2011): "The value of an educated population for an individual's entrepreneurship success", SCALES research reports, EIM Business and Policy Research.

Wiklund, J. and Shepherd, D. (2003): "Aspiring for, and achieving growth: the moderating role of resources and opportunities", *Journal of Management Studies*, **40**: 1919–1941.

5. Institutions, entrepreneurship, and regional growth in Indonesia (1994–2010)

François Facchini and Subandono

INTRODUCTION

The aim of this chapter is to explain the relationship between institutions, entrepreneurship, and economic growth. It contributes to the modern Austrian theory of economic development by developing an original theory of institutional flexibility. It suggests that the Schumpeterian figure of the innovator and the Kirznerian figure of the discoverer may only appear when the institutions of economic order are flexible. Its originality is in the definition of institutional flexibility. An institutional system is deemed flexible when it constructs an order that is neither contingent nor determinist. Private property rights, contracts, and money organize human behavior without determining it. By protecting economic freedom, people may believe that they can act to change the future to their advantage.

It describes two motivations, both empirical and theoretical. The empirical aim is to contribute to the debate on the role of entrepreneurship in developing and poor countries. Entrepreneurship is a vital force in the economics of developed countries (Audretsch and Keilbach, 2004). However, its role in developing and poor countries remains unclear. Empirically, van Stel et al. (2005) found that entrepreneurial activity has a positive effect on economic growth in developed countries, whereas the effect is negative for poor countries and remains unclear in developing countries. Thus, this study seeks to uncover empirically the role of entrepreneurship in Indonesia as a developing country. It considers not only the dichotomies in defining entrepreneurship (i.e. formal/informal, legal/illegal and necessity/opportunity), but also the existence of regional spatial dependency.

The theoretical motivation explains why economic freedom encourages the entrepreneur to act in a way conducive to economic development. Several studies have found a positive link between economic freedom and different measures of entrepreneurship (e.g., Bjornskov and Foss 2008;

Hall et al. 2012). How do we explain this positive relationship? Economic freedom is a particular institutional system.

Institutions are "rules of a game in a society or more formally are the humanly devised constraints that shape human interaction" (North, 1990, p. 3). The classical contributions to entrepreneurial economics suggest several determinants of entrepreneurship, including: the degree to which a person is "venturesome"; the ambition and intelligence to exercise leadership; and the institutions themselves (Bjornskov and Foss, 2008). If economic growth is the goal, attention should be paid to achieve the institutional mix that encourages the entrepreneurial aspect of human action. In this perspective, two approaches are possible: the first defines institutions as an incentive structure that affects the allocation of talent (Baumol, 1990); the second defines institutions by knowledge.

The economic problem of society is "how to secure the best use of resources known to any of the members of society, for ends whose relative importance only these individuals know" (Hayek, 1945, p. 520).

Information institution enables individuals to use more knowledge than that acquired alone, and to cross the ignorance frontiers through the experiences of their group (Hayek, 1994). It also limits possibilities (Heiner, 1983), uncertainty and ignorance, and facilitates cooperation (Hayek, 1986) and agent coordination. Free market institution and market price have decisive roles in solving the knowledge-dispersal problem due to the possibility of economic calculation.

In the Kirznerian perspective, alertness to profit opportunities is the essence of entrepreneurship (Harper, 2003). The entrepreneur recognizes something that others have failed to recognize. It has a cognitive function. Institutions have an effect on economic growth, if they affect entrepreneurial alertness. What are the sources of human propensity to be alert? Harper (2003) uses social psychology to answer this. Instead, here we mobilize Thomas Aquinas's philosophy of prudence. We define alertness as prudence and explain on this basis how economic institutions create a social order favorable for prudence and, *in fine*, favor entrepreneurial activity. This is our theoretical contribution to the literature about the relationship between institutions, entrepreneurship, and economic growth.

The rest of this chapter is organized as follows. The next section shows why entrepreneurship favors economic growth. Then we explain how the free market institution creates the natural condition of human freedom. We give an application. Finally, we discuss the empirical results and conclude.

ENTREPRENEURSHIP AND ECONOMIC GROWTH: KNOWLEDGE SPILLOVER ROLE

The driving forces of economic development are the innovation and coordination activity of the entrepreneurs who direct resources towards their most profitable uses. The effective causes of economic development lie not only in entrepreneurial innovative actions (Schumpeter, 1934) but also in the discovery of profit opportunities (Kirzner, 1973). Audretsch and Keilbach (2004) integrated these theoretical concepts and treated entrepreneurs as the drivers of the knowledge selection process that promotes economic growth. Not all innovation investment can be implemented as a new commercialized product/process, due to the existence of a knowledge filter which is a gap between potential and actual commercialized knowledge. The role of entrepreneurs is to select this potential knowledge by reducing its nature, which is characterized by uncertainty and information asymmetry, and which bears some transaction costs.

There are two major spillover channels. First, a firm engages in the research and development (RD) activities to create new innovation, and other firms adapt this innovation – hence spilling over knowledge (Audretsch and Keilbach, 2004 citing Cohen and Levinthal, 1989). The second channel refers to individuals rather than firms (Audretsch, 1995). Entrepreneurs transform potential economic knowledge into actual economic knowledge by starting up a firm. The selection process, which promotes knowledge spillover and increases the number of new startups, affects positively competition on new ideas and facilitates new entry bringing new innovation. Moreover, the increase of new-firm startups favors knowledge diversity due to the existence of various enterprises that may promote specialization, productivity, and growth. Knowledge exists, and entrepreneurs give value to this knowledge, after being alerted to its possible profitability. To explain economic development in this Misessian perspective, we must say why individuals change their posture *vis-à-vis* profit – why they are alert.

INSTITUTIONAL PREREQUISITES OF ENTREPRENEURIAL ACTIVITY

As Harper (2003, p. 35) writes, hypothesis about the principal determinants of entrepreneurship is "strongly conditioned by the particular set of disciplinary spectacles through which one looks" (see also Bjørnskov and Foss, 2008). If entrepreneurs are those persons endowed with alertness, an important line of enquiry is to explain the psychological determinants of individual differences in entrepreneurial alertness. Considering "what are the sources of human propensity to be alert?", Harper (2003, p. 35) argues that individuals' beliefs are a major determinant of alertness. Thomas Aquinas's theory of prudence is also a means to renew the answer to the question (Facchini, 2007).

The Entrepreneur and Prudence

Say (1971 [1803], p. 379) already stated that "ceux qui manquent de *prudence et de lumières*, ne font pas longtemps concurrence à ceux qui en sont pourvus". Aristotle also maintained that economy is the field of prudence (Ross, 1925). The prudent man is in moral philosophy a man like all the others (Aubenque, 1963). The prudent man is a man of action. He is not scientific and/or a philosopher. Prudence "is right reason applied to action" (Thomas d'Aquin, 1984, Q.47 art.8). A prudent man is one who is capable of taking good counsel (ibid., art.2). Counsel is about things that we must do in relation to some ends, and the reason that deals with things to be done for an end is a practical reason. The first act is "to take counsel", which belongs to discovery. This is an act of inquiry. The second act is "to judge of what one has discovered", and this is an act of speculative reason. But the practical reason, which is directed at action, goes further, and its third act is "to command", which implements the things that have been counseled and judged.

These three steps of prudence correspond to the debates surrounding the notion of alertness and Kirzner's defenses. Indeed, critics suggest that the essence of entrepreneurship can be sought in such qualities as imagination (White, 1976) or judgment (High, 1982). Kirzner (1994) attempted to meet some of these critics, and recognized that alertness in a world of uncertainty may call for good judgment and lively imagination.

Alertness is the prudence which leads individuals to know the consequence of their effort. We argue that only the institution that is neither contingent nor determinist serves the prudence posture. A determinist world is a world where the result of an action is determined *ex ante*. Individuals know that they will not have more than 100 Euros whichever way they act. Strict concrete rules frame an individual's actions. They determine exactly with whom and under what conditions an individual can exchange. They thus produce a deterministic order in which the future is completely certain. In contrast, institutions can create a contingent world if they do not define clearly a distribution rule *ex ante*. Without rules, nobody is constrained to follow any known and accepted rules. Order exists only for the master who has the power to allocate the rights of wealth. The coordination of human action is difficult because individuals do not follow any code of conduct to stabilize their behavior, facilitate cooperation, limit ignorance and reduce uncertainty.

Therefore, the implementation of rules that render the future completely certain atrophies the entrepreneurial spirit, which remains in a latent state. Institution can only create the required conditions for entrepreneurship to leave a pure contingent world. Economic development is thus conditioned by the more or less contingent nature of the institutional order. On this basis, we argue that economic freedom (i.e. private property rights, contracts, and money) creates an order that is neither determinist nor contingent, and respects the ontological conditions of human freedom.

Private Property Rights and Certainty about the Rules of the Game

Private property rights encourage the entrepreneur to promote economic development because they give an inalienable right to products. The exclusivity and transferability of property rights promote individuals to act in the most advantageous way for them and their group because "One takes more troubles, when it comes to acquiring something which is belong to one than if it is belong to the community or to a group" and because "human activity is more orderly, if each individual is responsible for one particular object" (Thomas d'Aquin, 1984, Q.66 art.2).

Thus, private property rights ensure that each person bears the costs and enjoys the benefits of their actions. It gives individuals the authority over how to use their possessions and how to determine the distribution of benefits and losses with the decision makers. It thus determines with certainty the beneficiaries of actions without determining *ex ante* the *ex post* amount of benefits. There is certainty of distribution rules (contracts), but uncertainty about the results (Hayek, 1986).

Exclusivity guarantees that entrepreneurs will profit from their actions, which in turn stimulates productivity, investment, and development (Dawson, 1998). Investment is determined by the institutional conditions of human action (Besley, 1995). Growth is determined by the investment level. It is thus connected to the respect of private property rights. Entrepreneurs invest because the rules guarantee their ownership of the expected profits even if they do not consume them (saving). It thus encourages individuals to undertake long-term projects, to improve production plans, and to adapt to future demand. Uncertainty about results, on the other hand, introduces an undetermined aspect. It also contributes to the process of development because it incites individuals to modify the exchange terms when they consider the latter unfavorable (Witt, 1987).

Private Property Rights are the Foundation of Contractual Freedom

Property rights are a condition of contractual freedom. In the market, it is the contracts freely agreed between agents that determine *ex ante* what each one will gain *ex post*. Contracts of exchanges are a form of private constitutional contract. Individuals constrain themselves mutually to restrict their future options. Freedom to contract is, in this sense, freedom to impose and self-impose restrictions on future behavior. For this reason, a contract produces a determined order. It defines the transaction *ex ante* what each party will gain *ex post*. Therefore, the rules that are produced by the contracts fix with certainty what an individual can rely on.

However, it is enough to withdraw from contracts to reopen the undetermined future. Free withdrawal from contracts without conditions is identical to disorder. For this reason a non-deterministic and non-contingent order is an order which regulates withdrawal without completely forbidding it. The right to withdraw enables individuals to remain free without rendering order impossible. Contracts thus form the foundation of a non-deterministic and non-contingent order that encourages productive activities favoring economic development.

Private Property Rights and Monetary Stability

Private property rights are also a condition of monetary stability by protecting each agent against inflation and currency risks (de Soto, 1998). It favors monetary stability for two reasons. First, it limits the generalization of fractional reserves. Second, it controls bankers through competition (Hayek, 1978). The right to choose a currency puts the creators of money (private banks in a free banking system) in competition with each other. Entrepreneurs can sanction bankers who exploit their currency value for political (in a central bank system) or economic reasons (in free banking and central bank systems). Thanks to the right to choose a currency, the currency creators are always under pressure from the users to secure their profits. It also prevents the currency creators from adopting inalienable rights over their share of the market – the discipline that forces bankers to guarantee price stability and development.

APPLICATION

Indonesia is a mixed system that is neither a fully free market nor an absolutely socialist one. The mixed system socializes only a portion of profits and gives entrepreneurs the possibility of negotiating the amount that must be allocated to society through a political process (democracy). First, we examine the hypothesis that entrepreneurs affect economic growth by spilling over knowledge. We complete Audretsch and Keilbach's (2004) model by the inclusion of public infrastructures for the case of developing countries. We argue that entrepreneurship increases the benefit value of infrastructures by mobilizing knowledge.

Hypothesis 1: Entrepreneurship influences positively economic growth through the interaction between knowledge and public infrastructures.

The effect of entrepreneurship on economic growth depends on the more or less contingent nature of the institutional order. So secondly, we test our proposition that economic freedom as a flexible institution has an effect on the entrepreneur's prudence posture. A freer economy allows individuals to view profit opportunities and promotes productive activities, whereas a less free economy encourages rent activities producing no wealth.

Hypothesis 2: Government size, tax regulation, public enterprise intervention, labor market regulation, business and corruption perception affect negatively an individual's prudence vis-à-vis profit opportunities, hence allowing individuals to perceive rent opportunities.

Estimation Model and Variable Description

We test the first hypothesis using the following growth equation:

$$\log (y_{i,t0} / y_{i,t-1}) = \alpha - \beta_1 \log(y_{i,t-1}) + \beta_2 X_{i,t-1} + \beta_3 E_{i,t-1} + \varepsilon_{i,t} \qquad (1)$$

Where $t=1994$–2010, $i=$region, y_i is labor productivity of region i, X_i is neo-classical growth variables (investment and labor force growth), and E_i is entrepreneurial measures.

Productivity and entrepreneurship may depend on a third variable that is the regional industry structure. We therefore include RD activities and public infrastructure, and consider entrepreneurship as a function of labor productivity and human capital (H_i).

$$E_{i,t0} = \int(y_{i,t-1}, H_{i,t-1}) \qquad (2)$$

Next, we estimate the effect of economic freedom on entrepreneurship using the following equation:

$$E_{i,t} = \alpha_i + \beta_1 G_{i,t} + \beta_2 G^2_{i,t} + \beta_3 X_{i,t} + \beta_4 Z_{i,t} + \varepsilon_{i,t} \qquad (3)$$

where E_i is entrepreneurial measures in region i, G_i is government size, X_i is economic freedom measures, and Z_i the control variables. Table 5.1 describes the panel statistics.[1]

We consider the possibility of spatial dependence (Anselin and Hudak, 1992), as the entrepreneurial activities of a region may induce effects on entrepreneurial activities in adjacent regions. Thus, we estimate the spatially autoregressive dependent variable (SAR) to measure spatial dependency on regional entrepreneurship. Our spatial weight matrix is constructed using longitude and latitude data.[2]

RESULTS

We estimate the relationship between entrepreneurship and economic growth by examining equations (1) and (2) as recursive models through three stages least squares. Table 5.2 reports the effect of self-employment (columns 1 and 2) and corporate density (columns 3 and 4) on productivity growth.

First, the coefficients of $log(y_{i,t-1})$ that refer to the initial productivity are negative, confirming the process of economic convergence. The investment and labor force growth coefficients have the expected sign according to predictions of neo-classical growth theory. The interactions between RD and public infrastructures have a positive impact on productivity growth, confirming that knowledge and infrastructure are the variables for which entrepreneurship and economic growth interact with one another. We distinguish entrepreneurship sector by general and manufacturing entrepreneurship. We argue that the manufacturing sector is more correlated to RD activities than the general sector to promote the knowledge selection process. The results show that the magnitudes of the effect of manufacturing entrepreneurship on productivity growth are positively greater than the general sector, confirming that entrepreneurship fosters the selection process of potential knowledge into commercialized knowledge. The bottom part of Table 5.2 shows that higher economic growth and human capital mean higher entrepreneurial capital.

Taking into account equation (3), we test the effect of economic freedom on entrepreneurship. Table 5.3 shows the estimation effect of economic freedom on self-employment and corporate density. Linear models (LM) and robust LM tests imply that the SAR estimations are more proper than OLS ones. They confirm the existence of spatial dependency on entrepreneurship between regions. Our control variables also have the effect suggested by previous studies. We confirm that economic freedom as a flexible institution induces effects on entrepreneurship. Squared terms of

Table 5.1 Panel descriptive statistics

Variables	Description	Mean	SD	Source
Regional entrepreneurship measures				
Self-employment	Self-employed excluding agricultural sector over labor force	1.53%	0.52%	BPS
Corporate density	Registered enterprises over labor force	1.13%	1.10%	IMoF
Regional economic growth measures				
Productivity	GDRP over labor force (1983 price)	€182.58	€17.98	
Investment	Investment over GDRP	21.47	6.89	BPS
Labor growth	Labor force growth	2.37%	1.12%	
Human capital	Secondary school enrollment	45.08%	10.01%	
RD	RD expenditures over labor force	€1.06	€1.21	IMoF
Infrastructures	Gov. capital spending over GDRP	0.034	0.013	
Regional economic freedom measures				
Government size	Gov. expenditure over GDRP	26.39%	17.62%	
(excl. central government)	Gov. consumption over total consumption	7.7%	3.7%	
	Gov. investment over total investment	11.12%	4.8%	IMoF
Taxes	Tax revenues over GDRP	0.77%	0.129%	
Public enterprises	Gov. enterprise revenue over local budget	0.55%	0.32%	
Labor market	Annual minimum wages over GDRP	2.1e-04	2.0e-04	IMoWT
	Gov. wages over GDRP	4.41%	2.74%	IMoF
Business quality	Weighted average of perception on business permits delivery	0.38	0.19	IFLS-RAND
Corruption	Weighted average of perception on corruption	0.53	0.14	

Notes: The Indonesian Central Bureau of Statistics (BPS) classifies self-employment by three categories: without help of workers; with help of temporary workers; with help of regular workers. Considering the dichotomies in defining entrepreneurship (i.e. formal/informal, legal/illegal, necessity/opportunity motif), we use only self-employed with help of regular workers (excluding the agricultural sector) as our measure of entrepreneurship. IFLS = Indonesia Family life Survey.

Table 5.2   Productivity growth and entrepreneurship

	Labor productivity growth			
$\log(y_{i,t-1})$	−0.017***	−0.016***	−0.018***	−0.019***
	(−3.31)	(−2.76)	(−3.41)	(−3.56)
Investment	0.0068***	0.0057**	0.0061***	0.0063***
	(3.36)	(2.33)	(3.62)	(3.66)
Labor growth	−0.053***	−0.053***	−0.053***	−0.053***
	(−11.41)	(−10.10)	(−11.67)	(−11.57)
RD*infrastructure	0.0065***	0.0065**	0.0039	0.0053*
	(2.48)	(2.49)	(0.87)	(1.68)
General SE	0.0064**			
	(2.06)			
Manufacturing SE		1.413*		
		(1.7)		
General corporate			0.283**	
			(2.0)	
Manufacturing corp.				8.744**
				(2.34)
F-stat	7.04***	6.92***	7.18***	7.14***

	Self-employment		Corporate density	
	General	*Manufacturing*	*General*	*Manufacturing*
$\log(y_{i,t-1})$	0.407***	0.0014	0.0143***	0.0005***
	(3.04)	(1.09)	(3.54)	(3.81)
Secondary school	1.44***	0.007***	0.034***	0.0012***
	(12.26)	(6.07)	(9.53)	(9.77)
F-stat	21.1***	9.37***	79.47***	269.23***

Note: ***, ** and * indicate significance at the 1 percent, 5 percent and 10 percent level, respectively.

local government consumption and investment have a negative effect on self-employment.[3] A more reasonable explanation is that private capital is not sufficient at the startup period to engage in the marketable sectors justifying public intervention. At times, government may nevertheless pass the threshold of *laissez-faire* when sufficient private capital already exists.

Local taxes, public enterprises, and public perceptions of business permit delivery have a negative effect on entrepreneurship. Local taxes and instability of taxation rules, which have changed four times between 1994 and 2010, are obstacles for startups. In addition, several private sector industries are still managed fully or partially by the government – for example some agricultural sectors, construction, and finance. Hence it

Table 5.3   Economic freedom and entrepreneurship

Variables	Self-Employment		Corporate Density	
	Coefficient	*t-stat*	Coefficient	*t-stat*
Gov. consumption	0.014	(1.086)	0.0382***	(3.692)
Gov. consumption^2	−0.0032	(−0.148)	0.0192	(1.149)
Gov. investment	0.0036***	(2.510)	0.0013	(1.239)
Gov. investment^2	−0.0005**	(−1.913)	−0.00008	(−0.358)
Tax revenue	−0.292***	(−2.739)	−0.291***	(−3.522)
Gov. enterprise rev.	−0.1186***	(−3.145)	−0.116***	(−3.982)
Minimum wage	−0.0117***	(−3.123)	0.0706**	(2.406)
Gov. wage spending	0.036	(1.514)	−0.0453***	(−2.463)
Business quality	−0.0062*	(−1.776)	−0.0179***	(−6.618)
Corruption	0.0004	(0.062)	−0.0235***	(−4.433)
Per capita GDRP	2e-06*	(1.827)	4e-06***	(4.989)
Unemployment	0.0079	(1.229)	−0.003	(−0.603)
Population density	4e-06**	(2.123)	1,5e-05***	(10.071)
Secondary enroll	0.0179***	(4.158)	0.0171***	(5.05)
Openness	0.0009	(0.642)	−0.0006	(−0.565)
Spatial auto	0.266***	(4.423)	0.202***	(3.699)
R-squared	0.6963		0.9323	
LM test	23.44***		11.81***	
Robust LM test	47.94***		5.75**	

Note: ***, ** and * indicate significance at the 1 percent, 5 percent and 10 percent level, respectively.

is hindering individuals viewing profit opportunity. Results suggest that individuals still perceive administrative procedures as barriers to startups, and this can be linked to the cost and complexity of obtaining business permission.

A minimum wage has a negative impact on self-employment but a positive effect on corporate density, which may indicate a greater ability of firms to pay the minimum wage than self-employed individuals, mainly SMEs. In addition, the effect of government wages on corporate density is negative, indicating that individuals are more interested in working in the public than the private sector.

The effect of corruption is unclear. Self-employed individuals and mainly SMEs may perceive corruption as business complexity interchangeably. However, when the measure of entrepreneurship is corporate density, we find a clear negative effect of corruption on entrepreneurship. Firms might perceive the existence of a hostile environment for their business. In general, these results indicate that the existing institutional order does not allow Indonesia to enjoy more economic growth than it should.

CONCLUSION

The essence of entrepreneurship is alertness to opportunities. Institutions will matter for economic growth if they have influence over the source of human propensity to be alert, i.e. prudence. Prudence that consists of imagination, judgment, and command is only served by the existence of flexible institutions, which are neither contingent nor determinist. On this basis, we believe that economic freedom (i.e. private property rights, contracts, and money) is a flexible institution that provides determinist rules *ex ante* without closing absolutely the future *ex post*. This proposition may renew the institutionalist theory of economic growth.

NOTES

1. We also employ several control variables—per capita gross domestic regional product (GDRP), unemployment rates, human capital, population density, and degree of open-ness—that are suggested by previous studies.
2. Longitude and latitude data are from Maps of World: http://www.mapsofworld.com/world-maps/world-map-with-latitude-and-longitude.html, consulted in 2014.
3. We consider the possibility of a non-linear relationship between government size and economic growth (Armey, 1995; Facchini and Melki, 2013) to uncover the effect of government consumption (unproductive) and investment (productive expenditure) on entrepreneurship.

REFERENCES

Anselin, L. and S. Hudak (1992), "Spatial econometrics in practice", *Regional Science and Urban Economics*, **22**(3), 509–536.
Armey, D. (1995), *The Freedom Revolution*, Washington, DC: Regnery.
Aubenque (1963), *La Prudence*, Paris: Presses universitaires de France.
Audretsch, D. (1995), *Innovation and Industry Evolution*, Cambridge, MA: MIT Press.
Audretsch, D. and M. Keilbach (2004), "Entrepreneurship capital and economic performance", *Regional Studies*, **38**, 949–59.
Baumol, W. (1990), "Entrepreneurship: Productive, unproductive, and destructive", *Journal of Political Economy*, **98**(5), 893–921.
Besley, T. (1995), "Property rights and investment incentives: Theory and evidence from Ghana", *Journal of Political Economy*, **103**(5), 903–937.
Bjornskov, C. and N. Foss (2008), "Economic freedom and entrepreneurial activity: Some cross country evidence", *Public Choice*, **134**(3), 307–328.
Dawson, J. (1998), "Institutions, investment, and growth: New cross-country and panel data evidence, *Economic Inquiry*, **36**(4), 603–619.

De Soto, J. (1998), *Money, Bank Credit, and Economic Cycles*, Auburn, AL: Ludwig von Mises Institute.

Facchini, F. (2007), "L'entrepreneur comme un homme prudent", *Revue Sciences de Gestion*, **4/5**(226–227), 29–39.

Facchini, F. and M. Melki (2013), "Efficient government size: France in the 20th century", *European Journal of Political Economy*, **31**, 1–14.

Hall, J., J. Pulito, and B. VanMetre (2012), "Freedom and entrepreneurship: New Evidence from the 50 states", Mercatus Center Working Paper, 12–13.

Harper, D. (2003), *Foundations of Entrepreneurship and Economic Development*, London: Routledge.

Hayek, F. (1945), "The use of knowledge in society", *American Economic Review*, **35**, 519–530.

Hayek, F. (1978), "Towards a Free Market Monetary System", *Journal of Libertarian Studies*, **3**, 1–8.

Hayek, F. (1979), *The Political Order of a Free People*, Chicago: University of Chicago Press.

Hayek F. (1986 [1976]), *Droit, Législation et Liberté, vol.2, Le mirage de la justice sociale*, collection libre échange, PUF: Paris. French translation by Raoul Audouin, *Law, Legislation and Liberty, Volume 2: The Mirage of Social Justice*, Chicago: University of Chicago Press.

Hayek, F. (1994 [1988]), *La présomption fatale: les erreurs du socialisme*, collection libre échange, Paris: PUF. French translation by Raoul Audouin, *The Fatal Conceit: The Errors of Socialism*, Chicago: University of Chicago Press.

Heiner, A. (1983), "The origin of predictable behavior", *American Economic Review*, **73**, 560–595.

High, J. (1982), "Alertness and judgment: Comment on Kirzner", in: Israel Kirzner (ed.), *Method, Process and Austrian Economics: Essays in Honor of Ludwig von Mises*, Washington, DC: Lexington, 161–168.

Kirzner, I. (1973), *Competition and Entrepreneurship*, Chicago: University of Chicago Press.

Kirzner, I. (1994), "Entrepreneurship", in: Peter Joseph Boettke (ed.), *The Elgar Companion to Austrian Economics*, Cheltenham, UK and Northampton, MA, USA: Edward Elgar Publishing, 103–110.

North, D. (1990), *Institutions, Institutional Change and Economic Performance*, Cambridge: Cambridge University Press.

Say, J. (1971 [1803]), *A Treatise on Political Economy or the Production, Distribution and Consumption of Wealth*, New York: Kelley.

Schumpeter, J. (1934), *The Theory of Economic Development*, Cambridge: Cambridge University Press.

Ross, W. (1925), *The Works of Aristotle: Ethica Nicomachea*, Oxford: Clarendon.

Thomas d'Aquin (1984), *Somme Théologique. Deuxième moitié de seconde partie*, Paris: Cerf.

Van Stel, A., M. Carree, and R. Thurik (2005), "The effect of entrepreneurial activity on national economic growth", *Small Business Economics*, **24**, 311–321.

White, L. (1976), "Entrepreneurship, imagination and the question of equilibrium", in: Stephen Littlechild (ed.), *Austrian Economics III*, Cheltenham, UK and Northampton, MA, USA: Edward Elgar Publishing, 87–104.

Witt, U. (1987), *Individualistische Grundlagen der evolutorischen Ökonomik*, Tübingen: Mohr/Siebeck.

6. Sub-national market-supporting institutions and export behaviors

Ngo Vi Dung and Frank Janssen

INTRODUCTION

The business environment of emerging and transition economies (EE&TE) is highly volatile and unpredictable, mainly because they lack strong formal market-supporting institutions, especially in their early phase of transition (McMillan, 1995; Peng, 2003). In this context, certain authors argue that a firm's strategy can be better explained and predicted by the institution-based view, followed by the industry-based view and the resource-based view (Hoskisson et al., 2000; Peng et al., 2008; Wright et al., 2005). Despite the fact that institutional conditions vary not only between countries but also within a country and between industries (Gao et al., 2010; Wright et al., 2005), prior studies often focus on national institutions and neglect the sub-national institutional level (Meyer and Nguyen, 2005). However, these lower institutional levels play an important role because they regulate firms' day-to-day activities (Luo and Junkunc, 2008). The current study aims to fill this gap by investigating the impact of the market-supporting institutions at the sub-national level on the export behaviors (i.e. export propensity, export mode choice, and export intensity) of firms in the context of an emerging economy in Southeast Asia, namely Vietnam (Arnold and Quelch, 1998; Ellis, 2010). By doing this, we also enlarge the scope of investigation of export studies beyond the usually studied emerging economies such as China, Brazil, Russia or other countries in Central and Eastern Europe (Aulakh et al., 2000; Gao et al., 2010; Shinkle and Kriauciunas, 2010).

EE&TE AND MARKET-SUPPORTING INSTITUTIONS

The market-supporting institutions can be defined as "the set of fundamental political, social and legal ground rules that establishes the basis for production, exchange and distribution" (Davis and North, 1971: 6), and that bases on and guarantees (supports) the principles of market mechanism and, more generally, economic freedom (Miller and Holmes, 2011). Emerging economies, including transition economies, are defined as economies that have "a rapid pace of economic development, and government policies favoring economic liberalization and the adoption of a free-market system" (Hoskisson et al., 2000: 63; see also Peng, 2003). Because of their transitional nature, EE&TEs often lack strong formal market-supporting institutions, which makes their business environment of EE&TE extremely volatile and unpredictable (Peng and Heath, 1996). In this context, informal market-supporting institutions play a very important role, and firms often rely on relationship-based strategies rather than resources-based or capabilities-based ones in order to gain an advantage (Peng and Heath, 1996; Peng et al., 2009).

The market-supporting institutions, both formal and informal, can have different types of impact on firms' behavior: they can be either facilitating/enabling or troubling/constraining forces of entrepreneurial behavior (Hoskisson et al., 2000; Welter and Smallbone, 2011), and their degree of impact varies between types of firms because each type—i.e. incumbent, entrepreneurial start-ups and foreign entrants—faces different degrees of institutional pressure (Peng, 2003). In developed economies, the impact of market-supporting institutions is almost invisible because the markets work smoothly; by contrast, in EE&TE, this impact is more conspicuous when the markets work poorly (McMillan, 2007).

HETEROGENEITY OF MARKET-SUPPORTING INSTITUTIONS AT SUB-NATIONAL LEVEL IN VIETNAM

Vietnam's transition from a centrally planned to a market-based economy formally started in 1986. The market-based legal framework has been incrementally built and improved for investment (Investment Law), business creation and doing business (Law of Enterprise, Law of Commerce, Competition Law, E-commerce Law, Bankruptcy Law, and Law of Audit) and property rights (Land Law, Law of Intellectual Rights). In addition, the international integration process of Vietnam became more and more intensive: in 1995, the country joined the Association of Southeast Asian Nations (ASEAN), and then Asia-Pacific Economic Cooperation (APEC) in 1998. The USA–Vietnam bilateral trade agreement (BTA) became effective in 2002, and in 2007 Vietnam officially became a member of the World Trade Organization (WTO).

Vietnam is politically homogeneous because its policy is based on a single-party regime. However, that does not mean that institutions in general and market-supporting institutions in particular are homogeneous within the country. Meyer and Nguyen (2005) argue that the heterogeneity of market-supporting institutions at the provincial level in Vietnam can be an effect of decentralizing the legal framework by giving more authority to provincial officials. For instance, the Investment Law (1996, 2005) gives provincial governments the right/responsibility to approve certain levels of foreign direct investment (FDI) projects (e.g., by capital size). On the other hand, central laws and regulations are not always clearly defined, and can thus be heterogeneously interpreted and implemented by local governments (Meyer and Nguyen, 2005). Nguyen et al. (2004) assert that southern provinces (Ho Chi Minh City and its provincial periphery) always achieved a higher economic growth rate than northern provinces (Ha Noi and its provincial periphery) because the informal market-supporting institutions (e.g., the attitude of local authorities toward the private sector and the autonomy of business associations) are more favorable in the former than in the latter. From a political science perspective, Malesky et al. (2011) argue that, contrary to China—which also has a single-party regime, but where the central authorities have total power—Vietnamese local leaders play an important role in the political selection processes of the country's Communist Party, and the Central Committee accepts local autonomy to a certain extent. In other words, the heterogeneity of the market-supporting institutions in Vietnam could also be an effect of political framework (Acemoglu et al., 2005).

SUB-NATIONAL MARKET-SUPPORTING INSTITUTIONS AND EXPORT BEHAVIORS

Exporting is the common internationalization strategy of firms, especially small- and medium-size enterprises (SMEs) and firms that come from EE&TE, because, compared to other internationalization strategies, it involves "fewer resources, lower risk, and less costs" (Leonidou et al., 2010: 78). In their study of 9,123 firms in 72 emerging economies, Luo and Junkunc (2008) focus on the negative impact of market-supporting institutions (i.e., the problem of bureaucracy that is ubiquitous in these economies) and find that firms could have two generic strategic responses: (i) a reactive strategy (engagement) in which entrepreneurs attempt to satisfy prevailing rules and regulations; and (ii) a proactive strategy (influence) in which entrepreneurs try to shape the rules and regulations. They also stress that the relationship between bureaucracy and firms' strategic responses is moderated by firms' entrepreneurial type, governance and location. In the context of China, Gao et al. (2010) focus on the positive impact of market-supporting institutions, and find that the development of free-market mechanisms and of intermediate institutions significantly and positively influences firms' export behaviors (i.e., export propensity and export intensity). However, they also find that this positive impact is not moderated by the firm's ownership, i.e., domestic private enterprises and foreign wholly owned subsidiaries. In their study on the interaction between provincial institutions and export strategy (export intensity) of Vietnamese firms, Nguyen et al. (2013) find that a province's state-owned enterprise (SOE) bias is significantly and negatively associated with the firm's export intensity: Vietnamese private manufacturing firms tend to increase their export sales when they face more province SOE bias. They also find that this negative impact of sub-national market-supporting institutions on export behavior of Vietnamese SMEs does not vary with the firm's attributes (age, size, industry).

In sum, the previous empirical studies successfully demonstrate that:

- Market-supporting institutions significantly influence a firm's behavior.
- Market-supporting institutions can be either positive or negative drivers of a firm's strategic choices in exporting.
- Sub-national market-supporting institutions matter to a firm's export behavior.

However, these studies also have some major shortcomings:

- They only focus on either positive or negative impacts of the market-supporting institutions, and fail to recognize that these institutions can be both facilitating and troubling forces of the firm's behaviors.
- They only investigate a limited number of aspects and elements of the market-supporting institutions that can have different types of impact on the firm's behaviors.
- Their findings on the moderating role of the firm's attributes (age, size, ownership, industry, etc.) are inconclusive.

The current study aims to fill these gaps by proposing that:

Hypothesis 1: The sub-national market-supporting institutions have both positive and negative impacts on the firm's export behaviors (i.e., propensity, mode choice, and intensity).

Hypothesis 2: These impacts vary with the firm's attributes (age, size, ownership, and industry).

DATA AND VARIABLES

In this study, we use the 2008 raw data of the Provincial Competitiveness Index (PCI) developed by the Vietnam Chamber of Commerce and Industry (VCCI). This dataset includes 7818 enterprises located in 64 cities/provinces of Vietnam. Among these 7818 firms are 719 that engage in exporting (about 9.2 percent of total sample population).

Dependent Variables

As in previous export studies, export propensity is measured as a dummy variable with "export" = "1" and "no export" = "0". Following Hessels and Terjesen (2010), we have classified firms that use both direct and indirect export modes in indirect export, and we measure export mode choice as a dummy variable, with "direct export" = "1" and "indirect" = "0". Following Gao et al. (2010), we measure export intensity as the percentage of export sales in the firm's total sales in the last year (2007).

Independent Variables

The PCI 2008 covers many dimensions of the sub-national market-supporting institutions that are measured by subjective methods (i.e., entrepreneurs' perception of their provincial institutional environment). A principal components analysis (PCA, varimax rotation) was performed and it reveals six institutional components with eigenvalues greater than one, explaining 58.7 percent of the variance:

- The first component contains six items concerning *provincial public services for business/private sector development (PC1)*.
- The second component also contains six items concerning *provincial attitude, bureaucracy, legal and informal charges (PC2)*.
- The third component contains four items relating to *provincial financial institutions (PC3)*.
- The fourth component contains three items concerning *provincial FDI bias (PC4)*.
- The fifth component contains three items relating to *provincial SOE bias (PC5)*.
- The sixth component contains two items concerning the *predictability of central and provincial laws and regulations (PC6)*.

The scores of these six components (factors), rather than individual variables, are used as independent variables within our models.[1]

Control Variables

Following many prior studies (e.g., Calof, 1994; Dosoglu-Guner, 2001), we use the firm's size (measured as an ordinal variable of its total number of employees in the last year, 2007);[2] its age (number of established years); its legal form (measured as a nominal variable with "Sole Proprietorship = 1", "Partnership = 2", "Limited Liability = 3", "Joint-Stock = 4", "Other = 5"); and its industry (a dummy variable with "manufacturing" = "1", "other sectors" = "0") as control variables.[3] In addition, in order to establish whether the impact of sub-national market-supporting institutions on the firm's export behaviors varies with different firm attributes, we created additional dummy variables in order to divide our sample into sub-groups by firm size ("SMEs < 250 workers" = "1" and "larger firms ≥ 250" = "0");[4] age ("younger firms ≤ 5 years" = "1" and "older firms > 5 years" = "0");[5] ownership ("with SOEs' or government agency shares" = "1" and "without SOEs' or government agency shares" = "0");[6] and industry (the same as control variable that is excluded in sub-group analysis).

RESULTS AND DISCUSSION

Because of their binary nature, following Hessels and Terjesen (2010), we use binominal or binary logistic regressions for export propensity and export mode choice. Export intensity varies within an interval of 0–100 and is skewed to the right (skewness = 4.02 and kurtosis = 15.08). Thus, following Gao et al. (2010), we use a tobit regression for export intensity. We tested for multicollinearity between the predictor variables by using variance inflation factors (VIFs). For all three models, the results show that all VIFs are well below 10: from 1.000 to 1.386 in model 1 (export propensity); from 1.011 to 1.397 in model 2 (export mode choice); and from 1.000 to 1.386 in model 3 (export intensity). The main results of regression analyses are presented in Table 6.1.

Our first major finding is that, among elements of the provincial market-supporting institutions, the firm's decision to export or not (export propensity) is mainly and negatively influenced by provincial financial conditions. Interestingly, unfavorable financial institutions, rather than favorable ones, will stimulate Vietnamese firms to internationalize (i.e., export). We also find that firms that often face financial difficulties in their domestic market (i.e., private, smaller, and younger firms rather than state-owned, larger and older firms) are more likely to choose exporting as a strategic response. But, as operating in overseas markets (i.e., exporting) theoretically requires more financial resources than operating in the

Table 6.1   Regression estimates

	Export propensity	Export mode choice	Export intensity
Control			
Firm age	−0.02	0.03	−1.06*
	(0.98)	(1.03)	(0.48)
Firm size	0.75***	0.12*	8.15***
	(2.11)	(1.13)	(1.33)
Firm legal form	−0.03	0.06	−1.64
	(0.97)	(1.06)	(1.85)
Firm industry	1.41***	−0.37*	−7.35
	(4.09)	(0.69)	(4.14)
Institutions			
PC1	0.07	0.19*	1.43
	(1.08)	(1.21)	(1.86)
PC2	−0.02	0.05	4.89*
	(0.98)	(1.05)	(1.95)
PC3	−0.13**	0.12	−3.14
	(0.88)	(1.13)	(1.75)
PC4	−0.08	0.01	0.00
	(0.92)	(1.01)	(1.81)
PC5	−0.03	0.02	1.52
	(0.97)	(1.02)	(1.76)
PC6	0.01	−0.07	−5.68**
	(1.01)	(0.93)	(1.89)
Constant	−5.26***	−0.66*	46.69***
Observation	6806	636	636
LR chi2	933.06	22.47	53.55
Prob > chi2	0.00	0.01	0.00
Pseudo R2	0.22	0.03	0.01
Log likelihood	−1646.33	−429.40	−2648.78

Notes: * p < 0.05; ** p < 0.01; *** p < 0.001. The values in parentheses are odds. The subgroup analyses can be requested from the authors.

domestic market, how can exporting become a strategic response to the difficult financial conditions in the domestic market?

Firstly, as several previous export studies have demonstrated (e.g., Leonidou, 1995), unsolicited orders from foreign customers are firms' most important export stimulus. We can suppose that this type of export stimulus is even more important for firms in EE&TE, especially SMEs, because they lack resources and capabilities that enable them to proactively identify their export clients. In this context, it seems that exporting is a *reactive* strategic response, but that its transaction costs could be lower than the ones doing business in domestic market. This is due to some external stimuli such as the pre-payment or on time-payment of foreign customers who *proactively* search and identify their supply sources. Thus, exporting can become a strategic choice of firms in order to respond to the difficult financial conditions in their domestic market.[7]

Secondly, among elements of the provincial market-supporting institutions, there is only little evidence about the positive impact of subnational market-supporting institutions (i.e. the provincial public services for business/private sector development) on the export mode choice of Vietnamese firms. The statistical results do not allow us to conclude that this positive impact varies with the firm's attributes. This is in line with the findings of other studies such as Hessels and Terjesen (2010), who argue that, in the Dutch context, the institutional theory perspectives are more appropriate to explain SMEs' decision to export rather than their export mode choice.

However, our results are also somewhat different from those of Hessels and Terjesen, who find no significant relationship between the firm's age, size, industry, or ownership and its export mode choice. In our study, the firm's size and industry do matter for its export mode choice. Nevertheless, Hessels and Terjesen's work was in the context of DE (the Netherlands), while the current study focuses on firms in EE&TE (Vietnam). We also tried to understand whether our finding is influenced by the measurement of the dependent variable (export mode choice): we performed an additional multinomial logistic regression in which firms that use both direct and indirect export are not grouped into a single group of indirect export. However, the statistical results do not significantly change. This allows us to question two things:

1. Is the institution-based view really appropriate to explain and predict the firm's export mode choice or do we need another theoretical perspective, as Hessels and Terjesen (2010) suggested?
2. Is the current measurement of export mode choice, either as a binary or multinomial variable, appropriate to capture the firm's export mode choice in reality?

Thirdly, among elements of the provincial market-supporting institutions, the export intensity of Vietnamese firms is mainly influenced by: (i) provincial attitude, bureaucracy, legal and informal charges (positive impact); and (ii) the degree of predictability of domestic laws and regulations (negative impact). While the positive impact of provincial attitude, bureaucracy, legal and informal charges is straightforward to understand—firms tend to export more when they face less burden of attitudinal discrimination, bureaucracy, legal, and informal charges (i.e. bribes)—the negative impact of the predictability of domestic laws and regulations is more complicated: the more likely firms are to predict the changes and implementation of domestic (national and provincial) laws and regulations, the less likely they are to increase their export intensity. Once again, logic is the same as for the first finding.

In the context of Vietnam, as well as in other EE&TE, the rules and regulations are rarely as well constructed as needed because of several reasons—mostly the lack of an efficient administrative system, of capable leadership, and of qualified government officials (Ohno, 2009). Laws and regulations often "can only be regarded as general guidelines, establishing the rough ambit of bureaucratic discretion" (Gillespie, 1993, cited in McMillan, 1995: 226). In this context, we can hypothesize that even if local entrepreneurs can predict the changes and implementation of domestic laws and regulations, this "knowledge" could incite the firm to use the "wait and see" strategy rather than immediately integrate this information into its export strategy (export intensity). In the best case, firms that can predict the changes and implementation of rules and regulations will profit from this by increasing their domestic sales while keeping their export sales stable or even decreasing these in order to avoid risk and uncertainty in overseas markets. By contrast, firms that cannot predict changes and implementation of rules and regulations—especially private, smaller, and younger firms that operate in manufacturing sectors, as our sub-groups analyses showed—will choose to increase export sales as a strategic response to the unpredictable rules and regulations in the domestic market.

CONCLUSION

This study demonstrates that sub-national (i.e. provincial) market-supporting institutions explain the export behaviors of Vietnamese firms to a certain extent. However, not all aspects and elements of these institutions have a similar impact on the firms' decisions in exporting, and not all types of firms behave in the same manner in responding to these institutional constraints. There are two major directions that future research could take to develop existing knowledge. Firstly, because exporting involves two markets, research on the influence of market-supporting institutions in both the home and the host market would bring more insightful results about the firm's export behaviors. Secondly, longitudinal and comparative future studies would be very helpful to conclude whether international entrepreneurship (i.e. export) can be considered as a last resort (Braunerhjelm, 2011) of entrepreneurs in EE&TE because of the institutional constraints in their domestic market.

NOTES

1. The items, their measurement, and the results of the principal components analysis can be requested from the authors.
2. 1 = fewer than 5 people, 2 = between 5 and 9 people, 3 = between 10 and 49 people, 4 = between 50 and 199 people, 5 = between 200 and 299 people, 6 = between 300 and 499 people, 7 = between 500 and 1000 people and 8 = more than 1000 people.
3. Manufacturing firms are defined as firms that have manufacturing revenue greater than 10 percent of their total revenue (Nguyen et al., 2013).
4. European Commission (EC) definition: http://ec.europa.eu/enterprise/policies/sme/facts-figures-analysis/sme-definition/index_en.htm.
5. Five years is a critical threshold of a firm's business life (Storey, 1997: 93).
6. PCI 2008 only includes Vietnamese firms, i.e., private and state-owned domestic firms.
7. A similar idea was proposed by Yamakawa et al. (2008), who argue that a regulative environment that favors large established firms (e.g., SOEs) and that discriminates against new ventures will motivate new ventures to internationalize from EE to developed economies, DE (proposition 7a).

REFERENCES

Acemoglu D, Johnson S, Robinson J. 2005. Institutions as a fundamental cause of long-run growth. In *Handbook of Economic Growth*, Aghion P, Durlauf SN (eds). Amsterdam: Elsevier; 385–472.

Arnold DJ, Quelch JA. 1998. New strategies in emerging markets. *Sloan Management Review* **40**(1):7–20.

Aulakh PS, Kotabe M, Teegen H. 2000. Export strategies and performance of firms from emerging economies: evidence from Brazil, Chile, and Mexico. *Academy of Management Journal* **43**(4):342–361.

Braunerhjelm P. 2011. Entrepreneurship, innovation and economic growth: interdependencies, irregularities and regularities. In *Handbook of Research on Innovation and Entrepreneurship*, Audretsch DB, Falck O, Heblich S, Lederer A (eds). Cheltenham, UK and Northampton, MA, USA: Edward Elgar Publishing; 161–213.

Calof JL. 1994. The relationship between firm size and export behavior revisited. *Journal of International Business Studies* **25**(2):367–387.

Davis LE, North DC. 1971. *Institutional Change and American Economic Growth*. Cambridge: Cambridge University Press.

Dosoglu-Guner B. 2001. Can organizational behavior explain the export intention of firms? The effects of organizational culture and ownership type. *International Business Review* **10**:71–89.

Ellis PD. 2010. International trade intermediaries and the transfer of marketing knowledge in transition economies. *International Business Review* **19**:16–33.

Gao GY, Murray JY, Kotabe M, Lu J. 2010. A "strategy tripod" perspective on export behaviors: evidence from domestic and foreign firms based in an emerging economy. *Journal of International Business Studies* **41**:377–396.

Hessels J, Terjesen S. 2010. Resource dependency and institutional theory perspectives on direct and indirect export choices. *Small Business Economics* **34**(2):203–220.

Hoskisson RE, Eden L, Chung ML, Wright M. 2000. Strategy in emerging economies. *Academy of Management Journal* **43**(3):249–267.

Leonidou LC. 1995. Export stimulation research: review, evaluation and integration. *International Business Review* **4**(2):133–156.

Leonidou LC, Katsikea CS, Coudounaris DN. 2010. Five decades of business research into exporting: A bibliographic analysis. *Journal of International Management* **16**:79–91.

Luo Y, Junkunc M. 2008. How private enterprises respond to government bureaucracy in emerging economies: the effects of entrepreneurial type and governance. *Strategic Entrepreneurship Journal* **2**:133–153.

Malesky E, Abrami R, Zheng Y. 2011. Institutions and inequality in single-party regimes: a comparative analysis of Vietnam and China. *Comparative Politics* **43**(4):409–419.

McMillan J. 1995. Markets in transition. In *Advances in Economics and Econometrics: Theory and Applications*, Kreps DM, Wallis KF (eds). Cambridge: Cambridge University Press; 210–239.

McMillan J. 2007. Market institutions. In *The New Palgrave Dictionary of Economics* (2nd ed.), Durlauf SN, Blume LE (eds). London: Palgrave.

Meyer KE, Nguyen HV. 2005. Foreign investment strategies and sub-national institutions in emerging markets: evidence from Vietnam. *Journal of Management Studies* **42**(1):63–93.

Miller T, Holmes KR. 2011. *Index of Economic Freedom, 2011*. Washington, DC: Heritage Foundation.

Nguyen DC, Pham AT, Bui V, Dapice D. 2004. *History or Policy: Why Don't Northern Provinces Grow Faster?* Hanoi: United Nations Development Programme.

Nguyen TV, Le NTB, Bryant SE. 2013. Sub-national institutions, firm strategies, and firm performance: a multilevel study of private manufacturing firms in Vietnam. *Journal of World Business* **48**(1):68–76.

Ohno K. 2009. Avoiding the middle-income trap: renovating industrial policy formulation in Vietnam. *ASEAN Economic Bulletin* **26**(1):25–43.

Peng MW. 2003. Institutional transitions and strategic choices. *Academy of Management Review* **28**(2):275–296.

Peng MW, Heath PS. 1996. The growth of the firm in planned economies in transition: institutions, organizations, and strategic choice. *Academy of Management Review* **21**(2):492.

Peng MW, Sun SL, Pinkham B, Chen H. 2009. The institution-based view as a third leg for a strategy tripod. *Academy of Management Perspectives* **22**(3):63–81.

Peng MW, Wang DY, Jiang Y. 2008. An institution-based view of international business strategy: a focus on emerging economies. *Journal of International Business Studies* **39**(5):920–936.

Shinkle GA, Kriauciunas AP. 2010. Institutions, size and age in transition economies: implications for export growth. *Journal of International Business Studies* **41**(2):267–286.

Storey DJ. 1997. *Understanding the Small Business Sector*. London: International Thomson Business Press.

Welter F, Smallbone D. 2011. Institutional perspectives on entrepreneurial behavior in challenging environments. *Journal of Small Business Management* **49**(1):107–125.

Wright M, Filatotchev I, Hoskisson RE, Peng MW. 2005. Guest editor's introduction: Strategy research in emerging economies: challenging the conventional wisdom. *Journal of Management Studies* **42**(1):1–33.

Yamakawa Y, Peng MW, Deeds DL. 2008. What drives new ventures to internationalize from emerging to developed economies? *Entrepreneurship Theory and Practice* **32**(1):59–82.

PART II

Entrepreneurial choice, orientation and success

7. Are French industrial establishments equally sensitive to the local atmosphere? An analysis resting upon a panel of manufacturing plants over the period 2003–2010

Nadine Levratto, Denis Carré and Luc Tessier

INTRODUCTION

Since the very beginning of the 2008 crisis, local authorities have been worrying about the consequences of firms closing down on employment. Many policy makers tried to implement measures and policies to prevent a massive increase in unemployment and loss of economic competitiveness. Quite new in a traditionally centralized country such as France, these local priorities, strengthened by an increase in the policy autonomy of local administration, jointly contributed to locally anchoring job creation and firms' development.

Looking at entrepreneurship and firms' trajectories at a regional level is not so new. Two branches of economics (new economic geography and industrial demography) already provide arguments in favour of such a perspective. Since the mid-1990s new economic geography has provided a theory on the emergence of large agglomerations which rely upon increasing return to scale and transportation costs (Baldwin, 1994). It also emphasizes links between firms and suppliers as well as between firms and customers. All these features result in providing a crucial advantage to geographical concentration of economic activity.

This local view long escaped industrial economists, whereas most of the research undertaken in this field seeks to provide a realistic explanation of firms' functioning. Although complex, rich and highly explicative, the numerous papers devoted to multivariate empirical analysis of firm growth still introduce location as a control variable (see Becchetti and Trovato, 2002 for example). However, an increasing number of scholars pinpoint that growth is a complex, multidimensional phenomenon and that a purely internal approach to its investigation, limited to the impact of resources, neglects the predictive potential of variables linked to the environment.

This chapter aims at contributing to the debate about the local determinants of firm growth. It differs from most previously published works by focusing not only on new entrepreneurial activities (Audretsch et al., 2012), turbulence (Nyström, 2007) or young firms (Hoogstra and van Dijk, 2004) but also on firms' trajectories. In addition to this first difference, which concerns the scope of the research, another original aspect of our approach comes from the method used to capture local specificities. Looking at the literature, it becomes quickly obvious that the major stake consists in finding the best proxies to capture the local business climate. Referring to economic geography, most studies use concentration, an index to measure entrepreneurial activities, and a demographic index alone or together with regional specialization to mirror a region's capacity to host new firms and growing industries. They are often complemented with indicators measuring educational level and industrial characteristics to describe properly the local context. Braunerhjelm and Borgman (2004) provide a quite exhaustive presentation of the different variables currently introduced in such a field of research, whereas Schimke and Teicher (2012) focus on the different ways to capture the composition and hence the quality of the local knowledge base. We continue in this way; but, instead of considering broad areas such as regions or counties, we increase the precision of the local level so that the statistical unit applied in this research is the employment area.

This study makes several contributions to the literature on firm growth. Firstly, it focuses on plants and not on companies, which makes it possible to analyse what happens at a precise local level. Secondly, we differentiate between independent and controlled establishments to determine to what extent sensitivity to local conditions can be affected by the governance structure. Thus, introducing indexes to illustrate the area performances enables us to assess their effect on plant growth rate of employment between 2003 and 2010. Population skills, business location, total number of employees, degree of autonomy, unemployment rate as well as a concentration index are all significant. Their role is confirmed whatever the model used since the different estimations demonstrate clear stability of the results.

The remainder of the chapter is organized as follows. The following section outlines a brief survey of the literature; it then depicts an empirical model to assess the influence of local considerations on firm growth, presenting the data and the sample studied. The results of estimations are then presented and discussed before the final section concludes.

LOCATION AS A DETERMINANT OF FIRM GROWTH

With the renewed interest in local phenomena resulting from the recognition that local factors matter, it is thus more and more frequently admitted that companies are not floating in the air but, on the contrary, are embedded in a local context able to shape their behaviour and performances. It is then of great importance to make a distinction between firm- and local-specific effects to understand better the growth process and provide policy makers with an efficient tool.

Theoretical Background

The theoretical framework linking growth to firms dates back to what has been characterized in the economics literature as Gibrat's law. The basic principle underlying this theory is that growth is normally distributed and occurs randomly since "the probability of a given proportionate change in size during a specified period is the same for all firms in a given industry – regardless of their size at the beginning of the period" (Mansfield, 1962, p. 1031). As comprehensive review articles by Caves (1998) and Sutton (1997) confirm, a plethora of studies has been accumulated; but, in fact, this literature consists almost exclusively of attempts to link firm-specific characteristics to firm growth (Santarelli et al., 2006).

More recently and coming from regional science, empirical research on agglomeration externalities has brought evidence about the role of local factors in regional employment dynamics. From Krugman (1991), it is broadly acknowledged that the role of location in firm growth follows a twofold logic: firstly, market opportunities as firms tend to locate in areas where consumers are willing to buy their products and resources; this applies to providers too, since firms are interested in being close to suppliers who are able to satisfy their organizational needs. In addition to this proximity effect, several types of external economies have been pointed out. The location of a firm is thus an important determinant of its growth performance due to factors like pooling of human capital and proximity to non-traded inputs and specialized goods, as well as easy access to markets (Audretsch et al., 2012). Variables such as human capital, the local labour market, product and process innovation, location, legal status and capital structure also intervene in their growth path.

According to Porter (1998), a concentration of industry activity in a geographic region affects firm performance because it introduces local competition which requires firms to innovate in order to remain competitive. These external economies for specialization are especially valid for innovative firms: provided that projects are location specific, and locations are known to differ in how profitable they can be, then firms with new ideas will initially implement these in the more profitable locations, and only then expand, at a slower pace, into less attractive locations. They are strengthened by knowledge spillover. As noted by Audretsch and Dohse (2007, p. 83), "firms using knowledge inputs will exhibit a superior performance if they are located in an agglomeration". Variables capturing the establishment's local environment may thus be introduced as explanatory factors in a firm growth equation.

The Econometric Model

Our basic econometric model comes directly from the multivariate model of firm growth (see Coad, 2009 for a survey). It begins with a standard definition of firm growth:

$$\text{GROWTH}_{i,t} = lnSIZE_{i,t} - lnSIZE_{i,t-1} \tag{1}$$

where GROWTH denotes the change in the number of employees in firm i at time t, and *SIZE* is the size of the firm. From the basic Gibrat model revisited, the best way to examine the origins of growth is to express it in a regression framework enriched with three sets of factors determining growth. The first are inherent to the firm and are sticky enough to remain the same in the short and medium term; the second are strictly exogenous as they depend on environment; and the third are endogenous in the sense that they are actively influenced by the strategy implemented by the management team. We refer to the resource-based view to introduce them as additional explanatory variables:

$$\text{GROWTH}_{i,t} = B_0 + B_1 \ln\text{Size}_{i,t-1} + B_2 \ln\text{Age}_{i,t} + \varepsilon_{i,t} \tag{2}$$

where firm growth, still defined by GROWTH, is a function of the lagged size in log ($\ln\text{Size}_{i,t-1}$) and of age ($\ln\text{Age}_{i,t}$). The estimator B_1 represents the effect of initial size on the subsequent growth rate, and B_2 measures the effect of age on growth. The term $\varepsilon_{i,t}$ is a stochastic error term. At this stage, all the variables are specific to the firm; and, as in most research, industry is included as a control variable only. Equation (2) may be presented in a shortened way as:

$$\text{GROWTH}_{i,t} = \beta_0 + \beta\text{Firm}_{i,t} + \varepsilon_{i,t} \tag{3}$$

where $\text{Firm}_{i,t}$ is a vector of variables representative of the firm's characteristics.

As in this chapter we intend to estimate the local influence on growth path, we extend this classical framework by considering location-specific determinants of growth as well. Equation (3) can then be extended introducing local characteristics, which results in a model mixing two families of variables. Some reflect the firm's characteristics, whereas others depict the environment in a given area j. The complete model then takes the form:

$$\text{GROWTH}_{i,j,t} = \beta_0 + \beta \text{Firm}_{i,t} + \gamma Loc_{j,t} + \varepsilon_{i,j,t} \qquad (4)$$

where $Loc_{j,t}$ is a vector of local variables characteristic of the area j at time t. If the traditional assumption according to which growth is randomly distributed holds, coefficients will not be significantly different from zero; but, if the locational factors play a role, which is the hypothesis proposed in this chapter, then the coefficients will not equal zero.

DATA DESCRIPTION

In order to capture the influence of local characteristics on variations in employment, we conduct the analysis at the establishment level. For information on this level, we use the *Connaissance locale de l'appareil productif* (CLAP) data set, which provides local knowledge of the productive system. Provided by the French National Institute of Statistics and Economic Studies (INSEE), this information system is exhaustive and includes enterprises and establishments that have had at least one day of economic activity in the financial year, whether they are employers or not. The following information is available on the enterprises and establishments:

- characteristics (number, size, sector of activity) and wages paid;
- employment offered – number of jobs, socio-professional category, gender, type of employment (including apprenticeships, subsidised contracts, interns);
- salaried employment measured in terms of "jobs" on 31 December (but also evaluated in terms of full-time equivalent over the year).

From these annual surveys, we compose a longitudinal dataset which includes establishments in the competitive manufacturing sector operating every year from 2003 to 2010. We omit any establishment that has missing data, is owned by the state, and that has not had at least one employee over the period considered. Having applied all these conditions to clean the data, our final sample contains 67,650 establishments.

Dependent Variable

The dependent variable measuring establishment growth is based on the total number of employees on 31 December of the respective year. This figure comprises full- and part-time employees entitled to social security. Short-term and part-time employees are converted into full-time equivalents according to INSEE. $GROWTH_{i,t}$ is thus the annual growth rate in the number of employees for the i-th firm from 2003 to 2010 measured by a difference of logarithms (Figure 7.1).

Explanatory Variables

Regarding our basic model of firm growth, several variables are introduced to display firm-specific and location-specific features.

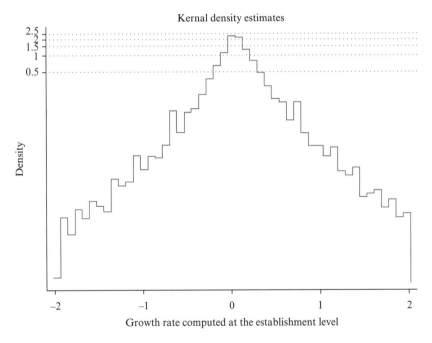

Note: Kernel = epanechnikov, bandwidth = 0.0200. The Kernel density is computed using Epanechnikov kernel. Y-axis is in log scale. The graph is estimated using the "kdensity package" available in STATA 12.1 software.

Figure 7.1   Distribution of the employment growth rate (2003–2010)

Firm-specific variables

Firm size, $Size_{i,t-1}$, is measured by the number of employees reported on the payroll at the end of every year. The value of this variable is taken in logarithmic form (noted $lnSize_{i,t-1}$) because it produces a better fit than the absolute value due to the lower dispersion. The general finding of empirical studies is that firms' growth is not proportional, since smaller firms grow at a higher rate compared with their larger counterparts. One should then stick to Caves' (1998) remarks that Gibrat's law holds for firms above a size threshold, while for smaller firms growth rates decrease with size.

These variables are complemented with two variables calculated at the establishment level. The first is $Age_{i,t}$, a classical variable in firm growth models (Coad, 2009), introduced in the analysis as a proxy for learning effects. It is measured as the difference between the year of observation and the year of enterprise creation. It is also introduced as a natural logarithm and written $lnAge_{i,t}$. The second has to do with corporate organization. Assuming that ownership structure is a relevant factor in determining performance, we introduce a variable named $Group\_n_{i,t}$ (n = 5), which describes the situation of any establishment given the ownership structure of the firms it is embedded in. Five possibilities are identified. An establishment can:

1. be included in an independent company;
2. belong to a company partially controlled by another;
3. belong to a subsidiary company of a French corporate group;
4. belong to a subsidiary company of a foreign corporate group; or
5. belong to a micro-group, i.e. a group of companies with headquarters in France employing fewer than 500 people.

Location-specific variables

The location-specific variables refer to the characteristics of the employment areas, a basic French territorial division, where the establishments are located. To appreciate the influence of local aspects on growth we consider a set of locally determined variables provided either by the Observatory of the Territories (which provides a selection of informative documents on local territories in France) or by INSEE through the CLAP dataset.

The location externalities are approached by two variables. The first approximates the role of available human capital in an area as a factor able to boost firm growth either as a resource or as a demand factor. As demonstrated by Hamermesh (1993), labour demand is highly interconnected with the qualification structure of the workforce. We use the difference in the share of white-collar employees among the total workforce in any capacity between 2003 and 2010 ($QUAL_{j,t}$) as an indicator of quality of the local workforce (Cooke, 2005).

Since the industrial specialization appears as a key factor of Marshall-Arrow-Romer externalities, one may admit that an over-representation of companies belonging to the same sector in a given period is an advantage for each firm (Martin et al., 2011). Named $INDUS_{j,t}$, this indicator is defined as the share of workers employed in the manufacturing industry in an employment area j with respect to the total number of employees in this area. It is expected to play a positive role in the individual growth process.

Local conditions are also captured, considering some specific features able to influence the business climate. The rate of unemployment ($UNEMP_{j,t}$) illustrates the economic trend at the employment area level. The associated sign is thus expected to be negative. Another factor able to determine establishment growth lies in competition intensiveness and capture effects. This is approximated by the rate of workers employed in the five biggest establishments ($C5_{j,t}$). The more concentrated, the less an economic system is open, which prevents the majority of establishments seizing growth opportunities. Finally, we also take into account an index of autonomy of decision at the local level. This consists of the ratio of the number of employees working in establishments belonging to an autonomous firm, i.e. completely independent or having one or more minority partnerships (each less than 50 per cent). The proximity between headquarters and the production level makes it possible to fit better to local conditions, to be more flexible and to be free from any corporate strategy and arbitrages between different plants. The sign associated with this variable is expected to be positive. Table 7.1 describes the distribution of the variables.

Table 7.1   Distribution of variables

	count	mean	sd	min	max
lnGrowth	473550	−0.008	0.276	−5.472	6.165
lnSize	541200	2.168	1.398	0.000	9.719
lnAge	541200	2.473	0.685	0.000	4.615
Group_0	541200	0.688	0.463	0.000	1.000
Group_1	541200	0.145	0.352	0.000	1.000
Group_2	541200	0.040	0.196	0.000	1.000
Group_3	541200	0.062	0.240	0.000	1.000
Group_4	541200	0.066	0.248	0.000	1.000
C5	541200	0.084	0.041	0.013	0.381
QUAL	541200	0.152	0.057	0.061	0.320
INDEP	541200	0.749	0.148	0.243	0.999
INDUS	541200	0.158	0.073	0.026	0.487
UNEMP	541200	8.503	1.984	3.600	16.400

ESTIMATION TECHNIQUE, RESULTS AND DISCUSSION

This section presents the results of the econometric analysis. Because of the strong correlation detected between *QUAL* and *INDEP* we estimated two models: one with the variable *QUAL* but without *INDEP*, and another with *INDEP* but without *QUAL*.[1] The results are reported in Table 7.2.

Hausman and White tests led us to adopt a fixed effect model. We used the robust version to solve problems raised by heteroskedasticity (see Table 7.2, columns 1 and 5). We also checked for possible endogeneity of the variable *INDUS* using the Durbin–Wu–Hausman test. We thus estimated the model using the lagged *INDUS* variable as an instrument (Table 7.2, columns 2 and 6). The results do not differ radically from the model where *INDUS* is measured at the same period as growth or other local variables. Finally, for comparison we estimated the models using OLS with and without industry as a control variable (Table 7.2, columns 3, 4, 7 and 8).

Whatever the model, the coefficients present the expected sign and are strongly significant. As expected, the coefficient on the lagged size variable (*lnSize*) is negative and statistically significant in any model. Larger firms tend to grow less than smaller ones. The same happens with age (*lnAge*), whose sign is always negative – which confirms that young firms create more jobs than older ones. The stability of the coefficient attests for the robustness of the estimator. Taking *Group_0* (establishments belonging to autonomous companies) as a reference, it is quite evident that being included in a group provides a great advantage as far as growth is concerned. This result confirms the view supported by Guzzini et al. (2012), that the advantage of business groups comes from their organizational and ownership structures.

In addition to these individual characteristics, local variables contribute to explain establishments' growth. Specialization approximated using variable *INDUS* plays a role in explaining job creation at the establishment level. The suspicion of endogeneity mentioned above led us to estimate the models using Hausman specification tests.[2] In each of them, the value of the coefficients is not very different. Since the coefficient associated with this variable is significantly positive, one confirms the hypothesis that a high degree of proximity between production units promotes growth (MAR version of agglomeration externalities).

As expected, concentration deters growth as *C5* is associated with a negative coefficient. An equitable allocation of labour force among the different establishments thus grants a better repartition of job creation than the concentration of workers in a small number of big units. Similarly, competitive pressure which corresponds to low levels of the *C5* ratio may

Table 7.2   The results

VARIABLES	(1) lnGrowth	(2) lnGrowth	(3) lnGrowth	(4) lnGrowth
lnSize_t−1	−0.587***	−0.587***	−0.0277***	−0.0285***
	(0.00429)	(0.00143)	(0.000418)	(0.000430)
lnAge	−0.00928***	−0.00668***	−0.0206***	−0.0204***
	(0.00300)	(0.00241)	(0.000699)	(0.000699)
Group_1	0.000540	0.000701	0.0378***	0.0381***
	(0.00350)	(0.00268)	(0.00127)	(0.00129)
Group_2	0.0140***	0.0141***	0.0341***	0.0340***
	(0.00436)	(0.00344)	(0.00231)	(0.00232)
Group_3	0.0354***	0.0356***	0.0603***	0.0601***
	(0.00583)	(0.00494)	(0.00193)	(0.00196)
Group_4	0.0269***	0.0271***	0.0526***	0.0510***
	(0.00650)	(0.00486)	(0.00181)	(0.00185)
C5	−0.341***	−0.359***	−0.00788	−0.0128
	(0.0674)	(0.0580)	(0.0121)	(0.0121)
INDEP	0.0412***	0.0414***	0.0204***	0.0194***
	(0.00860)	(0.00813)	(0.00301)	(0.00302)
INDUS	1.287***	1.373***	0.0464***	0.0462***
	(0.0617)	(0.0582)	(0.00640)	(0.00645)
UNEMP	−0.0120***	−0.0117***	−0.00163***	−0.00158***
	(0.000476)	(0.000495)	(0.000205)	(0.000205)
QUAL				
Sect				Yes
Constant	1.186***	1.166***	0.0824***	0.0867***
	(0.0206)	(0.0176)	(0.00326)	(0.00337)
Observations	473,550	473,550	473,550	473,550
R-squared	0.298		0.016	0.016
Number of ident	67,650	67,650		
model	fe	fe	ols	ols
R^2 within	0.298	0.298		
R^2 between	0.000224	0.000212		
R^2 overall	0.00946	0.00945		
F	2208	.	576.8	272.9
p	0	0		
R^2 adj.			0.0158	0.0164

(5) lnGrowth	(6) lnGrowth	(7) lnGrowth	(8) lnGrowth
−0.588***	−0.588***	−0.0277***	−0.0285***
(0.00428)	(0.00143)	(0.000418)	(0.000430)
0.00851***	0.0101***	−0.0205***	−0.0203***
(0.00317)	(0.00253)	(0.000701)	(0.000700)
0.00130	0.00140	0.0377***	0.0381***
(0.00350)	(0.00268)	(0.00128)	(0.00129)
0.0142***	0.0142***	0.0342***	0.0343***
(0.00436)	(0.00344)	(0.00231)	(0.00232)
0.0362***	0.0363***	0.0603***	0.0601***
(0.00583)	(0.00493)	(0.00193)	(0.00196)
0.0278***	0.0279***	0.0523***	0.0507***
(0.00650)	(0.00486)	(0.00181)	(0.00185)
−0.203***	−0.219***	0.0293**	0.0248**
(0.0675)	(0.0585)	(0.0122)	(0.0123)
1.054***	1.120***	0.0472***	0.0481***
(0.0630)	(0.0602)	(0.00667)	(0.00671)
−0.00656***	−0.00647***	−0.00151***	−0.00144***
(0.000582)	(0.000563)	(0.000207)	(0.000207)
1.106***	1.090***	0.00278	0.00797
(0.0614)	(0.0554)	(0.00887)	(0.00892)
			Yes
0.984***	0.973***	0.0931***	0.0957***
(0.0232)	(0.0194)	(0.00374)	(0.00377)
473,550	473,550	473,550	473,550
0.298		0.016	0.016
67,650	67,650		
fe	fe	ols	ols
0.298	0.298		
0.000137	0.000131		
0.00924	0.00924		
2270	.	572.9	271.2
0	0		
		0.0157	0.0164

Notes: Robust standard errors in parentheses; *** $p < 0.01$, ** $p < 0.05$, * $p < 0.1$

stimulate incumbent establishments' growth. This result goes in the same direction as the conclusion of the study by Burke and Hansley (2009), according to which industry concentration rates reduce the survival rate of new plants.

The model containing the variable *INDEP* concludes to the positive effect of the share of autonomous companies at the employment area level. The higher the proximity between decision and production centres, the more profitable it is for continuously operating establishments, which tends to comfort local policies aimed at promoting family business more intensively than big corporation attractiveness.

The positive and highly significant coefficient of human capital (*QUAL*) suggests that establishments experience higher growth rates in areas characterized by a high density of highly qualified employees. This conclusion is quite robust as the coefficient remains almost the same whatever the equation to be estimated is. This result is consistent with earlier studies conducted at the regional level. The closest confirmation comes with (Audretsch and Dohse, 2007), according to whom human capital exerts a positive effect on firm growth path.

CONCLUSIONS

This chapter aimed at explaining how local aspects influence employment changes at the establishment level by looking at a sample of French establishments operating in the manufacturing industry between 2003 and 2010. Thanks to the combination of individual and local variables measured at the employment area and yearly available in a fixed-effects models, we placed some emphasis on the importance of context on individual performance. Indeed, we demonstrate that the share of autonomous companies, the global contribution of manufacturing industry to employment, and the level of qualification of the workforce exert a positive effect on establishment growth. In contrast, the concentration of global activity in the five biggest establishments as well as unemployment rate, both measured at the employment area level, negatively affect individual growth. These results are robust regardless of the estimation technique implemented.

In addition to its contribution to research on the local determinants of economic activity, this study and its results can be of interest to economic decision makers. Putting some emphasis on the relationships between local characteristics and establishment growth, it draws the attention of policy makers to the necessary development of locally defined tools and objectives rather than transposing good practices, principles, receipts and generic tools defined at the national or European level.

Some limits apply stemming from the nature of the data used. Running the analysis at the establishment level prevents us incorporating accounting data collected at the company or legal entity level. One solution could be to consider only mono-establishment companies, which constitute the essence of the French productive system. This choice would, however, result in omitting business groups, which, in the recent context, constitute a major component to be taken into account.

NOTES

1. The correlation matrix gave a coefficient equal to -0.75 and significant at a 1 per cent level for these two variables (available on request).
2. Ivreg command in Stata 12.

REFERENCES

Audretsch, D. and Dohse, D. (2007), Location: a neglected determinant of firm growth, *Review of World Economics*, **143**(1): 79–107.
Audretsch, D., Grilo, I., and Thurik, A. (2012), "Globalization, entrepreneurship and the region", EIM research reports.
Baldwin, R. (1994), *Towards an Integrated Europe*, London: Centre for Economic Policy Research.
Becchetti, L. and Trovato, G. (2002), "The determinants of growth for small and medium sized firms: the role of the availability of external finance", *Small Business Economics*, **19**(4): 291–306.
Braunerhjelm, P. and Borgman, B. (2004), "Geographical concentration, entrepreneurship and regional growth: evidence from regional data in Sweden, 1975–99", *Regional Studies*, **38**(8): 929–947.
Burke, A. and Hansley, A. (2009), "Market concentration and business survival in static vs. dynamic industries", Working paper, Kiel Institute for World Economy, 1517: 1–21.
Caves, R. (1998), "Industrial organization and new findings on the turnover and mobility of firms", *Journal of Economic Literature*, **36**(4): 1947–1982.
Coad, A. (2009), *The Growth of Firms: A Survey of Theories and Empirical Evidence*, Cheltenham, UK and Northampton, MA, USA: Edward Elgar Publishing.
Cooke, P. (2005), "Regionally asymmetric knowledge capabilities and open innovation: Exploring globalisation 2 – a new model of industry organization", *Research Policy*, **34**(8): 1128–1149.
Guzzini E., Iacobucci D., and Rosa P. (2012), "Financial and organizational perspectives on small and medium-sized business groups", Working paper 1201, c.MET-05, Centro interuniversitario di Economia Applicata alle Politiche per L'industria, lo Sviluppo locale e l'Internazionalizzazione.
Hamermesh, D. (1993), *Labor Demand*, Princeton, NJ: Princeton University Press.
Hoogstra, G. and van Dijk, J. (2004), "Explaining firm employment growth: does location matter?", *Small Business Economics*, **22**: 179–192.

Krugman, P. (1991), "Increasing returns and economic geography", *Journal of Political Economy*, **99**(3): 483–499.

Mansfield, E. (1962), "Entry, Gibrat's law, innovation, and the growth of firms", *American Economic Review*, **52**(4): 1023–1051.

Martin, P., Mayer, T., and Maynerie, F. (2011), "Spatial concentration and plant-level productivity in France", *Journal of Urban Economics*, **69**(2): 182–195.

Nyström, K. (2007), "An industry disaggregated analysis of the determinants of regional entry and exit", *Annals of Regional Science*, **41**: 877–896.

Porter, M.E. (1998), *On Competition*, Cambridge, MA: Harvard Business School Press.

Santarelli, E., Klomp, L., and Thurik, A.R. (2006), Gibrat's law: an overview of the empirical literature. In Santarelli, E., ed., *Entrepreneurship, Growth, and Innovation: The Dynamics of Firms and Industries*, Boston, MA: Springer, 41–73.

Schimke, A. and Teicher, N. (2012), *Impact of Local Knowledge Endowment on Employment Growth in Nanotechnology*. Karlsruhe: KIT.

Sutton, J. (1997), "Gibrat's legacy", *Journal of Economic Literature*, **35**(1): 40–59.

8. The labor market and successful entrepreneurship

Jean Bonnet and Nicolas Le Pape

INTRODUCTION

Oxenfeldt (1943) was the first to recognize that unemployed individuals (or individuals with limited prospects for wage employment) may have an additional incentive to become self-employed in order to earn a living. In such cases the individual commits himself to an entrepreneurial activity because of a low opportunity cost. In a macroeconomic perspective, the *refugee effect* of unemployment can lead to new firm's formation,[1] while the *Schumpeter effect* conveys the fact that new firm formation reduces the rate of unemployment.[2] Several authors focus their research on measuring the extent of both the refugee and the Schumpeter effects. The refugee effect (also called the shopkeeper effect) is similar, from a microeconomic point of view, to the push effect in explaining entrepreneurial motives. Accordingly, individuals are driven to entrepreneurship mainly because they suffer from a poor position in the labor market and, consequently, face only low opportunity costs when deciding to become entrepreneurs (cf. Shapero and Sokol, 1982 or Noorderhaven et al., 2004, who underline the importance of "push" factors in entrepreneurship). For example Evans and Leighton (1989) and Acs et al. (1994) find significance to the push motive using American data.[3] In different European countries, unemployment is also a strong determinant, increasing the likelihood of an individual becoming an entrepreneur (Foti and Vivarelli, 1994 for Italy; Ritsilä and Tervo, 2002 for Finland; Abdesselam et al., 2004 for France).

On the other hand, "pull" (opportunity) motives refer to a set of positive motives (economic opportunity, valuation of a new idea or self-actualization). These motives refer to situations where new entrepreneurs are positively drawn to entrepreneurship. More precisely: "Pull entrepreneurs are those who are lured by their new venture idea and initiative venture activity because of the attractiveness of the business idea and its personal implication" (Amit and Muller, 1995, p. 65).

In this study, we empirically examine whether differences in the previous situation of the entrepreneur in the labor market interacts with his/her ability to implement successful product market strategies. More precisely, when distinguishing between *push* and *pull* entrepreneurs, one should expect that entrepreneurs sensitive to opportunity motives are more prone to implementing successful entrepreneurial market strategies, since the decision to set up a firm can be viewed as an unconstrained decision. Conversely since the push motive is mainly associated with a lack of alternatives, one can infer that the new entrepreneur was suffering from a depreciation of his/her own human capital in his/her previous occupation (Bhattacharjee et al., 2009). In that case, the entrepreneurial choice does not necessarily reveal some endowment in entrepreneurial abilities, and this may be an obstacle to the implementation of successful post-entry strategies.

This chapter is organized as follows. Section 1 presents the push and pull motives for entrepreneurship and the entrepreneurial orientation of new entrepreneurs. Section 2 examines the performance of the product market orientation of new firms according to pre-entry motives, and Section 3 concludes.

1. THEORETICAL BACKGROUND AND HYPOTHESES

1.1 Push and Pull Motives: A Reappraisal Based on the Previous Occupation of the Entrepreneur

Two types of new entrepreneur are classically distinguished:

- Entrepreneurs who are more responsive to negative motivations (push motives): avoiding depreciation in their human capital, with low opportunity cost to entrepreneurship. Setting up a firm is an option for individuals facing unemployment or a mismatch with their salaried position. Stoner and Fry (1982) examine if dissatisfaction in their previous job influenced whether entrepreneurs started their own ventures in a similar or different industry. They found that entrepreneurs who experienced dissatisfaction were more likely to start a new venture in a sector different from their previous job. They also found that entrepreneurs who had left their job to start a new venture in a similar sector of activity did so for the opportunities and growth that potential entrepreneurship provided.
- Entrepreneurs who are responsive to positive motivations, such as developing a new idea (innovation in the sense of Schumpeter, 1911),

or to business opportunities (innovation in a more incremental way in the sense of Kirzner, 1979, 1985) when their alertness enables them to take part in the clearing of markets.

From a macroeconomic perspective these two main types of motivation can be translated in the following way. When the labor market rewards individuals consistent with their productivity, the observed human capital of the individual gets paid, on average, its fair value and, in such cases, the setting up of a company by a salaried employee is rather a good signal since it may be expected that there is a new idea to develop or a market niche to exploit. Why go for a risky situation unless there is a profit expectation higher than one's wage? We consider that when new entrepreneurs set up their firm in their branch of salaried experience, they were well matched in the labor market. In such cases they had, a priori, good returns on their human capital (perceived wages reflected their productivity). If they decided to set up a firm, it might be due to information asymmetries concerning the actual quality of their ideas which did not allow them to pursue their idea within the firm where they were employed (Audretsch and Mahmood, 1995). In such cases self-employment mainly corresponds to pull motives (new ideas, innovation and so on). Wage earners go into entrepreneurship only whether they perceive that the potential failure of their project will not penalize them and that they can easily find the needed financial support and advice.

Conversely, an individual facing failure in the labor market (for instance the individual is unemployed or employed in an unsuitable job) results in one's human capital being paid less than it should on the labor market in the right position. The setting up of a company mainly results from low opportunity costs to entrepreneurship and/or the will to avoid depreciation of human capital (Bhattacharjee et al., 2006, 2009). Push motives are predominant in French entrepreneurship (Aubry et al., 2013), where the proportion of unemployed people among new entrepreneurs (setting up/ taking over) is around 3–4 times greater than the rate of unemployment.

Considering these two main motives as key determinants in the entrepreneurial decision, one can infer that new entrepreneurs will implement various post-entry strategies based on their previous occupation in the labor market, and that these strategies may also affect their likelihood of success. Within the set of different post-entry strategies, we focus then on the firm's competitive behavior or its willingness to overcome competitors to gain market share. This competitive entrepreneurial behavior includes all activities or attitudes aimed at overcoming rivals: willingness to increase activity, willingness to sub-contract and competitive aggressiveness (concerning prices, new customers and advertising strategy).

1.2 Entrepreneurial Orientation

Part of the management literature is shedding a light on what has been termed "entrepreneurial orientation" (EO): an entrepreneurial firm is one that "engages in product market innovation, undertakes somewhat risky ventures, and is first to come up with 'proactive' innovations, beating competitors to the punch" (Miller, 1983, quoted in Lumpkin and Dess, 1996, p. 139). The strategic orientation of the firm allows for a trade-off between growing fast in a competitive environment and establishing a market niche in order to ease the constraint of strong growth. Firm growth can be seen as a function of rivalry conditions and the competitive behavior of the firm on its product market. Smith et al. (2001) show that aggressive behavior spreading across firms in the same industry increases the degree of competition and, consequently, reduces the global profitability of the branch of industry. Yet these behaviors are beneficial for the firms initiating them. Moreover, it can be better to be the most aggressive in order to gain or maintain market leader status (Ferrier et al., 1999; Ferrier, 2001). The advantage of a proactive attitude may be expressed, in industrial organization literature, by the first mover advantage in a Stackelberg game (Lieberman and Montgomery, 1998). Firms attempt to capture market opportunities before rivals through the introduction of new products (Dess et al., 2003).

Covin and Covin (1990) define aggressiveness with respect to firm behavior in terms of three basic strategies: initiating action, introducing new products and adopting a very competitive stance. For newly created firms, they find that the more aggressive they are, the better they perform. Lumpkin and Dess (1996) identify five variables in order to specify the definition of the EO concept: proactiveness, competitive aggressiveness, willingness to take risk, autonomy and innovativeness.[4] We focus on the two first variables of proactiveness and competitive aggressiveness because we are interested in explaining the rivalry behavior and the product market's strategy of the new firms.

Proactiveness is defined by Lumpkin and Dess (2001, p. 429), as "how firms relate to market opportunities by seizing initiative in the market place; competitive aggressiveness refers to how firms react to competitive trends and demands that already exist in the market place." It is characterized by the anticipation of opportunities, the detection of future trends in the market and a high responsiveness to market signals that allows the firm to benefit from first mover advantages. The firm acts in advance to less responsive rivals, thus enabling it to be in a good position to seize market shares and to show superior performance over *rivals*. A proactive firm tends to shape its environment in its favor (Frese et al., 1996). It acts in anticipating future problems, needs or changes.

Competitive aggressiveness requires adopting tactics against competitors in order to weaken them or to benefit from their weaknesses. It also has to do with reactive behavior. In the case of new firms the aggressiveness posture is a means of establishing a position, a kind of legitimacy.

In the following section, we examine what kind of entrepreneurial strategies may improve the longevity of the firm. For this purpose, we distinguish between push and pull entrepreneurs by taking into account their previous situation in the labor market.

2. ENTREPRENEURIAL MOTIVES, POST-ENTRY STRATEGIES AND LONGEVITY OF NEW FIRMS: METHODOLOGIES AND RESULTS

2.1 Data, Measurement Issues and Methodology

In order to highlight the effect of post-entry strategies on the survival of new firms we used a French database of new entrepreneurs. Data is drawn from a 2002 survey (Sine 2002-1) conducted by the French National Institute of Statistical and Economic Studies (INSEE), which includes French firms set up or taken over during the first half of 2002. A follow-up survey, carried out in 2005 (Sine 2002-2), gives information about the status of the same firms three years later (closed down or still active). We integrate market policies during the last two years (2004–2005) into the discussion. Finally, with the last survey of the cohort in 2007 (Sine 2007-3), we consider the duration of the firms according to their strategies.

In order to have a homogenized population of new firms, we consider independent *ex-nihilo* start-ups (subsidiaries and takeovers are excluded) in French regions (overseas departments are excluded) with limited liability status. Theoretically firms evolving under limited liability are more prone to exit because exit costs are lower. This can be counterbalanced by the fact that this kind of status reflects a more business-oriented enterprise. Effectively in our sample the duration of the limited liability firms is slightly superior (57.10 percent against 55.10 percent). Harhoff et al. (1998) also suppose that growth rates are higher for survivor firms with limited liability since these firms undertake riskier projects.

2.1.1 Classes of entrepreneurial behavior

A variable is constructed so as to express the firm's entrepreneurial behavior (E.B.) in its market. The real behavior of the firm in its market can be spotted with five questions that represent the main dimensions of entrepreneurial behavior (Table 8.1). The competitive dynamism is naturally

Table 8.1   The questions from the SINE 2002–2 survey used to measure E.B.

What has been your global approach towards your firm over the last two years (2004–2005)?	**Global approach (GA)**
Increasing activity	1
Maintaining activity at its current level	0
Attempting to safeguard activity	0
Have you made advertising efforts over the last two years?	**Advertising effort (AE)**
Yes	1
No	0
Have you made efforts to attract new clients over the last two years?	**Client effort (CE)**
Yes	1
No	0
Have you made any effort on your prices over the last two years?	**Price effort (PE)**
Yes	1
No	0
Did you subcontract work (to other firms) over the last two years?	**Subcontracting work given (SWG)**
Yes	1
No	0

expressed by a decrease in price or an increase in production level. It also refers to several modes of winning market shares in a context of non-price competition: efforts to find new clients, advertising efforts (willingness to attract new clients or to sell new products) or subcontracting work to another firm. This last factor constitutes an indication of the firm's willingness to preserve its market share if it cannot respond immediately to new demand because of capacity constraints. It could also be a sign of the firm's willingness to increase its importance in subcontracting specialized work that could not be done inside the firm.

By summing these scores, we construct a global index of E.B. on a scale of 0–5: the higher the global index, the higher the E.B. index ascribed to the firm (Table 8.2).

We use a Cox model (proportional hazard model) in order to examine the impact of post-entry strategy on survival. Therefore we calculate the life span of the firm in months, and the duration model measures the

Table 8.2   The global index of E.B.

E.B.0: minimum level of E.B.	E.B.1: very weak level of E.B.
E.B.2: weak level of E.B.	E.B.3: medium level of E.B.
E.B.4: high level of E.B.	E.B.5: maximum level of E.B.

impact of the variables representing the nature and the level of entrepreneurial behavior on the life span of the firm. We also control with other variables that are commonly included in new firm survival analysis.

2.2   Empirical Results

We consider that pre-entry motives could be related to the individual ability to implement a successful proactive/aggressive strategy towards competitors. A dominant pull motive is expected to correspond to the category of people who do not change their branch of activity when they set up a firm. A dominant push motive is expected to be associated with the category of individuals unemployed for more than one year (see section 1). In the latter case, getting into entrepreneurship is a self-employment choice that probably conveys fewer growth-oriented strategies.

Descriptive statistics in Table 8.3 show that entrepreneurs who were previously long-term unemployed incur slightly higher levels of entrepreneurial behavior for the E.B.1 and E.B.3 classes. Surprisingly, we also find a higher proportion of firms that exhibit no entrepreneurial behavior in the population of previously salaried people. Concerning the effect of entrepreneurial behavior on duration, we observe that it is globally positive in the sense that it increases the life span of the new firm for the E.B.2, E.B.3 and E.B.4 classes of behavior – except for this last class for the category of entrepreneurs who were previously unemployed.

Pull entrepreneurs are, a priori, endowed with unobserved human capital (see section 1). These entrepreneurs have some personal abilities that allow them to adopt offensive positioning towards competitors or to be responsive to market signals. As a consequence they are more prone to adopt aggressive strategies that can improve the life span of the firm. Nevertheless in the population of push entrepreneurs, entrepreneurial behavior is still positive.

When differentiating by a combination of the different kinds of policies some interesting results appear (Table 8.4).

When we compare the two sets of entrepreneurs, a first result is that E.B. is more efficient in the case of those previously salaried in the same branch of activity (a larger range of combination of post-entry strategies

Table 8.3   Level of entrepreneurial behavior (E.B.) and survival of start-ups by entrepreneurs with experience in the same branch of activity or previously unemployed for over one year

Previously salaried same branch: dominant pull motive (n = 6238)

Index of entrepreneurial behavior	E.B.0	E.B.1	E.B.2	E.B.3	E.B.4	E.B.5
Number	1824	2055	1446	767	137	9
Share	29,24%	32,94%	23,18%	12,30%	2,20%	0,14%

Duration model/variables	Modalities	Coefficients	Effect on duration
	E.B.5	−9.996	n.s.
Level of entrepreneurial behavior	E.B.4	−0.525++	positive
	E.B.3	−0.451+++	positive
	E.B.2	−0.166+	positive
	E.B.1	0.029	n.s.

Long-term unemployed: dominant push motive (n = 1807)

Index of entrepreneurial behavior	E.B.0	E.B.1	E.B.2	E.B.3	E.B.4	E.B.5
Number	452	634	417	269	35	0
Share	25,01%	35,09%	23,08%	14,89%	1,94%	0,00%

Duration model/variables	Modalities	Coefficients	Effect on duration
Level of entrepreneurial behavior	E.B.5	x	x
	E.B.4	-0.739	n.s.
	E.B.3	-0.647^{+++}	positive
	E.B.2	-0.521^{+++}	positive
	E.B.1	-0.177	n.s.

Notes: The referential modality which is here E.B.0.
If $\beta<0$ and if $Pr>\chi^2$ is inferior to 10 percent the variable contributes significantly to increase the life span of the firm.
$^{+++}$, $^{++}$ and $^{+}$ indicate significance at the 1 percent, 5 percent and 10 percent level.
x: lack of data.
n.s.: not significant.

Table 8.4   Nature of entrepreneurial behavior (E.B.) and survival of start-ups by entrepreneurs with experience in the same branch of activity or previously unemployed for over one year

Previously salaried same branch: dominant pull motive (n = 6238)

Variables	Modalities	Coefficients	Effect on duration
Nature of entrepreneurial behavior	GA*CE*SWG	−0.669^{+++}	positive
	GA*CE*PE	−1.386^{+}	positive
	GA*AE*SWG	−1.021^{++}	positive
	AE*CE*PE	0.957^{+++}	negative
	GA*CE	−0.497^{+++}	positive
	GA*SWG	−0.484^{++}	positive
	AE*SWG	−1.594^{++}	positive
	PE*SWG	0.805^{+++}	negative
	CE*AE	0.502^{+++}	negative
	GA	−0.465^{+++}	positive
	CE	0.453^{+++}	negative
	PE	0.476^{++}	negative

Long-term unemployed: dominant push motive

Variables	Modalities	Coefficients	Effect on duration
Nature of entrepreneurial behavior	GA*CE*SWG	−0.550^{+}	positive
	GA*AE*CE	−1.152^{++}	positive
	GA*CE	−0.479^{+}	positive
	GA*SWG	−1.384^{+}	positive
	PE*SWG	1.941^{+}	negative
	CE*PE	−0.949^{+}	positive
	GA	−0.701^{+++}	positive
	PE	0.441^{+}	negative

Notes: All the combinatory variables are taken into account but only the significant modalities are presented (the results on control variables are available from the authors upon request). The interpretation of the coefficients is relative to no entrepreneurial behavior policy at all (E.B.0).
$^{+++}$, $^{++}$ and $^{+}$ indicate significance at the 1 percent, 5 percent and 10 percent level.

significantly impacts on survival and generally contributes to increasing life span of the new firm). A second result is that a global approach is always associated with successful strategies in the two populations.

Pull entrepreneurs (salaried and experienced in the same branch of activity) have more information, a priori, about the desired product and its characteristics, customers' tastes, and the rules of the competition in the product market (one can think that they have acquired this information from past experience). The two modalities – client effort (CE) and price effort (PE) – and their associated combinations with advertising effort (AE) are not efficient post-entry strategies that improve the duration of the new firm.

A possible explanation for these empirical results could be that these kinds of strategies do not reduce the information asymmetries between clients and the products or services supplied. When *pull* entrepreneurs implement such strategies it denotes an insufficient quality or completeness of the product/service with regard to the market. Nevertheless, advertising effort combined with subcontracting work given has a positive effect.

Push entrepreneurs (people who were unemployed) are more financially constrained (Crepon and Duguet, 2002); they create the smallest new ventures, and so below the minimum efficient size. One could imagine that E.B. allows the entrepreneur's business to reach the minimum efficient scale faster, and that a post-entry strategy based on growth favors longevity of their new firm. This is true for entrepreneurs driven by the desire to increase their activity – global approach (GA). Nevertheless not all the policies are favorable. Price effort combined with willingness to attract new clients is favorable for the survival of the firm. Yet, when combined with the subcontracting of work, it decreases the life span of the firm, probably because this strategy reduces the firm's price-cost margin.[5]

3.   CONCLUSION

In this study we investigate the complex relationships between an entrepreneur's previous position in the labor market, entrepreneurial behavior (intensity and nature) of the young firm and its survival chances. Empirical results are obtained from a sample of new French firms created in 2002 for which survival is examined during 2005–2007 after implementation of market policies in 2004–2005. The entrepreneur's previous position in the labor market is expected to be related to the main motive (pull or push) of their setting up a firm. We show that entrepreneurial orientation draws some interesting results that can go beyond the usual explanations of survival based on the initial conditions under which new firms are founded. More precisely, we find that being a *pull* entrepreneur is related to implementation of successful post-entry strategies, containing a higher level of entrepreneurial behavior, compared to *push* entrepreneurs. We also show that the entrepreneurial orientation of the new firm has a larger impact on its survival for the category of pull entrepreneurs. Maybe the entrepreneurial orientation (or the ability to implement proactive strategies) conveys some information about the "entrepreneurial human capital" of the individual which is, all things being equal, a determining factor in the survival of a new firm.

NOTES

1. People who are unemployed choose to create their own jobs (Thurik et al., 2008; Acs et al., 1994).
2. In an entrepreneurial society most new jobs are created by new-firm start-ups.
3. Storey (1991) finds a mixed effect with American data, as do Tervo and Niittykangas (1994) at the regional level for Finland and Audretsch et al. (2001) for Organisation for Economic Co-operation and Development (OECD) countries.
4. Lumpkin and Dess (1997) note that Covin and Slevin (1989, 1991) do not distinguish clearly the two concepts because they suggest that "proactive firms compete aggressively with other firms."
5. This is due to the association of a decrease in price and an increase in cost (outsourcing of production).

REFERENCES

Abdesselam, R., J. Bonnet, and N. Le Pape (2004). "An explanation of the life span of new French firms", *Small Business Economics*, **23**, 237–254.
Acs, Z.J., D.B. Audretsch, and D.S. Evans (1994). "Why does the self-employment rate vary across countries and over time?" CEPR Discussion Papers.
Amit, R., and E. Muller (1995). "'Push' and 'pull' entrepreneurship", *Journal of Small Business and Entrepreneurship*, **12** (14), 64–80.
Aubry M., Bonnet J., and P. Renou-Maissant (2013). "Business cycle and entrepreneurial behavior using French regional data". CREM Working Paper no. 4, January, http://ideas.repec.org/p/tut/cremwp/201304.html.
Audretsch, D.B., M.A. Carree, and A.R. Thurik (2001). "Does entrepreneurship reduce unemployment?" Tinbergen Institute Discussion Papers 01-074/3.
Audretsch, D., and T. Mahmood (1995). "New firm survival: new results using a hazard function", *Review of Economics and Statistics*, **77** (1), 97–103.
Bhattacharjee, A., J. Bonnet, N. Le Pape, and R. Renault (2006). "Inferring the unobserved human capital of entrepreneurs", in M. Van Praag (ed.), *Entrepreneurship and Human Capital*. Amsterdam: Amsterdam Center for Entrepreneurship, pp. 47–51.
Bhattacharjee, A., J. Bonnet, N. Le Pape, and R. Renault (2009). "Entrepreneurial motives and performance: why might better educated entrepreneurs be less successful?" TEPP Working Paper, FR CNRS 3126.
Covin, J.G., and T.J. Covin (1990). "Competitive aggressiveness, environmental context and small firm performance", *Entrepreneurship, Theory and Practice*, **14** (4), 35–50.
Covin, J.G., and D.P. Slevin (1989). "Strategic management of small firms in hostile and benign environments", *Strategic Management Journal*, **10**, 75–87.

Covin, J.G., and D.P. Slevin (1991). "A conceptual model of entrepreneurship as firm behavior", *Entrepreneurship, Theory and Practice*, **16** (1), 7–25.

Crepon, B., and E. Duguet (2002). "Prêt bancaire, aides publiques et survie des nouvelles entreprises: une analyse econométrique à partir des méthodes d'appariement sélectif sur données d'entrepreneurs", *Eurequa, Cahiers de Recherches*, **48**.

Dess, G.G., R.D. Ireland, S.A. Zahra, S.W. Floyd, J.J. Janney, and P.J. Lane (2003). "Emerging issues in corporate entrepreneurship", *Journal of Management*, **29**, 351–378.

Evans, D.S., and L.S. Leighton (1989). "The determinants of changes in US self-employment, 1968–1987", *Small Business Economics*, **1** (2), 111–119.

Ferrier, W.J. (2001). "Navigating the competitive landscape: the drivers and consequences of competitive aggressiveness", *Academy of Management Journal*, **44** (4), 858–877.

Ferrier, W.J., K.G. Smith, and C.M. Grimm (1999). "The role of competitive action in market share erosion and industry dethronement: a study of industry leaders and challengers", *Academy of Management Journal*, **42** (4), 372–388.

Foti, A., and M. Vivarelli (1994). "An econometric test of the self-employment model: the case of Italy", *Small Business Economics*, **6**, 81–94.

Frese, M., W. Kring, A. Soose, and J. Zempel (1996). "Personal initiative at work: differences between East and West Germany", *Academy of Management Journal*, **39**, 37–63.

Harhoff, D., Stahl, K., and Woywode, M. (1998). "Legal form, growth and exit of West German firms: empirical results for manufacturing, construction, trade and services industries", *Journal of Industrial Economics*, **46**, 453–488.

Kirzner, I.M. (1979). *Perception, Opportunity and Profit*. Chicago: University of Chicago Press.

Kirzner, I.M. (1985). *Discovery and the Capitalist Process*. Chicago: University of Chicago Press.

Lieberman, M.B., and D.B. Montgomery (1998). "First-mover (dis)advantages: retrospective and link with the resource-based view", *Strategic Management Journal*, **19**, 1111–1125.

Lumpkin, G.T., and G.G. Dess (1996). "Clarifying the entrepreneurial orientation construct and linking it to performance", *Academy of Management Review*, **21**, 135–172.

Lumpkin, G.T., and G.G. Dess (1997). "Proactiveness versus competitive aggressiveness: teasing apart key dimensions of an entrepreneurial orientation", in P. Reynolds et al. (eds), *Frontiers of Entrepreneurship Research*. Babson Park, MA: Babson College, pp. 47–58.

Lumpkin, G.T., and G.G. Dess (2001). "Linking two dimensions of entrepreneurial orientation to firm performance: the moderating role of environment and industry life cycle", *Journal of Business Venturing*, **16**, 429–451.

Miller, D. (1983). "The correlates of entrepreneurship in three types of firms", *Management Science*, **29**, 770–791.

Noorderhaven N., R. Thurik, S. Wennekers, and A. van Stel (2004). "The role of dissatisfaction and per capita income in explaining self-employment across 15 European countries", *Entrepreneurship, Theory and Practice*, **28**, 447–466.

Oxenfeldt, A.R. (1943). *New Firms and Free Enterprise: Pre-war and Post-war Aspects*. Washington, DC: American Council on Public Affairs.

Ritsila, J., and H. Tervo (2002). "Effects of unemployment on new firm formation:

Exploring the entrepreneurial society

micro-level panel data evidence from Finland", *Small Business Economics*, **19** (1), 31–40.

Schumpeter, J.A. (1911). *The Theory of Economic Development: An Inquiry into Profits, Capital, Credit, Interest, and the Business Cycle*. Cambridge, MA: Harvard University Press.

Shapero, A., and L. Sokol (1982). "The social dimensions of entrepreneurship", *Encyclopedia of Entrepreneurship*, pp. 72–90. Available at SSRN: http://ssrn.com/abstract=1497759.

Smith, K.G., W.J. Ferrier, and C.M. Grimm (2001). "King of the hill: dethroning the industry leader", *Academy of Management Executive*, **15**, 59–70.

Stoner, C.R., and F.L. Fry (1982): "The entrepreneurial decision: dissatisfaction or opportunity", *Journal of Small Business Management*, April, 39–44.

Storey, D.J. (1991). "The birth of new firms: does unemployment matter? A review of the evidence", *Small Business Economics*, **3** (3), 167–178.

Tervo, H., and H. Niittykangas (1994). "The impact of unemployment on new firm formation in Finland", *International Small Business Journal*, **13** (1), 38–53.

Thurik, A.R., M.A. Carree, A. van Stel, and D.B. Audretsch (2008). "Does self-employment reduce unemployment?", *Journal of Business Venturing*, **23** (6), 673–686.

9. The relationship between knowledge management and innovation level in Mexican SMEs: empirical evidence

**Gonzalo Maldonado Guzman,
Maria del Carmen Martinez Serna and
Domingo García-Pérez-de-Lema**

1. INTRODUCTION

The globalization of economy and high levels of market demand are pushing firms, mainly small- and medium-sized enterprises (SMEs), to restructure their business strategies in order to update them to current market demand. Similarly, different firms are considering knowledge management (KM) as a strategy that allows them to improve their level of competition (Audretsch and Thurik, 2000, 2001, 2004) because knowledge is considered essential to obtaining a higher level of competitiveness and innovation in organizations (Corso et al., 2003; Chirico, 2008). For this reason, SMEs have to improve their business skills in order to manage more efficiently the knowledge generated by their employees so they can adapt faster to the external and internal changes that will allow them to apply innovation activities and, as a consequence, improve their economic edge (Teece et al., 1997; Eisenhardt and Martin, 2000).

In this sense, the current business environment is changing rapidly from industrial based to knowledge based (Drucker, 1994; Van de Ven, 2004; Lu et al., 2008) by means of two essential elements. On one hand we have the globalization of economy (Lu et al., 2008), while on the other we have fast technological changes (Santos et al., 2004; Peng, 2006). Thus, this new business environment is requiring SMEs to build and improve their skills based on knowledge specialization and innovation in order to provide products that are more suited to their consumers than the ones provided by the competition (Lu et al., 2008).

As a result of these changes, KM is present in the current literature as one of the most important elements that enable the design and implementation of innovation activities as an integral part of firms' business strategies (Hitt et al., 1998; Lee and Grewal, 2004; Miller et al., 2007). Furthermore, the increase in innovation activities can be the result of more effective SME KM, particularly the activities of innovation in products, processes and management systems (Mohsen and Khadem, 2010).

In this sense, most studies that link KM and innovation have analyzed these elements from the perspective of large firms in developed countries; so there are few that have paid attention to SMEs (Thompson and Leyden, 1983; Acs, 1996), and even fewer that are related to the field of developing countries (OECD, 2003; Bozbura, 2007). Thus, one contribution of this chapter is the relationship between KM and SME innovation activities in a developing country (Mexico). Also, most researches based on these two characteristics have applied qualitative methods, and this study also contributes by providing information on how KM contributes to improving innovation activities in SMEs, by applying quantitative methods and using structural equation models.

2.   LITERATURE REVIEW

Knowledge management (KM) has been widely analyzed and discussed since the mid-2000s in different fields and contexts (Lopez et al., 2004) such as the construction industry (Maqsood and Finegan, 2009), pharmaceuticals (Normann and Ramirez, 1993), electronics (Sieloff, 1999), information and communication technology (ICT) (Rantapuska and Ihanainen, 2008) and manufacturing (Lu et al., 2008; Mohsen and Khadem, 2010).

The current literature shows different investigations where they directly relate to KM and SME innovation activities. One of the most cited papers is by Ruggles and Little (1997), which refers to the knowledge, personal experience and economic resources (such as the acquisition of equipment, tools and so on) that are accessible to all personnel. This model also refers to the people, who are considered as the seeds in which the new concepts can be generated and, at the same time, the main element of the innovation processes.

Another study, presented by Swan et al. (1999), postulated two perspectives termed *cognitive model* and *community model*. The cognitive model commonly denotes a perspective in which the generated knowledge can be picked up and codified by each employee in a firm (Sorensen and Lundh-Snis, 2001), whereas the community or social model is based on the development of technology.

The model presented by Van de Ven and Engleman (2004) considers four basic elements that are derived from the present relation between KM and innovation. The first is the *human* element, which consists in motivating the firm's employees to be more innovative by means of searching and developing both new and existing knowledge in SMEs. The second element is the *process*, which concerns how SME managers develop and implement new ideas in organizational processes. The third element refers to *structural problems*, which consists in the use of infrastructure between the company and its suppliers to obtain the knowledge that will help them generate, facilitate, support and promote innovation activities in SMEs. Finally, the fourth element, *leadership*, consists in the generation and adequate management of an environment that enables facilitation of innovation activities in the organization.

The model proposed by Tranfield et al. (2006) shows two stages in the KM–innovation relationship, which they called *discovery* and *realization*. The discovery stage consists in the need to look for and create ideal environments (both internal and external) to develop the innovation potential that lies within the organization. The realization stage consists in how the organization, along with available elements, can achieve the implementation and development of innovation by means of different steps that in the end allow either the development of new products and services or the development of new management processes or methods in the organization.

From the models discussed earlier, it can be inferred that innovation activities can be the most effective result of KM in which the innovations of products, processes and management systems are the essential components in the success and development of companies in the new millennium (Mohsen and Khadem, 2010). This is due to the fact that the new products and services obtained from the interaction between knowledge and technology are changing the way businesses deal and compete with each other in the new economic environment (Handzic, 2004). Hence, it has been demonstrated in the existing literature that innovation is a paramount element for the survival and development of SMEs as well as an important objective of KM activity (Ruggles and Little, 1997). Based on this information, the following hypotheses can be formulated:

Hypothesis 1: The higher the level of knowledge management, the higher the level of product innovation.

Hypothesis 2: The higher the level of knowledge management, the higher the level of process innovation.

Hypothesis 3: The higher the level of knowledge management, the higher the level of management systems innovation.

3. METHODOLOGY

In order to obtain the reference framework, the methodology used in this chapter consisted in obtaining a list of SMEs with between 20 and 250 employees. This was made possible through the 2009 directory from the Sistema de Información Empresarial de Mexico (Mexican Business Information System, or SIEM) for Aguascalientes State, which accounted for 130 manufacturing firms registered up to July 30, 2009. Also, a survey was designed to be answered by the SMEs' managers. It took the form of personal interviews with the 130 selected firms; however only 125 replied, giving a response rate of 96 percent. Knowledge management was measured by means of four dimensions:

- Employee training was measured with a scale of five items adapted from Bontis (2000) and OECD (2003).
- The scale for KM policies and strategies was adapted from Bozbura (2004, 2007) with 13 items.
- The scale for the creation and acquisition of external knowledge was adapted from OECD (2003) and Bozbura (2007) with five items.
- The scale for the effects of organizational culture was adapted from OECD (2003) and Bozbura (2007) with four items.

All the items were measured on a 5-point Likert scale, with 1 = Strongly disagree and 5 = Strongly agree.

In order to measure innovation, the survey required the managers to indicate whether their firm had implemented innovation activities during the two years prior to their application (1 = Yes; 0 = No). In order to measure the importance of the innovative activity, the survey asked the managers to evaluate the product innovation, the process innovation and the management systems innovation, where 1 = Not important and 5 = Very important (Zahra and Covin, 1993; Kalantaridis and Pheby, 1999; Frishammar and Hörte, 2005; Madrid-Guijarro et al., 2009).

In order to evaluate the reliability and validity of the measurement scales, a confirmatory factorial analysis (CFA) was carried out by the maximum likelihood method using EQS 6.1 software (Bentler, 2005; Brown, 2006; Byrne, 2006). This is presented in Table 9.1 and suggests that the theoretical model provides a good fit of data ($S\text{-}BX^2$ = 596.7760; df = 356; p = 0,000; NFI = 0.930; NNFI = 0.966; CFI = 0.971; RMSEA = 0.074). As evidence of the convergent validity, the results indicate that all the items of related factors are significant (p < 0.001); the size of all the standardized factorial loads are superior to 0.60 (Bagozzi and Yi, 1988); and the average of the standardized factorial loads exceeds the value of 0.70 (Hair et al., 1995).

Table 9.1 *Internal consistency and convergent validity*

Variable	Indicator	Factor Loading	Robust t-Value	Loading Average	Cronbach's Alpha	CRI	AVE
Training and mentoring employees of KM	BFT1	0.757***	1.000[a]	0.809	0.882	0.884	0.656
	BFT3	0.811***	9.342				
	BFT4	0.842***	10.074				
	BFT5	0.826***	10.886				
KM policies and strategies	BPE1	0.807***	1.000[a]	0.727	0.807	0.810	0.532
	BPE2	0.798***	12.260				
	BPE3	0.776***	13.257				
	BPE4	0.730***	13.118				
	BPE6	0.729***	10.672				
	BPE7	0.647***	8.240				
	BPE9	0.678***	11.370				
	BPE12	0.618***	11.523				
	BPE13	0.757***	18.705				
Knowledge capturing and acquisition from outside	BKO1	0.750***	1.000[a]	0.730	0.849	0.851	0.535
	BKO2	0.776***	12.382				
	BKO3	0.764***	10.143				
	BKO4	0.651***	9.855				
	BKO5	0.709***	11.534				

Table 9.1 *(continued)*

Variable	Indicator	Factor Loading	Robust t-Value	Loading Average	Cronbach's Alpha	CRI	AVE
Effects of organizational culture	BOC1	0.821***	1.000[a]	0.835	0.896	0.903	0.701
	BOC2	0.819***	13.459				
	BOC3	0.923***	19.383				
	BOC4	0.778***	11.299				
Product innovation	INP1	0.888***	1.000[a]	0.907	0.904	0.903	0.824
	INP2	0.927***	15.081				
Process innovation	INR1	0.962***	1.000[a]	0.954	0.952	0.953	0.911
	INR2	0.947***	32.240				
Management systems innovation	ING1	0.946***	1.000[a]	0.957	0.969	0.971	0.917
	ING2	0.980***	35.109				
	ING3	0.946***	27.378				

$S\text{-}BX^2$ (df = 356) = 596.7760; p = 0.000; NFI = 0.930; NNFI = 0.966; CFI = 0.971; RMSEA = 0.074

Note: *** = p < 0.01.

With regard to the evidence of discriminant validity, the measurement is given in two ways, as shown in Table 9.2. First, with a confidentiality interval of 95 percent, none of the individual elements of the latent factors from the correlation matrix contain the value 1.0 (Anderson and Gerbing, 1988). Second, the variance extracted between each pair of constructs is superior to its corresponding AVE (Fornell and Larcker, 1981). Based on these criteria, it can be concluded that the different measurements used in this study show sufficient evidence of reliability as well as convergent and discriminant validity.

The diagonal represents the average variance extracted (AVE), while above the diagonal the shared variance (squared correlations) are represented. Below the diagonal the 95 percent confidence interval for the estimated factors correlations is provided.

4.   RESULTS

The theoretical model was analyzed in this research using the structural equations model (SEM) with EQS 6.1 software. In order to obtain the statistical results of the hypotheses, a SEM was carried out with the same variables to prove the structure of the model and obtain the results that could allow the contrast of the established hypotheses. The nomological validity of the theoretical model was analyzed by the chi-square performance test in which the theoretical model was compared with the measurement model. The results indicate that the non-significant differences of the theoretical model are good in the explanation of the relations observed between the latent constructs (Anderson and Gerbing, 1988; Hatcher, 1994). The final results obtained from SEM are presented in Table 9.3.

With regard to H1, the results obtained (shown in Table 9.3) – $\beta = 0.320$, $p < 0.001$ – indicate that KM has significant and positive effects in product innovation. With regard to H2, the results obtained, $\beta = 0.380$, $p < 0.001$, indicate that KM has significant and positive effects in process innovation. Finally, with regard to H3, the results obtained, $\beta = 0.456$, $p < 0.001$, indicate that KM has significant and positive effects in management systems innovation. To sum up, it can be proved that KM has significant and positive effects in SME innovation activities.

5.   DISCUSSION AND CONCLUSIONS

The results show that KM encourages innovation activities in three ways. First, it helps SMEs to locate innovative knowledge in the external

Table 9.2 Discriminant validity

Variable	1	2	3	4	5	6	7
1 Training and mentoring employees of KM	**0.656**	0.171	0.139	0.194	0.128	0.094	0.104
2 KM policies and strategies	0.268–0.560	**0.532**	0.166	0.164	0.109	0.145	0.107
3 Knowledge capturing and acquisition from outside	0.236–0.512	0.278–0.538	**0.535**	0.126	0.115	0.141	0.149
4 Effects of organizational culture	0.305–0.577	0.267–0.543	0.229–0.481	**0.701**	0.108	0.126	0.098
5 Product innovation	0.211–0.507	0.169–0.493	0.200–0.480	0.148–0.512	**0.824**	0.648	0.454
6 Process innovation	0.158–0.458	0.212–0.552	0.240–0.512	0.171–0.539	0.649–0.961	**0.911**	0.583
7 Management systems innovation	0.174–0.474	0.172–0.484	0.205–0.569	0.146–0.482	0.514–0.834	0.654–0.874	**0.917**

Table 9.3   Structural equation model results

Hypothesis	Path	Standardized Path Coefficients	Robust t-Value
H1: Higher knowledge management, higher product innovation	Knowledge management → product innovation	0.320***	8.313
H2: Higher knowledge management, higher process innovation	Knowledge management → process innovation	0.380***	9.188
H3: Higher knowledge management, higher management systems innovation	Knowledge management → management innovation	0.456***	10.573

$S\text{-}BX^2$ (df = 357) = 267.5603; p = 0.000; NFI = 0.894; NNFI = 0.948; CFI = 0.965; RMSEA = 0.074

Note: *** = p < 0.01.

environment of the firm, to own that knowledge and to transfer it to all personnel and incorporate it efficiently into productive activities. This generates changes or improvements to the products created. Thus, the knowledge generated in universities, research centers, government institutions and other organizations that produce similar or identical products allows SMEs to acquire and develop knowledge that turns into superior human resources (HR) skills, which results in an improvement of the competitive advantage of firms by means of the generation of new products in the target market. Similarly, in a market that is ever more globalized and highly competitive, such as the one where most SMEs are currently established, the survival and development of this kind of firm depends on the constant change or improvement of the products made to adapt them to the constant preferences and needs of consumers; and, in order to do this, they need the knowledge generated outside the firms.

Second, KM helps SMEs improve their level of competitiveness by enhancing the production processes because it gets, assimilates and uses the innovative knowledge from the external environment in favor of the organization. KM usually promotes and regulates the adoption cycle of firms' innovation activities, mainly production processes, because, on one hand, it requires important monetary investments for the automation of production by acquiring new technology; and, on the other hand, it needs an efficient record of the production and predictive, corrective maintenance of machinery and equipment. Similarly, it is necessary to have innovative initiatives in delivery methods; higher levels of cooperation with suppliers to diminish risks; and a more efficient and effective production schedule. Hence, SMEs require external innovative knowledge that is spread throughout the industry, and KM allows this process into the organization in order to generate new knowledge. This will facilitate its fast internal dissemination of firms' operational processes, which will cause changes or improvements in the production processes.

Third, KM helps SMEs achieve better development by means of change or improvement in management systems. The limited use of explicit or processual knowledge that exists inside SMEs, as well as the tacit knowledge that is in people's skills and experience, affects the specific behavior of employees and the organizational culture, which usually means that different SMEs do not accept new knowledge that is outside the firm. That is why managers will have to put into effect changes or improvements in the management systems of SMEs to facilitate the transference of explicit and tacit knowledge among all the employees in the organization. Thus, the changes or improvements in the management systems will have to guarantee the optimal use of the available knowledge (both inside and outside the organization) because the use of internal knowledge can create a high demand for the available external knowledge that would directly result in improving the management systems in order to use such knowledge efficiently. This could be perceived in better output and a higher level of innovation in the firms. In order to take external knowledge and incorporate it with the existing knowledge in SMEs it is necessary to improve and upgrade the KM process and provide the skills necessary for the firms to become learning organizations.

This research has some limitations. Firstly, the sample only considered manufacturing SMEs with 20–250 employees in Aguascalientes (Mexico), so further investigations might take into account smaller firms, from other sectors and from other countries. Secondly, the research only considered four dimensions or factors in order to measure KM; further investigations might consider other variables such as HR, aptitude, creativity, level of education and working experience, among others. Similarly, the research could include moderating variables such as the characteristics of the industry, ownership of the firms, competitive strategy and the structure of the organization. Finally, another limitation of this research is the fact that the survey only included SME managers. It would be interesting for future investigations to consider in the survey the employees, clients and suppliers of the organization in order to obtain the opinion of other participants in the firms.

REFERENCES

Acs, Z.J. (1996), Small firms and economic growth, In *Small Business in the Modern Economy*, Acs, Z.J., Carlsson, B. and Thurik, A.R. (eds.), Padstow: T.J. Press, 1–62.

Anderson, J. and Gerbing, D. (1988), Structural equation modeling in practice: a review and recommended two-step approach, *Psychological Bulletin*, **13**, 411–423.

Audretsch, D. and Thurik, R. (2000), Capitalism and democracy in the 21st century: from the managed to the entrepreneurial economy, *Journal of Evolutionary Economics*, **10**, 17–34.

Audretsch, D. and Thurik, R. (2001), What's new about the new economy: sources of growth in the managed and entrepreneurial economies, *Industrial and Corporate Change*, **19**, 759–821.

Audretsch, D. and Thurik, R. (2004), A model of entrepreneurial economy, *International Journal of Entrepreneurship Education*, **2**(2), 143–166.

Bagozzi, R.P. and Yi, Y. (1988), On the evaluation of structural equation models, *Journal of the Academy of Marketing Science*, **16**(1), 74–94.

Bentler, P.M. (2005), *EQS 6 Structural Equations Program Manual*, Encino, CA: Multivariate Software.

Bontis, N. (2000), Intellectual capital and business performance in Malaysian industries, *Journal of Intellectual Capital*, **1**(1), 85–100.

Bozbura, F.T. (2004), Measurement and application of intellectual capital in Turkey, *The Learning Organization: An International Journal*, **11**(4/5), 357–367.

Bozbura, F.T. (2007), Knowledge management practices in Turkish SMEs, *Journal of Enterprise Information Management*, **20**(2), 209–221.

Brown, T. (2006), *Confirmatory Factor Analysis for Applied Research*, New York: Guilford Press.

Byrne, B. (2006), *Structural Equation Modeling with EQS, Basic Concepts, Applications, and Programming* (2nd edn), London: LEA Publishers.

Chirico, F. (2008), Knowledge accumulation in family firms: evidence from four case studies, *International Small Business Journal*, **26**(4), 433–462.

Corso, M., Martini, A., Pellegrini, L. and Paolucci, E. (2003), Technological and organizational tools for knowledge management: in search of configurations, *Small Business Economics*, **21**(4), 397–408.

Drucker, P. (1994), The age of social transformation, *Atlantic Monthly*, **274**, 53–80.

Eisenhardt, K. and Martin, J. (2000), Dynamic capabilities: what are they?, *Strategic Management Journal*, **21**, 1105–1121.

Fornell, C. and Larcker, D. (1981), Evaluating structural equation models with unobservable variables and measurement error, *Journal of Marketing Research*, **18**, 39–50.

Frishammar, J. and Hörte, S. (2005), Managing external information in manu-facturing firms: the impact of innovation performance, *Journal of Product Innovation Management*, **22**, 251–266.

Hair, J.F., Anderson, R.E., Tatham, R.L. and Black, W.C. (1995), *Multivariate Data Analysis with Readings*, New York: Prentice Hall.

Handzic, M. (2004), *Knowledge Management through the Technology Glass*, Singapore: World Scientific Publishing.

Hatcher, L. (1994), *A Step-by-Step Approach to Using the SAS System for Factor Analysis and Structural Equation Modeling*, Cary, NC: SAS Institute.

Hitt, M., Keats, B. and DeMarie, S. (1998), Navigating in the new competitive landscape: building competitive advantage and strategy flexibility in the 21st century, *Academy of Management Executive*, **12**, 22–42.

Kalantaridis, C. and Pheby, J. (1999), Processes of innovation among manufacturing SMEs: the experience of Bedfordshire, *Entrepreneurship and Regional Development*, **11**, 57–78.

Lee, R.P. and Grewal, R. (2004), Strategic responses to new technologies and their impact on firm performance, *Journal of Marketing*, **68**, 157–171.

Lopez, S.P., Montes-Peon, J.M. and Vazquez-Ordas, C.J. (2004), Managing knowledge: the link between culture and organizational learning, *Journal of Knowledge Management*, **8**(6), 93–104.

Lu, Y., Tsang, W.K. and Peng, M.W. (2008), Knowledge management and innovation strategy in the Asia Pacific: toward an institution-based view, *Asia Pacific Journal of Management*, **25**, 361–374.

Madrid-Guijarro, A., García-Pérez-de-Lema, D. and Van Auken, H. (2009), Barriers to innovation among Spanish manufacturing SMEs, *Journal of Small Business Management*, **47**(4), 465–488.

Maqsood, T. and Finegan, A.D. (2009), A knowledge management approach to innovation and learning in the construction industry, *International Journal of Managing Projects Business*, **2**(2), 297–307.

Miller, D., Fern, M. and Cardinal, L. (2007), The use of knowledge for technological innovation within diversified firms, *Academy of Management Journal*, **50**, 308–328.

Mohsen, S.A. and Khadem, S.A. (2010), The relationship between knowledge management practices and innovation level in organizations: case study of sub-companies of selected corporations in the city of Esfahan, *Journal of Business Case Studies*, **6**(1), 89–97.

Normann, R. and Ramirez, R. (1993), From value chain to value constellation: designing interactive strategy, *Harvard Business Review*, **71**(4), 65–77.

OECD (2003), *Measuring Knowledge Management in the Business Sector*, Paris: Organisation for Economic Co-operation and Development/Statistics Canada.

Peng, M.W. (2006), *Global Strategy*, Mason, OH: South-Western Cengage.

Rantapuska, T. and Ihanainen, O. (2008), Knowledge use in ICT investment decision making of SMEs, *Journal of Enterprise Information Management*, **21**(6), 585–596.

Ruggles, R. and Little, R. (1997), Knowledge management and innovation: an initial exploration, Working Paper, Ernst & Young Center for Business Innovation.

Santos, J., Doz, Y. and Williamson, P. (2004), Is your innovation process global?, *Sloan Management Review*, **45**(4), 31–37.

Sieloff, C.G. (1999), 'If only HP knew what HP knows': the roots of knowledge management at Hewlett-Packard, *Journal of Knowledge Management*, **3**(1), 47–53.

Sorensen, C. and Lundh-Snis, U. (2001), Innovation through knowledge codification, *Journal of Information Technology*, **16**, 83–97.

Swan, J., Newell, S., Scarbrough, H. and Hislop, D. (1999), Knowledge management and innovation: networks and networking, *Journal of Knowledge Management*, **3**(3), 262–275.

Teece, D.J., Pisano, G. and Shuen, A. (1997), Dynamic capabilities and strategic management, *Strategic Management Journal*, **18**(7), 509–533.

Thompson, J.H. and Leyden, D.R. (1983), The United States of America, in *The Small Firm: An International Survey*, Storey, D.J. (ed.), London: Croom Helm, 7–45.

Tranfield, D., Young, M., Partington, D., Bessant, J. and Sapsed, J. (2006), Building knowledge management capabilities for innovation projects, in *From Knowledge Management to Strategic Competence: Measuring Technological, Market and Organisational Innovation*, Tidd, J. (ed.), London: Imperial College Press, 126–149.

Van de Ven, A. (2004), The context-specific nature of competence and corporate development, *Asia Pacific Journal of Management*, **21**, 123–147.

Van de Ven, A. and Engleman, R. (2004), Central problems in managing corporate innovation and entrepreneurship, *Advances in Entrepreneurship, Firm Emergence and Growth*, **7**, 47–72.

Zahra, S. and Covin, J. (1993), Business strategy, technology policy and firm performance, *Strategic Management Journal*, **14**(6), 451–478.

PART III

Entrepreneurial behaviors

10. Entrepreneurial opportunity recognition and exploitation in academic spin-offs

Ugo Rizzo

1. INTRODUCTION

Academic spin-offs (ASOs) – firms whose business is the exploitation of research results developed within the academic environment – are important elements of the technological change and economic growth of the local contexts in which they are formed (Vincett 2010). These entities are important vehicles capable of bringing highly technological knowledge to the market (Fontes 2005). Consequently, they have been significantly incentivised by policy makers, and investigated by innovation scholars.

Literature on ASOs has mostly been directed towards describing the phenomenon in terms of its characteristics (e.g. Chiesa and Piccaluga 2000; Pirnay et al. 2003; Fontes 2005): up to recent times studies were mostly atheoretical (Djokovic and Souitaris 2008) and based on: identifying the determinants of the creation and development of ASOs (e.g. Di Gregorio and Shane 2003; Perez and Sanchez 2003); detecting the obstacles and challenges such firms need to face (e.g. Chiesa and Piccaluga 2000); and delineating policy implications aimed at fostering the phenomenon (e.g. Roberts and Malone 1996).

Although "the phenomenon is becoming more mature" (Djokovic and Souitaris 2008, p. 242) and theory-based investigations have recently been increasing, in order to further the comprehension of the phenomenon, researchers should continue to produce theoretically driven works (Djokovic and Souitaris 2008). An important element that is still to be explored with respect to the creation and development of ASOs regards the recognition and exploitation of entrepreneurial opportunity (Djokovic and Souitaris 2008). Few studies have addressed the issue at the level of high technology-based firms (an exception is Park 2005). However, theories on opportunity recognition and development are still at an embryonic stage and remain an underdeveloped topic in entrepreneurship research (e.g. McMullen et al. 2007). In order to understand entrepreneurship, investigating how opportunities are recognised and exploited remains a priority (Shane and Venkataraman 2000). This chapter aims to contribute to the investigation of the ASO phenomenon by linking the process of creation and development of ASOs to the insights developed by research into entrepreneurial opportunity.

The chapter is structured as follows: Section 2 reviews the main theoretical foundation of the concept of entrepreneurial opportunity; Section 3 develops the research questions we deal with and outlines the methodological procedures, data collection and empirical qualitative analysis; finally, Section 4 provides some concluding thoughts.

2.   THEORETICAL FRAMEWORK

The aim of this section is to delineate what is meant by entrepreneurial opportunity and how this concept can be employed in order to better understand the process of creation and development of ASO firms. The theoretical framework on which this chapter is mostly based is the analysis of Alvarez and Barney (2007) and Alvarez et al. (2010), who differentiate entrepreneurial opportunity into discovery opportunity and creation opportunity.

Investigating entrepreneurial opportunity remains at the heart of understanding the process of entrepreneurship and is an important task for entrepreneurship research (Shane and Venkataraman 2003). Recognising and exploiting an opportunity is about introducing new goods and services to the market (Shane 2003). In this chapter we limit opportunity to the introduction of new goods and services by means of the creation of new firms.

The most widespread view of opportunity is based on the works of Kirzner, and assumes that opportunities need to be discovered as they already exist when the entrepreneur finds them and puts them to work (Shane 2000, 2003; Grégoire and Shepherd 2012). In this perspective, opportunities are objective entities in nature, often brought to life by changing elements in the environment such as new technologies or regulations.

Scholars following this view have mostly concentrated on investigating the reasons why some individuals discover the opportunity and why others do not, contributing to the delineation of the entrepreneur versus non-entrepreneur profile. The "alertness" concept introduced by Kirzner (1973) is one of the main elements that differentiates between entrepreneur and non-entrepreneur. However, it has been noted that alertness and personal characteristics must be accompanied by prior knowledge related to the opportunity – possessing related information and knowledge is a necessary requisite in order for an entrepreneur to recognise and exploit an opportunity (Shane 2003).

More recently, scholars have started to contrast this view by claiming that it may be that opportunities are not always objectively in the marketplace and need only to be discovered, and that it is the human activities and the social landscape in which the potential entrepreneur is embedded that shape and lead to the generation of an opportunity. Opportunities are conceptualised not as available in the environment but as created by the actions and relations of individuals (Alvarez and Barney 2007; Sarasvathy et al. 2010). From this perspective, opportunities arise because of the actions of individuals (Buenstorf 2007): they are "social constructions that do not exist independent of entrepreneurs' perceptions" (Alvarez and Barney 2007, p. 15). Therefore, in this interpretation of entrepreneurial opportunity, a main element is represented by the feedback process between the entrepreneurial action and the environment in which such action is undertaken – recognising and exploiting an entrepreneurial opportunity is a dynamic process in which the opportunity itself and the entrepreneur are both shaped by means of market and environmental feedback.

While the first framework of interpretation highlighted has been labelled "discovery opportunity", the latter has been called "creation opportunity" (Alvarez and Barney 2007). The two frameworks depart from a different conception of what an opportunity is – something exogenous and objective versus something endogenous and subjective – and how such an opportunity is put to work: discovering and exploiting it versus a trial and error process. Although very different in nature, as scholars claim (Sarasvathy et al. 2010; Buenstorf 2007; Companys and McMullen 2007; Alvarez and Barney 2007), the two frameworks are not substitutes, but need to be integrated in order to better comprehend the entrepreneurship phenomenon.

In other words, both frameworks (or contexts) may be instructive in order to appreciate how different opportunities are transformed into new products or into new businesses. To this end, Alvarez and Barney (2007) show how it is essential not to distinguish cases by linking them to one typology of opportunity context rather than another. Instead, if the aim is to comprehend the nature of entrepreneurial opportunity, it could be informative to distinguish and connect the two contexts in respect to the distinguishing traits that characterise the two typologies of opportunity.

In this regard, literature highlights that when a new organisation is formed in order to exploit a discovered opportunity, we may expect the new organisational form to resemble existing organisational forms in an already present population (Alvarez et al. 2010); we may expect such a new organisation to bear risk rather than to create uncertainty (Alvarez and Barney 2007; Companys and McMullen 2007); and we may expect such a new organisation to contribute to solving some already identified problems (Ardichvili et al. 2003). On the contrary, the authors claim that an opportunity-creation process leads to the formation of an organisation that is differentiated from existing ones (Alvarez et al. 2010), that bears more uncertainty than risk (Alvarez and Barney 2007; Companys and McMullen 2007) and that needs to find a problem to an identified solution (Ardichvili et al. 2003).

In this chapter we seek to connect the insights derived from the theoretical literature on entrepreneurial opportunity to the processes of creation and development of ASOs. Academic spin-offs have been recognised as heterogeneous entities, and the aim of this chapter is to shed light on their heterogeneity by investigating how they differ according to the processes of opportunity recognition and exploitation.

3. RESEARCH DESIGN

The goal of this chapter is to explore whether different ASOs may have been formed and developed according to a process of discovery rather than the creation of entrepreneurial opportunity. Based on the literature presented in the previous section, we therefore distinguish between two groups of ASO:

- In the first group ASOs are firms that replicate other firms in the population, that bear risk rather than uncertainty and that seek a solution to a well-known problem.
- In the second group we consider ASOs that enter non-existing markets, that bear uncertainty and that have a solution to a problem which is not yet clear-cut.

The heterogeneity of ASOs has been widely explored (e.g. Mustar et al. 2006; Druilhe and Garnsey 2004). Consequently, we have witnessed a flourishing of taxonomies and classifications of different ASOs. The aforementioned differentiation seems to resemble the not yet investigated commercial versus non-commercial type of spin-off (Hayter 2010). A non-commercial ASO is a firm whose business deals with the development of patents, which is based on the securing of venture capital investments and whose mission is the generation of a strong protected technology. On the other hand, commercial ASOs are firms which are generated with the aim of producing revenues as quickly as possible and whose main activity regards a product's place in the market, both in the form of a good and a service.

Based on this distinction, we conjecture that the commercial type of ASO is generated and developed according to a process of creation opportunity, while the non-commercial ASO is formed and developed following a process of discovery opportunity. In order to test this hypothesis, we employ a multiple case study research and provide evidence that the two different types of firm behave according to the set of actions described by Alvarez and Barney (2007, p. 17) – leadership, human resource practices and strategy.[1]

This chapter concerns theory building, and therefore case study research is the most suitable method of investigation (Eisenhardt 1989). Moreover, the investigation regards particular decision processes: the questions we pose are in the *why* and *how* form, and therefore need to be investigated in a qualitative way (Yin 1994). We thus conducted six face-to-face interviews, selecting firms according to the two typologies previously described. Therefore three of the firms we interviewed were not commercialising any product and were only investing in the development of technology through private investments, while the other three firms put the first product on the market very soon after its creation.

The interviews were conducted with ASOs of the University of Manchester in the UK. This university has been active in the generation of ASOs since the sixties, and in 2008 – according to the Higher Education Funding Council for England report (HEFCE 2009), there were almost 120 active ASOs generated by this university. The context is therefore ideal to test our research conjectures as it allows us to rely on a wide and heterogeneous population of firms. In order to strengthen our analysis we selected heterogeneous firms in terms of sector and age.

The interviews were based on open-ended questions and were developed according to the firms' specificities during the conversation. The aim was to investigate the detailed evolution processes through which firms formed and developed from the initial business idea of their founders. We therefore sought to speak to at least one of the founders. We did this in all but one case where, instead, we spoke to a manager who had entered the firm very soon after its creation. We triangulated our data with interviews of technology transfer office (TTO) staff, and an independent author visualised the transcribed material in order to check for misinterpretation of the data (Yin 1994).

3.1 Data Analysis

The data analysis is based on two levels. The first regards the identification of the opportunity in order to check if the two typologies of ASO – commercial versus non-commercial – respect the three main foundations of the two types of entrepreneurial opportunity frameworks as previously described (new versus non-new organisation; uncertainty versus risk; providing solution versus seeking problem). The second level of analysis refers to the entrepreneurial actions that Alvarez and Barney identify to characterise the two different entrepreneurial opportunity frameworks – leadership, human resource practice and strategy. Table 10.1 summarises the firms' characteristics.

Concerning the first level of analysis, the data at hand confirms that the two typologies of firms resemble the discovery and creation context of entrepreneurial opportunity. More specifically, we can affirm that the entrepreneurial opportunity framework on which non-commercial ASOs are generated – that is those firms whose business is focused on the development of a protected technology and that have no revenues but live on the investment of private investors – resembles the discovery context. In fact, the firms we interviewed clearly demonstrated that: they were acting as new firms of an existing population whose only mission was the development of a specific technology; that the business was risky because they had only a limited degree of success, although the path to follow was clear and mostly planned both in terms of timing and activities; and that the technology they were developing had a specific problem waiting for a solution.

With respect to this point, Firm C of our sample clearly highlighted how the business and the mission are clear-cut. Its founder commented:

> Patents in drugs discovery are very clear and specific – this molecule here has potential for this disease . . . We never sold anything – a company of drugs discovery doesn't sell anything until the product is ready for the market and this usually takes around 15 years. We generate value in the IP.

Conversely, the three commercial firms were clearly behaving according to the creation opportunity framework: they were looking to sell a product for which there was no market, therefore there were no direct competitors; they were bearing uncertainty more than risk because they were continually adapting their behaviour to the evolving situations; and they did find a solution to a still non-defined problem.

For example, the founder of Firm E clearly highlights how uncertain and new the business they wanted to create was when the business idea was set up in a firm:

> We got the idea of starting the business before knowing exactly what the business would be about . . . Then we started the business [two years later]. We

Table 10.1   Description of firms and entrepreneurial opportunity identification framework

Firm	Activity description	Type of ASO	Entrepreneurial opportunity framework
Firm A	Generated in 2002, the firm operates in hardware support, in particular concerned with the designing process of microchips to manage very complex data	Non-commercial	Discovery context
Firm B	Founded in 2006 for developing a breakthrough printing technology based on nanotechnology	Non-commercial	Discovery context
Firm C	Drug development company, constituted in 2001, that produces small molecule aggregation inhibitors especially for Alzheimer's	Non-commercial	Discovery context
Firm D	Created in 2004; initially a consulting firm but now also developing software in the building services sector and from 2007 especially concerned with energy issues	Commercial	Creation context
Firm E	Business psychology company created in 2001. Now the core business is specific software consultancy services concerning workplace wellbeing	Commercial	Creation context
Firm F	Constituted in 2002, the core product is software for monitoring applications and control systems. Since 2007 the business has expanded into specific applications for the pharmaceutical sector	Commercial	Creation context

knew it was about some kind of consultancy but we still did not know what the core focus of the business would be about. We were in a kind of testing phase.

The second level of analysis, as mentioned, concerns the entrepreneurial actions that, according to Alvarez and Barney (2007), refer to the two entrepreneurial opportunity frameworks – creation and discovery. The authors distinguish the behaviour of entrepreneurial actions with respect to leadership, human resources (HR) practices and strategy.

The authors claim that when an entrepreneurial opportunity emerges as a discovery process, leaders will be expert people in dealing with that market. By contrast, in opportunity creation contexts leaders are charismatic persons whose mission is transforming a business idea into a firm in the market. In our sample of firms we note that while non-commercial ASOs, formed on the discovery of an opportunity, shaped their development on the recruitment of expert managers from the industrial world, the managers of the commercial ASOs were always the academics who had had the business idea. These scientist-entrepreneurs shaped and adapted their ideas according to the market feedback, as seen in a constructionist approach.

The second entrepreneurial action refers to how human resources are managed. The authors claim that in the discovery scenario the recruitment of personnel regards specific skills and competences broadly available in the market. Conversely, the recruitment processes in the creation framework are mostly embedded in the social network of the entrepreneurs. In our sample of firms a clear difference emerges between commercial and non-commercial ASOs. While the former mostly recruit personnel from the parent department from which the ASO span off, the recruitment processes of the non-commercial ASOs were mostly undertaken by means of an external recruitment agency. In other words, the competences needed by the non-commercial ASOs were generally available in the marketplace, while the skills sought by the commercial ASOs were not; and the firms were recruiting people whose background was as close as possible to that of the entrepreneur. The founder of Firm D stated more than five years after constitution: "At this stage university has a marginal role, but still important for recruitment."

The third set of entrepreneurial actions analysed regard the strategy of the firm. Alvarez and Barney (2007) argue that we should expect a very flat and unchanging strategy in the discovery opportunity scenario, while the strategy should be adapted and evolve significantly in the entrepreneurial creation framework. We clearly observe this distinction in our two types of ASO. Commercial ASOs continually adapt their business idea to the feedback of the external environment. We register several changes in the direction of the core business in the very early stages of the firms' development. The interviews provided evidence that the definition of a core business emerged only after several years of trial and error. The founder of Firm F stated:

> Initially we were thinking of building the software and sell[ing] it alone, but very soon we realised that a sort of consultancy service to the company adopting the software was a central part of the product because of the inability of the company of using the software straightaway. The software sales have never really materialised and the consultancy part was growing because of the continuous need of the companies in dealing with it.

In contrast, the objective and mission of the non-commercial ASOs were clear and well-defined since before the firms were created.

The analysis provided in this chapter has two main outcomes. First of all, we have seen how commercial and non-commercial ASOs are very different in nature – they are the output of very different processes of knowledge exploitation. They are based on different types of entrepreneurial opportunity contexts: one in which the entrepreneur discovers an opportunity and the mission is straightforward in its exploitation; and the other in which the entrepreneur creates the opportunity in a trial and error interaction process with the external environment.

The second outcome regards the consequences that discovering or creating an opportunity have on the development of the firm – that is, on the entrepreneurial actions we investigated. We have in fact seen how the development of commercial ASOs is uncertain and needs to be flexible in order to be able to adapt to the environment, to define a problem to which the entrepreneur has seen the solution and therefore to create a market.

4.   CONCLUDING THOUGHTS

This chapter has explored how ASOs differ in terms of the entrepreneurial opportunities they bring to the market. The analysis supports the argument that commercial and non-commercial ASOs are different entities, and we have explored the issue with respect to the processes by which entrepreneurial opportunities are recognised and exploited in the two types of ASO.

This chapter supports the theoretical argument that discovery and creation contexts mirror different entrepreneurship processes (Alvarez and Barney 2007; Alvarez et al. 2010). We have also provided evidence that both are informative in order to understand how business ideas are brought to the market, and also how new firms are formed and developed. Our work is therefore in line with the argument that in order to build a theory of entrepreneurship it is necessary to build on the complementarity of the two frameworks (Buenstorf 2007).

This chapter has investigated two very different types of ASO firms, and the literature on the ASO phenomenon clearly highlights the wide heterogeneity between these firms. Therefore, the distinction pursued in this exploratory work is not exhaustive of all types of ASO, and we believe that further research should be conducted in order to explore whether the creation and development of ASO firms may be the result of mixed entrepreneurial opportunity contexts.

However, some important implications may be derived from this chapter. Comprehending the differences between commercial and non-commercial ASOs may be informative when it comes to supporting and advising scientist-entrepreneurs in the creation and development processes of their ASO. For example, TTO staff could target with greater precision the supporting tools provided to the ASO, taking into consideration the nature of their entrepreneurial opportunity context.

NOTE

1. Alvarez and Barney highlight other elements of actions that we do not take into account here as they are partly included in the definition of commercial and non-commercial ASOs.

REFERENCES

Alvarez S.A., Barney J.B. (2007), "Discovery and creation: alternative theories of entrepreneurial action", *Strategic Entrepreneurship Journal* **1**, 11–26.

Alvarez S.A., Barney J.B., Young S.L. (2010), "Debates in entrepreneurship: opportunity formation and implications for the field of entrepreneurship", in Acs Z.J., Audretsch D.B. (eds), *Handbook on Entrepreneurship Research*, New York: Springer.

Ardichvili A., Cardozo R., Ray S. (2003), "A theory of entrepreneurial opportunity identification and development", *Journal of Business Venturing* **18**, 105–123.

Buenstorf G. (2007), "Creation and pursuit of entrepreneurial opportunities: an evolutionary economics perspective", *Small Business Economics* **28**, 323–337.

Chiesa V., Piccaluga A. (2000), "Exploitation and diffusion of public research: the case of academic spin-off companies in Italy", *R&D Management* **30**, 329–339.

Companys Y.E., McMullen J.S. (2007), "Strategic entrepreneurship at work: the nature, discovery, and exploitation of entrepreneurial opportunity", *Small Business Economics* **28**, 301–322.

Di Gregorio D., Shane S (2003), "Why do some universities generate more start-ups than others?", *Research Policy* **32**, 209–227.

Djokovic D., Souitaris V. (2008), "Spinouts from academic institutions: a literature review with suggestion for further research", *Journal of Technology Transfer* **33**, 225–247.

Druilhe C., Garnsey E. (2004), "Do academic spin-outs differ and does it matter?", *Journal of Technology Transfer* **29**, 269–285.

Eisenhardt K.M. (1989), "Building theories from case study research", *Academy of Management Review* **14**, 488–511.

Fontes M. (2005), "The process of transformation of scientific and technological knowledge into economic value conducted by biotechnology spin-offs", *Technovation* **25**, 339–347.

Grégoire D.A., Shepherd D.A. (2012), "Technology-market combinations and the identification of entrepreneurial opportunities: an investigation of the opportunity-individual nexus", *Academy of Management Journal* **55**, 753–785.

Hayter C.S. (2010), "In search for the profit-maximizing actor: motivations and definitions of success from nascent academic entrepreneurs", *Journal of Technology Transfer* **36**, 340–352.

HEFCE (2009), *Higher Education: Business and Community Interaction Survey 2007–2008*, Bristol: Higher Education Funding Council for England.

Kirzner I.M. (1973), *Competition and Entrepreneurship*, Chicago: University of Chicago Press.

McMullen J.S., Plummer L.A., Acs Z.J. (2007), "What is an entrepreneurial opportunity?", *Small Business Economics* **28**, 273–283.

Mustar P., Renault M., Colombo M.G., Piva E., Fontes M., Lockett A., Wright M., Clarysse B., Moray N. (2006), "Conceptualising the heterogeneity of research-based spin-offs: a multi-dimensional taxonomy", *Research Policy* **35**, 289–308.

Park J.S., (2005), "Opportunity recognition and product innovation in entrepreneurial hi-tech start-ups: a new perspective and supporting case study", *Technovation* **25**, 739–752.

Perez M.P, Sanchez A.M. (2003), "The development of university spin-offs: early dynamics of technology transfer and networking", *Technovation* **23**, 823–831.

Pirnay F., Surlemont B., Frederic N. (2003), "Toward a typology of university spin-offs", *Small Business Economics* **21**, 355–369.

Roberts E.B., Malone D.E. (1996), "Policies and structures for spinning out new companies from research and development organizations", *R&D Management* **26**, 17–48.

Sarasvathy S.D., Dew N., Velamuri S.R., Venkataraman S. (2010), "Three views of entrepreneurial opportunity", in Acs Z.J., Audretsch D.B. (eds), *Handbook on Entrepreneurship Research*, New York: Springer.

Shane S. (2000), "Prior knowledge and the discovery of entrepreneurial opportunity", *Organization Science* **11**, 448–470.

Shane S. (2003), *A General Theory of Entrepreneurship: The Individual-Opportunity Nexus*, Cheltenham, UK and Northampton, MA, USA: Edward Elgar Publishing.

Shane S., Venkataraman S. (2000), "The promise of entrepreneurship as a field of research", *Academy of Management Review* **25**, 217–226.

Vincett P.S. (2010), "The economic impacts of academic spin-off companies, and their implications for public policy", *Research Policy* **39**, 736–747.

Yin R.K. (1994), *Case Study Research: Design and Methods* (3rd edition), London: Sage.

11. Firm location choice in the New Economy: exploring the role of entrepreneurial work-lifestyles of neighbourhood entrepreneurs in the business location decision*

Anne Risselada and Veronique Schutjens

1. INTRODUCTION

The flexible knowledge-based and networked character of an information communication and technology (ICT)-driven economy brings new types of jobs and entrepreneurs, different mobility patterns and changing work–life combinations leading to structural changes in cities, regions, and the global economy. Many macro-level studies conceptualise the manner in which this changing economic configuration relates to the spatial and economic structures in (urban) society, the changing connectivity in economic transactions or the emergence of new production sites (Castells, 1999; Gospodini, 2006). However, this New Economy (Hutton, 2004) has also opened up a variety of work-lifestyle configurations for individuals. Still, thus far only limited academic attention has been given to these changing work practices and their confluence with entrepreneurial strategies and business decisions of entrepreneurs at the micro level.

Even in studies on firm location processes, in which the entrepreneur is the decisive actor, the influence of work-lifestyle is largely omitted. However, a growing number of entrepreneurs display varied work–home combinations in which entrepreneurial preferences and the choices for business property are closely and inseparably linked to the private home situation of entrepreneurs, and thus to the choice of their personal dwelling. For example, recent studies show that a growing number of New Economy enterprises in the knowledge, personal services and consumer sectors are home-based businesses (HBBs), and that for a majority of these entrepreneurs running the business from home is a deliberate choice (Mason et al., 2011).

We suggest that, due to changing economic configurations, entrepreneurs make increasingly diverse business decisions, for instance with respect to work-lifestyles, growth ambitions and profit-maximising behaviour. This means that firm location choices and their explanations have changed as well. Unless this heterogeneity among entrepreneurs is addressed, scholars investigating the determinants of firm location decisions may arrive at incorrect conclusions which provide a weak basis for local economic policy aiming to facilitate and stimulate economic activity and business investments in neighbourhoods.

This study aims to answer the following question: To what extent is the choice to run an HBB related to the work-lifestyle characteristics of the entrepreneur?

To answer this question we study the location choice of firms in residential neighbourhoods and consider these neighbourhoods as the micro scale in which spatial economic alternatives are being judged and weighted according to the individual preferences of entrepreneurs. In the Netherlands, approximately 40 per cent of all jobs are located in urban residential neighbourhoods, housing 35 per cent of all private firms (Raspe et al., 2010). These (mostly) small local firms are underrepresented in the academic literature on firm location decisions and behaviour (Mason et al., 2011; Phillips, 2002; Green et al. 2000).

2. THEORY

Factors that influence the location choices of firms can be categorised as either internal or external. Firm-internal factors are associated with firm characteristics or entrepreneurial characteristics, such as age, education and lifestyle preferences of the entrepreneur. External location factors are the characteristics of the specific site and surroundings of the firm. These can be firm specific, for example business property characteristics and parking facilities at the firm's premises; or they can cover the wider economic or social environment, including the distance to markets and the quantity and quality of the local labour force (Brouwer et al., 2004).

Empirical studies on the effects of firm-internal factors on firm location decisions incorporate firm-level factors such as age, size and growth or industrial sector. Thus far, the literature on firm location decisions hardly acknowledges the entrepreneur's personal characteristics, professional ambitions, strategies and choices with respect to the balance between work and private life. This omission has often been caused by the absence of registration data on entrepreneurs and on firms, for example business location characteristics and (changing) addresses as a result of relocation.

We argue that whether the choice for the business property is residential or commercial depends on the work-lifestyle characteristics of the entrepreneur, even when controlling for features of the previous business property and characteristics of the current location.

Rational profit-maximising economic behaviour is conditioned by an individual's context, as defined by one's social networks and embodied, objectified and institutionalised cultural dispositions (Bathelt and Glückler, 2003; Bourdieu, 1984; Granovetter, 1985). The contribution of such general theoretical insights to the understanding of firm relocation can best be illustrated and tested by looking at the actual spatial behaviour of individual firms, the underlying entrepreneurial decisions and their drivers. For entrepreneurs making firm location decisions, the conditioning role of social and institutional contexts means that the effect of pure rational profit maximisation on the decision's outcome is mitigated by other factors such as: personal or relational networks (Dahl and Sorenson, 2009; Schutjens and Völker, 2010); the image, identity of place and attachment to neighbourhood (Raspe et al., 2010); and bounded information and other private concerns (Greenhalgh, 2008; Mackloet et al., 2006).

We explore four indicators of entrepreneurial work-lifestyles that typically fit the flexible knowledge-based and networked character of the New Economy and that are expected to influence the likelihood of entrepreneurs choosing to run their businesses from home. The first indicator is the extent to which the entrepreneur has firm growth ambitions. The second indicator is related to whether the entrepreneur aims to combine his/her professional career with caretaking tasks. The third and fourth indicators are related to whether the entrepreneur is responsible for the main household income, and the number of work hours of the entrepreneur.

(Non-)Ambitious Entrepreneurship

Many suggest that the relationship between entrepreneurship and firm ownership is blurred. On the one hand, entrepreneurship is not limited to the establishment of a firm; it can also be considered in terms of intrapreneurship, or one's display of entrepreneurial traits as an employee (Bosma et al., 2010). On the other hand, not all firm owners are entrepreneurs. The demand for flexible, highly skilled labour has given rise to many 'firms' created by self-employed freelancers. These freelancers might not by definition have an intrinsic drive to 'work for themselves' and be entrepreneurial. Tentatively, one can make a distinction between the behavioural perspective and an occupational definition of entrepreneurship as primarily involving the ownership or creation of an enterprise (Stam et al., 2012). Taking this occupational perspective as a starting point leads to the need to define a degree of entrepreneurial ambitiousness as a distinctive lifestyle characteristic.

Stam et al. (2012) distinguish several motives that characterise ambitious entrepreneurs based on their need for achievement (McClelland, 1961). This need for achievement makes ambitious entrepreneurs likely to show growth ambitions with regard to employment, innovation and turnover, and to behave accordingly. Non-ambitious entrepreneurs show neither similar growth ambitions nor the ambition to develop innovative products. Studies by Mackloet et al. (2006) and Mason et al. (2010) have shown that HBB owners do show some growth ambitions in terms of revenue, but they are primarily content with the situation of their business and want neither to outgrow their home base nor to hire employees (Pratt, 1999). Therefore, it is expected that non-ambitious entrepreneurs are more likely to be home based.

Hypothesis 1: The degree of ambitiousness of the entrepreneur is negatively related to the likelihood of being a home-based business (HBB).

Caring Tasks

Self-employment enables an individual to work part-time and to meticulously plan professional activities all by herself/himself during the day, week or month (Hanson and Pratt, 1988; Thompson et al., 2009). Pratt (1999) used US Bureau of Census data to show that family responsibilities played a minor role in starting a business, but were significantly more important for HBBs compared to non-HBBs. In a more gender-specific study by Walker and Webster (2004) the 'balance of work and family' and the 'flexibility of working hours' were among the most commonly mentioned reasons for women becoming self-employed. Although these are also important reasons for men, they are significantly less so than for women. Firms often have their start-up location at home, mostly to accommodate start-up costs and to overcome initial economic hurdles (Mackloet et al., 2006). However, in a study on HBBs in the United Kingdom, it was found that more than a quarter were started from home foremost to accommodate family needs (Mason et al., 2011). Based on these findings we hypothesize the following:

Hypothesis 2: Entrepreneurs performing caring tasks are more likely to be home based than those not performing caring tasks.

Primary Income and Working Hours

The studies of Pratt (1999) and Mason et al. (2011) have shown that HBBs are more often a source of second income than firms based in commercial property. Moreover, entrepreneurs of HBBs consistently work fewer hours than entrepreneurs of firms in commercial property (FCPs). This finding is also confirmed in the study on female home-based entrepreneurs (Thompson et al., 2009). These two lifestyle factors – which are most likely, but not necessarily, related – also influence the likelihood of being an HBB.

Hypothesis 3: Entrepreneurs who do not provide the primary family income are more likely to be home based than entrepreneurs who do provide the primary family income.

Hypothesis 4: The average workweek hours of the entrepreneur is negatively related to the likelihood of being a home-based entrepreneur.

In the analysis on which factors influence the likelihood of being an HBB, we control for other factors such as the gender of the entrepreneur, firm sector, firm age and firm size. We also control for two other firm-internal factors relating to the use of business property: the amount of work time the entrepreneur spends at the property and the degree to which the property functions as a place to meet clients or costumers. Moreover, based on the finding that an entrepreneur's valuation of property factors influences location choice, we control for the relative importance of business property factors (Risselada, 2013). We also account for routine choices and control for the fact that being home based before influences the likelihood of being currently home based.

3.   DATA AND METHOD

The empirical analysis is based on information from 370 entrepreneurs operating in 41 residential neighbourhoods of five Dutch cities (Amsterdam, Dordrecht, Leiden, Utrecht and Zoetermeer) which was gathered from a survey conducted between May and July 2011. Zoetermeer, Dordrecht and Leiden are medium sized, with approximately 120,000 inhabitants, while Amsterdam and Utrecht are larger, with 767,000 and 306,000 inhabitants in 2010 respectively. All cities belong to the Randstad region, the conurbation in the west of the country which is often considered as functioning as one regional economy. The cities offer a broad array of Dutch urban residential environments differing in size, physical structure, age and economic background (for elaboration on the fieldwork design see Risselada, 2013).

To answer the research question a dichotomous variable was constructed measuring the location choice (i.e., their current business property) for an HBB (1) and the choice of a commercial property (0). To analyse the influence of lifestyle aspects on the choice to run the business from home, a logistic regression model was performed. Table 11.1 shows that almost 67 per cent of the firms in the sample are home based. The work-lifestyle variable measuring the entrepreneur's ambition is a scale variable in which four statements about the wish for future firm growth are taken into account, namely: the desire to reduce firm activity or to quit the business; the desire to stabilize current firm activity; the ambition to innovate or for growth in turnover; and the desire for growth in sales, floor space or employees.

In the analyses it is important to control for internal characteristics that can cause sorting effects (Brouwer et al., 2004). Table 11.1 also displays the used control variables. We control for the 'usual suspects' in explaining the firm location choices – that is firm size, firm sector and firm age – and also control for the gender of the entrepreneur. Firm size is an important factor in explaining the likelihood of being home based. Because there is a large correlation between firm size and the likelihood of being home based, this control factor will not be considered in the first two computations. With regard to firm size, the share of home-based entrepreneurs is 61 per cent, of which 20 per cent have at least one employee. Of the firms based in commercial property, 76 per cent have at least one employee. We control for firm sector as firms that supply larger geographic markets are more flexible in their location choice, serving markets less dependent on physical distance.

As recent studies have shown that firm location choices are influenced by firm-related factors (Risselada et al., 2013), we also include three specific business property factors. The first is the degree to which the business site is used to meet with business contacts; the second is the extent to which the entrepreneur works mainly at the business site. In addition, we include a variable indicating whether a firm was previously home based: Entrepreneurs are 'routine agents': over time they tend to stick to their choice of running their firm from home. The two neighbourhood factors measuring prosperity and liveability were constructed by means of principal component analysis (PCA) in which two components from seven indicators of the socio-economic neighbourhood status were constructed (Folmer and Risselada, 2012). Neighbourhood prosperity is a construct that measures the economic power, or market potential, of a neighbourhood. Neighbourhood liveability is a construct that measures the social status of a neighbourhood.

Table 11.1 Summary of dependent and key independent variables

	%	Mean	SD
Dependent variable			
Choice for current location			
Firm in Commercial Property (FCP)	33.2		
Home-based Business (HBB)	66.8		
Key independent variables (work-lifestyle)			
Ambition		1.51	.71
Care tasks			
Yes	36.8		
No	63.2		
Not primary income			
Yes	30.3		
No	69.7		
Number of work hours per week		41.07	17.86
Control variables			
Firm-internal factors			
Firm age (log)		.31	.49
Firm size (log)		.28	.44
Sector			
Industry, transport, wholesale and car repair	10.8		
Public sector and healthcare	23.9		
Consumer services	33.4		
Financial services	6.9		
Business services	25.0		
Gender			
Male	62.0		
Female	38.0		
Business property related factors			
Relative importance of real estate factors		.44	.89
Previous location			
HBB	22.8		
FCP or firm start-up	77.2		
Working more than 50% of time at the business property			
Yes	69.1		
No	30.9		
Business property is place for face-to-face contact with business relations			
Yes	39.7		
No	60.3		
Firm-external factors			
Neighbourhood prosperity		.49	1.37
Neighbourhood liveability		.07	.92

4. RESULTS

Table 11.2 shows to what extent the likelihood of being an HBB relates to internal firm factors and entrepreneurial-related factors. In model 1, we put forward only firm and business property-related factors. In model 2, we add the four key factors explaining the likelihood of being home based: the work-lifestyle characteristics. In models 3 and 4, we add control variables for firm size and neighbourhood characteristics. Model 2 shows that work-lifestyle factors significantly impact the likelihood of being home based, even when other gender, firm and business property factors are included. In fact, the work-lifestyle factors take away the significant effect of gender in model 1. However, firm size and current neighbourhood characteristics (models 3 and 4) mitigate some of the work-lifestyle effects. By adding the control for firm size the explanatory power of the model increases quite significantly. As expected, the choice to locate the HBB is strongly driven by the size of the firm: Only small firms can be run easily from home. The effect of neighbourhood controls shows that in areas characterised by high liveability scores the likelihood of being an HBB is higher.

Are effects of the separate work-lifestyle factors as expected? In model 2, the business growth ambition of the entrepreneur significantly and negatively relates to the likelihood of being an HBB, which was expected (hypothesis 1). The effect disappears when we control for firm size; but when adding neighbourhood controls the effect becomes significant again, confirming the first hypothesis. Entrepreneurs who perform caring tasks are more likely to be home based, even when we control for firm size and neighbourhood features ($p < .05$), which confirms the second hypothesis. The third hypothesis is confirmed as well: If the household income does not primarily come from the firm, the entrepreneur is more likely to have an HBB. Finally, contrary to expectations, the number of hours per week an entrepreneur invests in his/her firm does not relate to running the firm from home when controlled for other factors, which leads us to reject the fourth hypothesis.

In short, there are three work-lifestyle factors that matter to whether neighbourhood firms are home based. Running the firm from home is negatively associated with the growth ambition of the entrepreneur, and is positively associated with firms in which the entrepreneur performs caring tasks and with firms that do not provide the primary household income.

Table 11.2 *Logistic regression on the likelihood of being an HBB*

	Model 1			Model 2			Model 3			Model 4 [a]		
	B	Sig.	S.E.	B	Sig.	S.E.	B	Sig.	S.E.	B	Sig.	S.E.
Firm and entrepreneurial characteristics (control)												
Gender (female = 1)	.939	***	.336	.285		.384	.351		.435	.405		.458
Firm age	-1.519	***	.333	-1.742	***	.358	-1.279	***	.391	-1.331	***	.410
Industry: transport, wholesale and car repair	.224		.578	.334		.618	.152		.656	.256		.687
Consumer services	.204		.370	.269		.401	.050		.444	.272		.479
Financial services	1.006		.660	1.027		.708	1.129		.778	1.451	*	.783
Business services	.900	**	.442	.901	*	.475	1.020	*	.538	1.193	**	.571
Business property-related factors (control)												
Previous location HBB	1.073	***	.370	1.172	***	.398	1.079	**	.440	.933	**	.451
Business property is meeting place (F2F contact)	-1.667	***	.315	-1.347	***	.338	-1.035	***	.375	-1.027	***	.390
% of work time spent at business property	-.482		.549	-.888		.606	-1.157	*	.682	-1.309	*	.708
Relative importance of business property factors	-.240		.161	-.223		.177	.053		.208	.141		.232
Work-lifestyle characteristics												
Ambition				-.674	***	.249	-.388		.267	-.472	*	.282
Care tasks				1.085	***	.361	.668	*	.397	.809	*	.421
Not primary income				.868	**	.441	1.092	**	.545	1.027	*	.585
Hours per weekly spent on firm				-.023	**	.010	-.012		.012	-.014		.013

150

Variable	Model 1	Model 2	Model 3	Model 4	Model 5	Model 6
Firm characteristic (control)						
Firm size			−2.757 ***	.505	−2.732 ***	.535 ***
Neighbourhood characteristics (control)						
Neighbourhood prosperity (pull)					.235 *	.136 *
Neighbourhood liveability (pull)					.857 ***	.229 ***
Constant	.375	.684	1.196	1.220	1.417	1.476
Model summary	Nagelkerke R^2	Nagelkerke R^2	Nagelkerke R^2	Nagelkerke R^2	Nagelkerke R^2	Nagelkerke R^2
	.205	.352	.467	.581	.624	.909
	N	N	N	N	N	N
	294	294	294	294	294	294

Notes: [a] Because two variables at neighbourhood level were added, we also tested a multilevel model. The logistic regression coefficients proved to be robust and, for the sake of clarity and comparison with previous models, the results of the logistic computation are put forward in model 4.
*** = $P<0.01$; ** = $P<0.05$; * = $P<0.1$

5.   CONCLUSION

A new type of economy is increasingly enabling people to adopt entrepreneurial lifestyles or workstyles, allowing entrepreneurs to display varied work–home combinations. In firm location studies, little attention has been given to the fact that these changing work practices lead to changes in the business property requirements and location choices of entrepreneurs.

Our results show that work-lifestyle indicators influence the likelihood of basing the firm at the entrepreneur's home, even when controlling for other internal and external factors and for the former choice of location. The effects are small but remain significant after controlling for other factors, and have the expected sign. Three of the hypotheses concerning work-lifestyle factors are confirmed: When the firm's revenue is not the primary household income, or when the entrepreneur also performs caring tasks, the firm is more likely to be home based. These findings hold when we control for firm size, the main driver of the decision to run a firm from home. An interesting finding is also that adding the work-lifestyle factors takes away the gender effect, suggesting that it is not so much gender that plays a role in choosing to be home based, but rather that work-lifestyle indicators prove more valuable in explaining the likelihood of having an HBB.

These results show that the lifestyle of the entrepreneur matters in the firm location choice. For many small neighbourhood entrepreneurs firm location is based on maximisation of private life and work, and not only on a monetary profit utility function. As Pratt notes in her study on HBBs in the US: 'The choice of a home-based or non-home-based business comes down to balancing economic needs with lifestyle choices' (1999: viii).

A firm's location decision is based on a complex array of factors and considerations significant to entrepreneurs, which could not all be accounted for in our study. First, because of the cross-sectional fieldwork design, no information was available on entrepreneurial work-lifestyle characteristics that have changed over time. This static approach might have caused us to miss certain triggers of location behaviour, especially if household composition or location preferences have changed or as the recent economic recession affected the income sources of many households and entrepreneurs. The same problem applies to several firm-internal factors that we had to assume to be stable over time. Second, despite the above-average fieldwork response, the number of cases was limited. This justifies a follow-up study that either draws on a larger group of respondents or uses in-depth interviews to deepen the insights into how changing work-lifestyles interact with processes of firm location choice.

NOTE

* Many thanks go to those entrepreneurs willing to fill in the questionnaire, and to the LISA register (National Information System of Employment). A preliminary version of the chapter was presented at the AAG conference in New York and the Third Entrepreneurship, Culture, Finance and Economic Development Workshop in Namur, Belgium. Thanks go to the participants of those conferences for their comments. This study was funded within the research project 'Dynamic neighbourhoods in dynamic urban economies' led by Prof. Dr R. Kloosterman, AISSR, University of Amsterdam. The project team included Prof. Dr J. Rath and E. Folmer (AISSR) and Prof. Dr V. Schutjens, Prof. Dr F. van Oort and A. Risselada, URU, Utrecht University.

REFERENCES

Bathelt, H. and J. Glückler (2003) Toward a relational economic geography, *Journal of Economic Geography* 3(2), pp.117–144.
Bosma, N., E. Stam and S. Wennekers (2010) *Intrapreneurship: An International Study*, Zoetermeer: EIM.
Bourdieu, P. (1984) *Distinction: A Social Critique of the Judgement Taste*, Cambridge, MA: Harvard University Press.
Brouwer, A.E., I. Mariotti and J.N. Van Ommeren (2004) The firm relocation decision: An empirical investigation. *Annals of Regional Science*, 38(2), pp.335–347.
Castells, M. (1999) *The Information Age: Economy, Society and Culture*, Oxford: Blackwell.
Dahl, M.S. and O. Sorenson (2009) The embedded entrepreneur, *European Management Review* 6(3), pp.172–181.
Folmer, E. and A. Risselada (2012) Planning the neighbourhood economy: Land-use plans and the economic potential of urban residential neighbourhoods in the Netherlands. *European Planning Studies*, pp.1–22. DOI: 10.1080/09654313.2012.722965.
Gospodini, A. (2006) Portraying, classifying and understanding the emerging landscapes in the post-industrial city, *Cities* 23(5), pp.311–330.
Granovetter, M. (1985) Economic action and social structure: The problem of embeddedness, *American Journal of Sociology* 91(3), pp.481–510.
Green, H., A. Strange and H. Trache (2000) The homeworking revolution: Considering the property dimension, *Regional Studies* 34(3), pp.303–307.
Greenhalgh, P. (2008) An examination of business occupier relocation decision making: Distinguishing small and large firm behaviour, *Journal of Property Research* 25(2), pp.107–126.
Hanson, S. and G. Pratt (1988) Reconceptualizing the links between home and work in urban geography, *Economic Geography* 64(4), pp.299–321.
Hutton, T.A. (2004) The new economy of the inner city, *Cities* 21(2), pp.89–108.
Mackloet, A., V. Schutjens and P. Korteweg (2006) *Starten vanuit huis: Bittere noodzaak of verkozen lifestyle?* (36th ed.), Utrecht: DGW/NETHUR.
Mason, C.M., S. Carter and S. Tagg (2011) Invisible businesses: The characteristics of home-based businesses in the United Kingdom, *Regional Studies* 45(5), pp.625–639.
McClelland. D. (1961) *The Achieving Society*, New York: Free Press.

Phillips, B.D. (2002) Home-based firms, e-commerce, and high-technology small firms: Are they related?, *Economic Development Quarterly* **16**(1), pp.39–48.

Pratt, J. H. (1999) *Homebased Business: The Hidden Economy*, Dallas: Office of Advocacy, United States Small Business Administration.

Raspe, O., A. Weterings, M. v. d. Berge, F. van Oort, G. Marlet, V. Schutjens et al. (2010) *Bedrijvigheid en leefbaarheid in stedelijke wijken*, The Hague/Bilthoven: Planbureau voor de Leefomgeving (PBL).

Risselada, A.H. (2013) *Housing the Mobile Entrepreneur*, Amsterdam: AUP.

Risselada, A.H., V. Schutjens and F. Van Oort. (2013) Real estate determinants of firm relocation in urban residential neighbourhoods, *Tijdschrift voor Economische en Sociale Geografie* **104**(2), pp.136–158.

Schutjens, V. and B. Völker (2010) Space and social capital: The degree of locality in entrepreneurs' contacts and its consequences for firm success, *European Planning Studies* **18**(6), pp.941–963.

Stam, E., N. Bosma, A.Van Witteloostuijn, J. De Jong, S. Bogaert, N. Edwards and F. Jaspers (2012) *Ambitious Entrepreneurship: A Review of the Academic Literature and New Directions for Public Policy*, The Hague: Advisory Council for Science and Technology Policy (AWT).

Thompson, P., D. Jones-Evans and C. Kwong (2009) Women and home-based entrepreneurship: Evidence from the United Kingdom, *International Small Business Journal* **27**(2), pp.227–239.

Walker, E. and B. Webster (2004) Gender issues in home-based businesses, *Women in Management Review* **19**(8), pp.404–412.

12. How to explain gender differences in self-employment ratios: towards a socioeconomic approach

Dieter Bögenhold and Uwe Fachinger

INTRODUCTION

A main reason for the growing relevance of self-employment can be seen in the employment shift from the industrial to the service sector. To a large extent this sector is characterized by personnel-intensive or technologically innovative fields of work, often requiring flexible organizational arrangements. In light of this, the more or less steady growth of the service sector mirrors changes within the category of self-employment. One of those fundamental changes is the increase in female solo self-employment, as there is prima facie evidence that the rise of self-employment is mostly a rise of micro-firms and solo self-employment, of which especially solo self-employment is a female domain. Enterprises owned and run by women are one of the fastest growing entrepreneurial populations in a world of growth ratios (Brush et al. 2009). But it is not clear whether the development is primarily driven by necessity in order to take part in the labour market or if these activities reflect new modes of labour market integration revealing new opportunities and markets which are, in great part, especially due to the service and health care sectors.

However, those developments raise the question whether self-employment can be seen as a strategy for women to achieve work–life balance, and whether these changes in the organization of work are leading to an improvement in the quality of (working) life. One of the most consistent findings in studies on women's labour force participation is the negative effect of the presence of young children on the probability of participation. It could be argued that difficulties in combining work and family enhance the transition to or entry into self-employment.

Solo self-employment may deliver possibilities for women to use their strengths to overcome weaknesses, and it opens up opportunities helping to counter threats (Bögenhold and Fachinger 2013, 2015; Bögenhold and

Klinglmair 2015). In particular, solo self-employment may deliver options that could lessen the constraints that family care places on women's employment. It may also be the case that women place a higher value on nonwage aspects of self-employment than men do, and that women with greater family responsibilities may trade earnings for the family-friendly aspects of self-employment. Therefore self-employment may reflect the development of more or less successful strategies for coping with the conflicts arising from the difficult balance of self-employment and family life. However, can female solo self-employment be seen as a representation of a new paradigm of employment, which does not fit the well-known traditional type of self-employment? We will examine the influence of personal characteristics, household and labour market characteristics for both mothers and fathers in a family context, and their probability of being self-employed as compared to parents who have chosen formal, gainful employment.

The chapter combines conceptual thoughts on the development of self-employment within stratified modern societies with empirical reflections based on public census data for Germany. The analysis is based upon microcensus data from the Federal Statistical Office, which are available for the period 1989–2009 (see Statistisches Bundesamt 2012).

COMPETING APPROACHES TO DEAL WITH GENDER-RELATED LABOUR MARKET DISPARITIES

When analysing social structures and patterns of inequality, gender is one of the items that highlights social disparities. Disparities are sometimes interpreted as indicators of discrimination practices, and the literature reports four problems of gender segregation (Charles and Grusky 2004). Regarding the fact that divisions of social structure show significant differences in gender participation and in gender distribution, discussion has to evaluate carefully the reasons for those gender gaps (Verheul et al. 2012).

In public, but also in academic gender discourse, different explanations regarding gender imbalances exist, which factors can be held responsible and whether we are witnessing a declining significance of gender (Blau et al. 2006: 3–33). A more fundamental feminist explanation interprets female over- or underrepresentation as a mirror of male power strategies in society, and as proof of the limited power of women to obtain the same positions in the same percentages as held by men. While this position is close to a model of gender domination, a competing position argues more moderately by claiming that the gender division of different social classes and labour market categories is itself a reflection of more complex factors, to which different patterns of gender decisions in education and further education also belong (England et al. 2007). In particular, we see that gender decisions for different university study subjects are obvious, which initialize the result that engineering and many natural sciences are overwhelmingly male domains while the teaching profession is dominated by women (Leoni and Falk 2010). Gender-based discussion is very rich in showing divergent sets of academic argumentation in that respect (Minniti 2010; Hesse-Biber 2014).

Finally, one can interpret the landscape of social and occupational (asymmetrical) distribution not only as a result of societal discrimination practices or divergent individual decisions by gender but also as a mirror of complex *household* decisions rather than individual actors' decisions. When following that line of thought, households gain a status as acting subjects who appear to have their own distinct rationality to make occupational decisions and to organize the structure and philosophy of life-courses. When employing this perspective, patterns of explanation become more diverse than simple dichotomic black–white modes usually offer; and cause and effect become difficult to separate, which also has to be reflected when teaching entrepreneurship (Heinonen and Hytti 2010).

Based upon evaluations of German census data, Tables 12.1 and 12.2 show a range of reasons for working part time. The relevance of these reasons differs depending on whether people are employees or self-employed. Furthermore, fundamental differences between men and women are visible.

To obtain more reliable information about the factors behind these statements, it is necessary to explore the relationship between self-employment, partner's employment, household and children. Our analysis examines the influence of personal as well as household and labour market characteristics for men and women in a family context, and their probability of being self-employed as compared to parents who have chosen formal, gainful employment. Observing labour market data at the household level allows an investigation of the forms of work hybridity (Folta et al. 2010) as a strategy to combine different income sources of different household agents with a common whole on a rational basis.

Data in Table 12.2 shed light on the family and/or household background of those entrepreneurial agents who were treated as full-time or part-time entrepreneurs in our previous discussion. Now, when turning to the perspective of households, completely new horizons emerge. While solo self-employed women and female employees contribute to a household income in about 48 per cent of the cases (compared to 27 per cent for

Table 12.1   Reasons for working part time

Men

	Solo Self-Employed	Self-Employed with Employees	Employees
Full-time employment not available	17.2	5.8	38.8
Education	8.8	3.8	14.6
Illness, accident	3.3	3.8	7.0
Private or family commitments	5.1	7.7	5.1
Full-time employment not possible or not wanted	39.8	53.8	23.5
Caring for child or disabled person	2.9	1.9	3.1
n.a.	23.0	23.1	7.8
All	100.0	100.0	100.0

Women

	Solo Self-Employed	Self-Employed with Employees	Employees
Full-time employment not available	10.9	5.9	20.1
Education	5.3	1.5	3.5
Illness, accident	1.8	2.9	2.1
Private or family commitments	20.8	23.5	23.8
Full-time employment not possible or not wanted	27.1	25.0	21.0
Caring for child or disabled person	21.7	25.0	26.3
n.a.	12.4	16.2	3.2
All	100.0	100.0	100.0

Source: Own calculations based on the scientific use file of the Microcensus 2009 of the Federal Statistical Office Germany.

self-employed people with employees), which is not the primary income source of the household, one can interpret the data in the sense that a relativly large proportion of female agents simply want to gain additional income in order to contribute to the overall volume of household income. Taking together reasons for working part time (Table 12.1) and information provided in Table 12.2, the interpretation comes to mind that female part-time entrepreneurship especially is led by a rationality geared towards

Table 12.2   Relationship between main income earner and the reference person representing the household

Men

	Solo Self-Employed	Self-Employed with Employees	Employees
Main income earner is the reference person and is an independent farmer	5.9	4.4	0.0
Main income earner solely achieves highest income class	59.6	70.1	75.2
Main income earner achieves the highest income class jointly with additional person	5.4	4.1	5.0
Other main income earner (reference person in the household)	7.0	8.2	3.6
Person in the household with main income earner is an independent farmer (full time)	0.3	0.1	0.2
Person achieving the highest income class, but not main income earner	1.3	0.9	2.1
Person declaring income, but not in the highest income class	15.2	6.5	12.2
Person does not declare income, but other household members provide details of individual incomes	4.6	4.9	0.9
Person does not declare income; no other household members declare income	0.7	0.8	0.8
Total	100.0	100.0	100.0

Women

	Solo Self-Employed	Self-Employed with Employees	Employees
Main income earner is the reference person and is an independent farmer	0.3	0.4	0.0
Main income earner solely achieves highest income class	34.9	46.6	38.0

Table 12.2   (continued)

Women

	Solo Self-Employed	Self-Employed with Employees	Employees
Main income earner achieves the highest income class jointly with additional person	1.5	2.0	1.7
Other main income earner (reference person in the household)	2.8	4.0	1.3
Person in the household with main income earner is an independent farmer (full time)	1.3	1.1	0.4
Person achieving the highest income class, but not main income earner	4.3	9.3	6.2
Person declaring income, but not in the highest income class	47.4	27.1	48.7
Person does not declare income, but other household members provide details of individual incomes	4.0	3.8	0.6
Person does not declare income; no other household members declare income	3.6	5.8	3.0
Total	100.0	100.0	100.0

Source: Own calculations based on the scientific use file of the Microcensus 2009 of the Federal Statistical Office Germany.

generating additional income for the household's financial package. An argument that highlights different gender aspects in entrepreneurship by emphasizing new meanings of reliability and risk-moderation may find specific proof here (Hytti 2005).

SOME RESULTS FROM THE BINARY LOGISTIC REGRESSION

Employees and Self-Employment

Over the past decades, a restructuring of the labour market has taken place which has led to diminishing differences between employees and the self-employed – due on the one hand to outsourcing, and on the other hand to more possibilities for taking up a business, especially as in the services sector high start-up capital is not necessary. Binary logistic regression was undertaken to gather more information about the significance of the explanatory variables (Bögenhold and Fachinger 2013). In the first step, we looked at the differences between self-employed workers and employees. Employment status was coded as 0 = employees and 1 = self-employed. The following variables were chosen as predictors:

- Economic sector – services; agriculture, forestry, fishing; industry; domestic trade, accommodation, transport
- Gender
- Age
- Highest level of education according to the International Standard Classification of Education (ISCED97)
- Actual working time
- Number of children below the age of three.

According to the scientific use file for 2009, the labour force consists of around 38.64 million people, with 45.8 per cent women. Most people work in the service sector (51.4 per cent). In 22.3 per cent are employed the industry sector, and only 2.3 per cent in the primary sector. Regarding the highest level of education, most people in Germany have a level of ISCED 3b (45.8 per cent). For the regression we chose the following reference categories:

- Services for economic sector
- ISCED 6 for highest level of education
- Male for gender
- Three children.

Table 12.3 gives the statistics for each predictor. The Wald statistic for most of the variables is quite high, indicating some relevance of predictors. However, the number of children and some ISCED values for education have a low Wald statistic and are not significant. Factors of relevance are economic sector, age, working time and gender.

Table 12.3   Variables in the equation, Step 1

Economic sector	B	S.E.	Wald	df	Sig.	Exp(B)
Services			837.570	3	.000	
Agriculture, forestry, fishing	1.186	.086	191.839	1	.000	3.273
Industry	−1.181	.062	357.661	1	.000	.307
Domestic trade, accommodation, transport	.489	.042	136.598	1	.000	1.630
Age	.047	.002	848.417	1	.000	1.048
Actual working time	.034	.001	836.379	1	.000	1.034
Female	−.408	.039	109.694	1	.000	.665
ISCED 1			614.176	9	.000	
ISCED 2	−.155	.163	.901	1	.342	.856
ISCED 3a	−1.357	.456	8.857	1	.003	.257
ISCED 3b	1.019	.174	34.475	1	.000	2.770
ISCED 3c	.018	.151	.014	1	.907	1.018
ISCED 4a, b	.610	.161	14.305	1	.000	1.840
ISCED 5a	.906	.155	34.044	1	.000	2.475
ISCED 5b	.860	.153	31.418	1	.000	2.364
ISCED 6	1.219	.180	46.061	1	.000	3.384
n.a.	.481	.405	1.410	1	.235	1.617
3 children			36.092	3	.000	
No children	.445	.077	32.955	1	.000	.560
1 child	.499	.273	3.347	1	.067	1.647
2 children	.941	1.303	.522	1	.470	2.563
Constant	−5.653	.176	1030.768	1	.000	.004

With respect to economic sector, the possibility of being self-employed is higher for the primary sector and the sector with domestic trade, accommodation and transport, and lower for industry than for the service sector. People are also more likely to be self-employed if they are older. The positive sign for actual working time indicates that, on average, self-employed people are working longer. Regarding education, it can be seen that for people with a low level the possibility of being self-employed is low. However, for ISCED 2 and 3a the Wald statistic is low, therefore those variables are not statistically significant. In contrast, there are two statuses in particular, ISCED 3b and ISCED 6, where the B values indicate that people with those levels of education are very likely to be self-employed.

However, the binary logistic regression regarding the differences between being self-employed and being an employee shows a rather weak model fit (Bögenhold and Fachinger 2013). This indicates that there are no major differences between the two statuses.

However, in the literature it is argued that the group of self-employed people is very heterogeneous, and that sometimes being solo self-employed or working for a company is nearly the same as regards individual characteristics – those solo self-employed are sometimes characterized as *scheinselbständig* (self-employed in name only). Therefore, differences may occur when comparing the solo self-employed with self-employed people with employees.

Self-Employment and Solo Self-Employment

To get a better understanding of the self-employed, we took a closer look at the differences between self-employed and solo self-employed people (Bögenhold and Fachinger 2013). In the sub-sample only people who are self-employed are included. Employment status is coded as 0 = self-employed with employees and 1 = solo self-employed.

The dependent variable which measures solo self-employment is equal to 1 if the respondent is solo self-employed and 0 otherwise. The logistic regression model is used to estimate the factors that influence solo self-employment if someone is self-employed. A logistic regression analysis was conducted to predict solo self-employment using the following as predictors:

- Economic sector: services (reference category); agriculture, forestry, fishing; industry; domestic trade, accommodation, transport
- Gender
- Age
- Age squared
- Highest level of education (ISCED97)
- Actual working time
- Number of children below three.

However, in a first estimation, age squared and number of children was not significant regarding Wald statistics (Bögenhold and Fachinger 2013). Therefore, as the inclusion of irrelevant variables can result in a poor model fit, we omitted those variables for the final estimation.

In 2009 the number of self-employed people in Germany was around 4.2 million, with 31.2 per cent women. Most self-employed people work in the service sector (53.1 per cent). The number of self-employed in the industry sector (8.1 per cent) is quite low. The figure of 2.3 per cent in the primary sector is an expression of the structural changes in the economy. Regarding the highest level of education, most people have a level of ISCED 3b or 5, the first stage of tertiary education (34.1 and 42.9 per cent respectively). For the regression we chose the following reference categories:

Table 12.4   Variables in the equation, Step 1

Economic sector	B	S. E.	Wald	df	Sig.	Exp(B)
Services			95.474	3	.000	
Agriculture, forestry, fishing	.283	.144	3.844	1	.050	1.327
Industry	−.723	.130	30.986	1	.000	.485
Domestic trade, accommodation, transport	−.627	.082	59.133	1	.000	.534
Age	−.015	.003	23.624	1	.000	.985
Actual working time	−.032	.002	290.873	1	.000	.968
Female	.133	.078	2.939	1	.086	1.142
ISCED 1			112.707	9	.000	
ISCED 2	.318	.328	.942	1	.332	1.375
ISCED 3a	−.104	.956	.012	1	.914	.902
ISCED 3b	.689	.354	3.776	1	.052	1.991
ISCED 3c	.340	.303	1.259	1	.262	1.405
ISCED 4a, b	.262	.323	.659	1	.417	1.300
ISCED 5a	−.314	.309	1.032	1	.310	.731
ISCED 5b	.099	.308	.104	1	.747	1.104
ISCED 6	−1.265	.352	12.895	1	.000	.282
Constant	2.439	.345	49.910	1	.000	11.463

- Services for economic sector
- ISCED 1 for highest level of education
- Male for gender.

Table 12.4 shows the statistics for each predictor. The Wald statistic for most of the variables is quite high, indicating the relevance of predictors. Regarding economic sector, the results indicate that the possibility of being solo self-employed in industry and in the domestic trade, accommodation and transport sectors is lower. That means that it is more probable that we can find solo self-employed people in the service sector. With respect to age, the negative sign shows that, on average, solo self-employed people are younger than self-employed people with employees. Actual working time for the solo self-employed is lower than for self-employed people with employees. This is also a plausible result, as the solo self-employed more often work part time, as the descriptive analysis has shown.

Gender also contributes to the model, as the positive B value indicates that the solo self-employed group tends to have significantly more females than males. Concerning education level, the results show that those with a higher level of education are more likely to have employees. It can be also seen that people with a special form of education (e.g. ISCED 3b and c as well as 4a and b) are more likely to be solo self-employed. Especially interesting is the negative B value for ISCED 6 as this group consists in large part of 'free professions' (lawyers, physicians, auditors, tax advisors and related professions), which need a high level of education.

CONCLUSIONS

While gender disparities can be found and are discussed at many different levels, this chapter restricted the level of observation to the division of labour market segregation and, especially, to gendered aspects of participation and representation within self-employment. Our results indicate that the general trend of growing female integration into the labour market is true for the specific field of self-employment. However, since women are engaged more than average in the service sector and in solo self-employment there is no real trend that gender differences, such as pay gaps, are closed because in those fields, for example, lower working hours and lower wage rates exist.

Our results indicate that not only the division of labour but also the division of engagement in self-employment depends highly on a rationality of labour market participation. People's intentions to engage to a specific extent and with specific degrees of motivation reflect diverse areas of the organization of private life. The rationality of private duties, needs, challenges and aspirations belong to the factors which influence the decisions. All these areas can be subsumed under the idea of the 'social context of entrepreneurship' (Welter 2011). A crucial impact on those decisions is made by the background of the household members and what the household looks like. Issues of business partnership and marital status, and the existence of children (and their age) or elder relatives are factors which provide different life-worlds which set relevant parameters to engage in the labour market. This engagement is often a struggle between different preferences and conditions to acknowledge so that decisions are framed and led by different social contexts.

All in all, the household as the entity of different interests, motivations, needs and obstacles proves to be the real 'actor' rather than the individual. Individuals seem to be embedded in wider logics of life-world sense, including all factual restrictions, wants and needs. Therefore, above average participation of women in solo self-employment may reflect growing needs for flexibility in terms of time sovereignty despite lower incomes. Understanding the variability in gender segregation (Charles and Grusky 2004) needs also to get to grips with household rationalities to understand that different divisions of gender participation are not only a reflection of discrimination but also mirror the different social constraints in the context of the organization of business and society (Charles and Bradley 2009).

REFERENCES

Blau, Francine D., Brinton, Mary C., and Grusky, David B. (eds). 2006. *The Declining Significance of Gender?* New York: Russell Sage Foundation.
Bögenhold, Dieter, and Fachinger, Uwe. 2013. Rationality of self-employment: do female and male entrepreneurs differ?, *Journal of Business and Finance*, **1** (2), 42–62.
Bögenhold, Dieter, and Fachinger, Uwe. 2015. Unternehmerinnen: Kontextuelle Faktoren der Zunahme von weiblicher Selbständigkeit und Entrepreneurship, *Sozialer Fortschritt*, **64** (9–10), 227–233.
Bögenhold, Dieter, and Klinglmair, Andrea. 2015. Female solo self-employment: features of gendered entrepreneurship, *International Review of Entrepreneurship*, **13** (1), 47–58.
Brush, C.G., de Bruin, A., and Welter, F. 2009. A gender-aware framework for women, *International Journal of Gender and Entrepreneurship*, **1** (1), 8–24.
Charles, Maria, and Bradley, K. 2009. Indulging our gendered selves? Sex segregation by field of study in 44 countries, *American Journal of Sociology*, **114**, 924–976.
Charles, Maria, and Grusky, David B. 2004. *Occupational Ghettos: The Worldwide Segregation of Women and Men*. Stanford: Stanford University Press.
England, Paula, Allison, P., Li, S., Mark, N., Thompson, J., Budig, M. and Sun, H. 2007. Why are some academic fields tipping toward female? The sex composition of U.S. fields of doctoral degree receipt, 1971–2002, *Sociology of Education*, **80**, 23–42.
Folta, Timothy, Delmar, Frédéric, and Wennberg, Karl. 2010. Hybrid entrepreneurship, *Management Science*, **56**, 253–269.
Heinonen, Jarna, and Hytti, Ulla. 2010. Back to basics: the role of teaching in developing the entrepreneurial university, *Journal of Entrepreneurship and Innovation*, **11** (4), 283–292.
Hesse-Biber, Sharlene Nagy (ed.). (2014). *Feminist Research Practice: A Primer*. London: Sage.
Hytti, Ulla. 2005. New meanings for entrepreneurs: from risk-taking heroes to safe-seeking professionals, *Journal of Organizational Change Management*, Special Issue: Change in the feminine: women in change, **18** (6), 594–611.
Leoni, Thomas, and Falk, E. Martin. 2010. Gender and field of study as determinants of self-employment, *Small Business Economics*, **34**, 167–185.
Minniti, Maria. 2010: Female entrepreneurship and economic activity, *European Journal of Development Research*, **22**, 294–312.
Statistisches Bundesamt. 2012. *Mikrozensus. Bevölkerung und Erwerbstätigkeit. Stand und Entwicklung der Erwerbstätigkeit. Deutschla*nd, 2010, Fachserie 1, 4.1.1, Wiesbaden.

Verheul, Ingrid, Thurik, Roy, Grilo, Isabel, and van der Zwan, Peter. 2012. Explaining preferences and actual involvement in self-employment: gender and the entrepreneurial personality, *Journal of Economic Psychology*, **33**, 325–341.
Welter, Friederike. 2011. Contextualizing entrepreneurship: conceptual challenges and ways forward, *Entrepreneurship, Theory and Practice*, **35** (1), 164–184.

PART IV

Entrepreneurial finance, growth and
economic crises

13. Entrepreneurship and Schumpeterian growth

Paolo E. Giordani

1. INTRODUCTION

Economic theory identifies technological progress as the main engine of economic growth. In particular, in the endogenous innovation-driven growth literature (Romer, 1990; Grossman and Helpman, 1991b), technological progress is the result of "voluntary" investment decisions taken by profit-maximizing economic agents. This literature, however, disregards the role of *strong* uncertainty (Knight, 1921) in the investment decisions concerning innovation. The implicit assumption in all these models is that of a perfectly assessable investment horizon, implied by the existence of transparent and well-organized financial markets. In a world of "measurable" uncertainty, there is no room for the Schumpeterian entrepreneur-innovator, that is, for someone who has "the capacity to see things in a way, which afterwards proves to be true, although it cannot be proven at the time" (Schumpeter, 1934, p. 85).

On the other hand, as suggested by early insights by Knight and Schumpeter himself, the decision to devote time and resources to innovative activities is taken under conditions of severe uncertainty on their expected returns.[1] Innovations are unique events, and the process aimed at producing them is—both by logic and by historical inspection—an intrinsically uncertain economic activity. The key role played by uncertainty to understand the dynamics of technical change has also been explicitly recognized by economists and economic historians of innovation (Scherer and Harhoff, 2000; Rosenberg, 1996), and is largely confirmed by the empirical evidence on firm behavior (Freeman and Soete, 1997, Ch. 10). Finally, a large number of experimental studies conducted in psychology and decision-making sciences (Bhidé, 2000; Busenitz, 1999; Hansemark, 2003), as well as more recent empirical evidence (Hvide and Panos, 2013), have suggested that the choice of starting up an innovative venture is crucially affected by the agents' tolerance of uncertainty.

The purpose of this chapter is to introduce a role for Knightian uncertainty into a modern Schumpeterian growth framework (Aghion and Howitt, 1992; Grossman and Helpman, 1991a), and to give a theoretical foundation to the micro-evidence suggesting a relationship between entrepreneurial choice and attitude towards uncertainty.

In the class of Schumpeterian growth models, the arrival of innovation is governed by a Poisson process whose parameter—capturing the instantaneous probability of innovation—is constant and known to economic agents. We remove this hypothesis and investigate the possibility that agents are strongly uncertain about this probability. We draw on the recent advancements in the theory of decision making under uncertainty to model an agent's attitude towards uncertainty, sometimes referred to as *ambiguity* (Schmeidler, 1989). In particular, we follow a generalization of the "multiple prior" approach, pioneered by Gilboa and Schmeidler (1989) and inspired by the Ellsberg (1961) paradox, which provides a clear and "operational" distinction between risk and uncertainty.[2] The idea of the multiple prior approach to uncertainty is that, in highly uncertain choice scenarios, the decision maker's information is too vague to be represented by a single probability distribution. In such cases, decision makers have multiple priors whose extension captures the level of uncertainty of the choice scenario. To compute their expected payoff, they then select one of them; and whether they select a relatively more "optimistic" or "pessimistic" prior defines their attitude towards uncertainty.

We consider the realistic possibility that agents are heterogeneous in their attitude towards uncertainty, in the sense that some individuals may be more uncertainty seeking than others. In the framework of a Schumpeterian growth model, we then study the occupational choice of economic agents along the balanced growth path. We find that, in equilibrium, a threshold value for the individuals' uncertainty aversion exists such that all those with a higher uncertainty aversion become salaried workers, while all those with lower uncertainty aversion become entrepreneurs. In this respect, the "entrepreneurial spirit" resides in the individuals' attitude towards uncertainty. The implications for the economic performance of the system are powerful: given that the balanced growth path of an economy is positively related to the amount of resources devoted to entrepreneurial innovation, which in turn depend on uncertainty attitude, then in the long run, and other things equal, societies populated by individuals more tolerant towards uncertainty tend to grow faster than societies populated by more uncertainty-averse individuals.

This work is closely related to the theoretical literature on the determinants of the entrepreneurial choice. Two alternative theories exist that attempt to identify the behavioral key feature of the entrepreneur. One, inspired by the early work of Lucas (1978), suggests that entrepreneurs are those with relatively higher abilities than the rest of the population. The other, originally proposed by Kihlstrom and Laffont (1979), claims that entrepreneurs are those with the relatively stronger propensity towards risk. Both explanations have been largely debated and criticized by studies in experimental psychology and decision sciences. Experimental evidence has convincingly shown that entrepreneurs are *not* on average more risk seeking than the rest of the population.[3] We propose an alternative explanation of entrepreneurial choice based on the attitude towards uncertainty, the inspiring argument being strikingly simple: if the entrepreneur makes her distinctive choice—that of venturing into an innovative enterprise— under conditions of uncertainty, then her distinctive trait is not her attitude towards risk but her attitude towards uncertainty.

This work also connects to the literature on Schumpeterian growth theory (Aghion and Howitt, 1992; Grossman and Helpman, 1991a, b; Aghion and Howitt, 1998). Our specific contribution to this stream of literature is to have introduced strong uncertainty into the innovation process, and to have given a role to the Schumpeterian entrepreneur. In this respect, a close piece of research is the one by Cozzi and Giordani (2011), who also consider the possibility that the innovation process be subject to strong uncertainty. Their model, however, is a representative agent model that neglects completely the occupational choice of economic agents and, hence, has nothing to say about the theoretical foundations of entrepreneurship, which represent a major focus of the present analysis.

The rest of the chapter is organized as follows. In the next section we present the model. Section 3 characterizes the stationary equilibrium, while Section 4 concludes with a few remarks.

2.   ENTREPRENEURSHIP IN THE NEO-SCHUMPETERIAN FRAMEWORK

In this section we introduce the economic agents' occupational choice into the simplest Schumpeterian growth framework (Aghion and Howitt, 1992). Time is continuous, and there exists a *continuum* of infinitely lived households with identical intertemporally additive preferences, with r representing the rate of time preference. To simplify matters, and without loss of generality, we assume a linear instantaneous utility.[4] Households are endowed with flow units of skilled or unskilled labor time which they supply inelastically in a perfectly competitive market.

2.1 The Final Good Sector

There is a perfectly competitive final sector in which output is produced according to a constant returns to scale (CRS) technology. For simplicity, we assume a Cobb–Douglas specification:

$$y_t = A_t x^\theta_t N_t^{1-\theta} = A_t x^\theta_t \quad 0<\theta<1$$

where y is final output, x is the intermediate good and N, normalized to 1, is the total mass of unskilled labor. A is the productivity parameter that reflects the current quality of the intermediate good and which is assumed to evolve according to the following rule:

$$A_{t+1} = \gamma A_t \text{ for } \gamma>1 \text{ and } t = 0,1,2. \ldots$$

Notice that subscript t does not refer to calendar time (which is instead indexed by τ), but to the generation of the intermediate product that is being used. Whenever a new intermediate product is introduced into the market, the economy *jumps* by γ. Hence, γ measures the size of the *vertical* innovation. Finally, the price of the final output acts as numeraire: $p(y_t) = 1$.

2.2 The Intermediate Good Sector

The intermediate good x is produced through a one-to-one technology from skilled labor. Hence, x also denotes the amount of labor currently employed in the intermediate sector. Skilled labor, however, can also be employed in research to generate innovations (as we will see in Subsection 2.4). The model determines how the total amount of skilled labor resources, denoted by L, is allocated between these two alternative uses.

Before describing the dynamics of the innovation process, let us illustrate what happens when a new quality is discovered: as soon as a new intermediate product is introduced, it is automatically protected by a perfect and infinitely lived patent, which allows the inventor (or whoever buys the blueprint) to temporarily *monopolize* the market. With the assumption that innovations are drastic, monopoly profits can be easily obtained from the profit-maximizing condition:[5]

$$\max\lfloor \pi_t = A_t \theta \, x_t^{\theta-1} x_t - x_t w_t \rfloor,$$

where w_t is the skilled labor wage. This maximization gives the optimal value of x_t as:

$$x_t = \left(\frac{w_t}{A_t\theta^2}\right)^{\frac{1}{1-\theta}}.$$

Maximum profits can then be written as:

$$\pi_t = \frac{1-\theta}{\theta}x_t w_t.$$

2.3 Uncertainty in the Innovation Process

In the class of Schumpeterian growth models, the innovation process is governed by a Poisson process. A unit of skilled labor devoted to innovation produces an instantaneous probability λ_t of discovering the next innovation vintage (we here follow the common practice of referring to λ_t as the flow probability of discovering vintage $t+1$). We now remove the hypothesis that economic agents know exactly this probability, and consider the possibility that they hold *ambiguous* prior beliefs about it. In particular, we make the weaker assumption that, for each vintage t, agents only know that λ_t takes a strictly positive finite value between a minimum and a maximum value—that is to say: $\lambda_t \in [m, M]$ $\forall t$, where $m, M \in]0,+\infty[$ and $M>m$.[6] The width of the interval represents the extension of priors, and it is a measure of the uncertainty perceived by the agents.

To capture the agents' attitude towards uncertainty we follow a multiple prior approach and, in particular, a decision rule axiomatized by Ghirardato et al. (2004) called $\alpha-MEU$ decision rule (where MEU stands for maxmin expected utility). This rule is a generalization of the classical Hurwicz (1951) α−pessimism index criterion, and it computes a α−weighted sum of the *maxmin* expected utility (obtained via the selection of the worst prior) and the *maxmax* expected utility (obtained via the selection of the best prior). The $\alpha-MEU$ criterion has the advantage of allowing a clear and simple distinction between uncertainty, which is measured by the extension of priors, and uncertainty aversion, which is instead (positively) measured by the coefficient $\alpha \in [0,1]$.

2.4 The Occupational Choice

The total mass of skilled workers L are heterogeneous in their attitude towards uncertainty α. In particular, assume that this attitude is distributed along the interval $[0,1]$ according to a known distribution function F. Denote the generic agent by $l \in [0,L]$, and her uncertainty aversion coefficient by α_l.

What determines the occupational choice of skilled worker l in the economy? She has two options. On the one hand, she can work in the intermediate good sector as a salaried worker, thus earning w_t. Alternatively, she can devote her unit of skilled labor time to entrepreneurship, thus gaining a probability λ_t of coming up with the innovation vintage $t+1$, whose value is denoted by V_{t+1} (and is explicitly characterized in the next subsection). Given that λ_t is strictly uncertain, each agent l evaluates her expected returns from entrepreneurship by computing an α_l-weighted average of the maxmin level (also called "security level", mV_{t+1}) and the maxmax level (also called "optimism level", MV_{t+1}), thus obtaining $[\alpha_l m + (1-\alpha_l)M] V_{t+1}$. By comparing this payoff with the secure wage associated with manufacturing, this agent decides to become an entrepreneur if $[\alpha_l m + (1-\alpha_l) M]V_{t+1} > w_t$, and to work in manufacturing if the opposite inequality holds.

2.5   The Value of the Innovation

The entrepreneurial sector is perfectly competitive. The value of the vintage $t+1$ innovation is the present discounted value of the (monopoly) profits associated with the new intermediate good. To characterize this value, we follow the standard practice of analyzing the investment decisions of households. Two investment options are available: investing in risk-free assets or in shares of monopolistic firms. At equilibrium, and given that instantaneous utilities are assumed linear, agents must be indifferent about the two options. The value V_{t+1} must then satisfy the following *asset equation*:

$$rV_{t+1} = \pi_{t+1} - \lambda^l_{t+1} n_{t+1} V_{t+1},$$

where rV_{t+1} is the return from investing in risk-free shares; π_{t+1} is the flow of profits corresponding to vintage $t+1$; n_{t+1} is the endogenous number of entrepreneurs involved in the discovery process of vintage $t+2$; and $\lambda^l_{t+1} n_{t+1} V_{t+1}$ is the expected capital loss due to the introduction of vintage $t+2$ and embodies Schumpeter's idea of the *creative destruction* process.

The expected capital loss depends on the degree of uncertainty aversion of economic agents. Decision makers following the $\alpha-$MEU criterion compute an $\alpha-$weighted average of the maxmin level ($Mn_{t+1}V_{t+1}$) and the maxmax level ($mn_{t+1}V_{t+1}$). Notice that, in contrast to the decision problem analyzed in the previous subsection, agents are here evaluating a potential loss, and thus m and M are now respectively associated with the maxmax level and the maxmin level. In equilibrium, it must then be $rV^l_{t+1} = \pi_{t+1} - [\alpha^l M + (1+\alpha^l)m]n_{t+1} V^l_{t+1}$, from which we obtain the expression for V^l_{t+1} as

$$V^l_{t+1} = \frac{\pi_{t+1}}{r + [\alpha^l M + (1 - \alpha^l)m]n_{t+1}} \qquad (1)$$

stating that the value to an investor of the monopolistic firm producing vintage $t+1$ is the flow of profits that it generates, discounted at her subjective, obsolescence-adjusted interest rate.

3. ENTREPRENEURIAL INNOVATION ALONG THE BALANCED GROWTH PATH

Given that the mass of workers is continuously distributed along the uncertainty aversion interval [0,1], there must exist a worker who is exactly indifferent about being employed in manufacture and venturing into innovation. More formally, there must exist a threshold value of uncertainty aversion α^* such that

$$[\alpha^* m + (1 - \alpha^*)M]V^*_{t+1} = w_t$$

The equation above is usually referred to as the *research arbitrage equation* in that it determines the mass of workers devoting to innovation and the mass of workers devoting to manufacture. Moreover, in our framework (in which workers are heterogeneous), this condition also allows us to establish *who* becomes entrepreneur and who becomes employee. All agents whose α^l is lower than α^* become entrepreneurs, since for them the expected return from entrepreneurial innovation is strictly higher than the wage they can earn in the manufacturing sector. Their number is $F(\alpha^*)L$. All agents whose α^l is higher than α^* become salaried workers for the opposite reason. Their number is $[1-F(\alpha^*)]L$.

More formally, the stationary equilibrium is defined by the triple (α^*, n, x) that solves the following system:

$$\begin{aligned}
[\alpha^* m + (1-\alpha^*)M]V^*_{t+1} &= w_t \\
F(\alpha^*)L &= n \\
[1-F(\alpha^*)]L &= x,
\end{aligned} \qquad (2)$$

where the expression for V^*_{t+1} is given in (1). Figure 13.1 provides a graphical representation of the occupational distribution of skilled workers in this economy under the hypothesis of uniform distribution of skilled workers along the uncertainty aversion interval. We also provide an illustrative example at the end of this section.

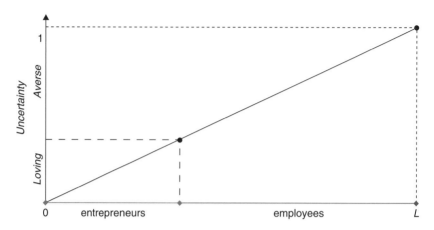

Figure 13.1   The occupational distribution of skilled workers

In this class of models, the instantaneous growth rate of the economy is given by the number of innovations per unit of time multiplied by the size of the step ahead brought about by each of them, that is, $g^*_t = \lambda_t F(\alpha^*) L \ln \gamma$. The performance of an economy is then positively affected not only by its "innovativeness", as dictated by its fundamentals (λ and γ), but also by the endogenous number of entrepreneurs ($F(\alpha^*)L$). Given that this number depends on tolerance towards uncertainty, we can conclude that, *ceteris paribus*, an economy populated by uncertainty-seeking individuals will grow faster than an economy populated by uncertainty-averse individuals.

Finally, notice a final implication of our entrepreneurial theory based on tolerance towards uncertainty. The equilibrium value of α^* that is obtained from system (2) depends on the profitability conditions of the economy. This implies that there are no "genetic" entrepreneurs: the choice as to whether or not to devote to entrepreneurial innovation reflects the incentives provided by the economy so that, say, an agent opting for salaried work in one country might well have become an entrepreneur in a more favorable entrepreneurial climate. This stands in contrast with the main result in Rigotti et al. (2008), who also propose, in a different framework, a theory of entrepreneurial choice based on uncertainty attitude. In their model, however, an *ex ante* distinction is made between two types of agent: bulls, who become entrepreneurs; and bears, who opt for more secure jobs. In our model, instead the two groups and their sizes are determined endogenously.

Example: For the sake of illustration, assume now that skilled workers are uniformly distributed along the uncertainty aversion interval [0,1], from the most uncertainty seeking ($\alpha=0$) to the most uncertainty averse

(α=1). After plugging the expression for V^*_{t+1} as given in (1) and using the fact that, in steady state, the expression for monopolistic profits in $t+1$ is given by $\pi_{t+1} = \gamma\pi_t = \gamma(1-\theta)/\theta.x_t w_t$, the steady-state system of our economy can be rewritten as

$$[\alpha^*m + (1-\alpha^*)M]\dfrac{\gamma\dfrac{1-\theta}{\theta}x}{r + [\alpha^*M + (1-\alpha^*)m]n} = 1$$

$$\alpha^*L = n$$

$$(1-\alpha^*)L = x,$$

where the last two equations of the system exploit the uniform distribution assumption. Using them to substitute for the expressions of n and x into the first equation and rearranging, we obtain a quadratic equation in α^* admitting two closed-form solutions of α^* only one of which is acceptable (as the other is negative) and is given by

$$\alpha^* = \dfrac{\left\{\left[1 + (2M-m)\gamma\dfrac{1-\theta}{\theta}\right]^2 - 4(M-m)\left(1-\gamma\dfrac{1-\theta}{\theta}\right)\left(\dfrac{r}{L}-\gamma\dfrac{1-\theta}{\theta}M\right)\right\}^{\frac{1}{2}} - 1 - 2(M-m)\left(1-\gamma\dfrac{1-\theta}{\theta}\right)}{2(M-m)\left(1-\gamma\dfrac{1-\theta}{\theta}\right)}$$

This value of α^* defines the level of uncertainty aversion that makes the worker exactly indifferent to the two job options: all workers with a more optimistic perception of uncertainty ($\alpha^l < \alpha^*$) will devote themselves to entrepreneurial innovation, while all workers with a more pessimistic perception of uncertainty ($\alpha^l < \alpha^*$) will become employees.

4.   CONCLUDING REMARKS

In this chapter, we have extended the class of innovation-driven growth models to consider the possibility that economic agents ignore the exact probability of arrival of the next innovation. We have proposed a theory of occupational choice to link the subjective innovative spirit of individuals to their tolerance of uncertainty. We have explicitly characterized the balanced growth path of the economy and shown that entrepreneurial ventures are launched by the relatively more uncertainty-seeking individuals. Moreover, a more positive attitude towards uncertainty induces a higher amount of resources devoted to entrepreneurial innovation, and thus it improves the economic performance of the whole economy.

The policy implications from this type of analysis can be valuable. For a country, growth-enhancing policies are those that favor its entrepreneurial climate. The extent of entrepreneurial innovation, however, is crucially affected by the citizens' tolerance of uncertainty, which, as empirical evidence suggests, may differ substantially from country to country (Hofstede, 2001; Giordani et al., 2010). As a result, policy intervention should be tailored to the special characteristics of the countries themselves. A simple but illuminating example on bankruptcy law is provided by Gerard Roland (2005, p. 6):

> For example, in an economy where agents are very risk [uncertainty]-averse and display little taste for entrepreneurship, a bankruptcy law should not be too punitive towards failed entrepreneurs, whereas bankruptcy laws should be tougher towards debtors in an economy where agents are both very entrepreneurial and prone to cheating to make a quick buck.

Hence, knowing the determinants of entrepreneurship is key to designing more accurate and effective growth policies.

NOTES

1. It must also be stressed that, while Schumpeter regarded innovative activity as highly uncertain, he was not convinced that the distinctive trait of the entrepreneur was risk attitude. To use his own words: "risk bearing is no part of the entrepreneurial function. It is the capitalist who bears the risk. The entrepreneur does so only to the extent to which, besides being an entrepreneur, he is also a capitalist, but qua entrepreneur he loses other people's money" (1939, p. 104).
2. The two-urn version of the paradox goes as follows: two urns are given, each of which contains ten balls. One of them is known to contain five white balls and five black balls, while no information is given about the balls' colors in the other. The decision maker is asked to bet on the color of the first ball drawn at random from either urn, and must decide which urn she prefers. The paradox arises because people usually prefer to bet on the 'known' urn (that is, the one containing five white and five black balls). This choice behavior cannot be explained by the standard subjective expected utility framework, since there is no subjective (additive) probability distribution that supports these preferences.
3. Early works include Brockhaus (1980) and Wärneryd (1988). More recent evidence can be found in Shane et al. (2003) and Wu and Knott (2003).
4. This assumption, and the fact that capital markets are perfect, implies that r is also the equilibrium interest rate.
5. Under the assumption of non-drastic innovation, the monopolist simply applies a limit pricing strategy. Nothing changes for our purposes.
6. This assumption is meant to exclude the uninteresting cases in which the agent is either totally hopeless about the possibility of innovating ($\lambda_t = 0$) or absolutely sure of producing an innovation in the exact instant in which she invests ($\lambda_t \to +\infty$). Moreover, in our setting agents have no possibility of improving their knowledge upon the parameter via a learning process, since innovations are unique events—the probability distribution changes from one innovation to another—and, hence, there is no statistical basis for embarking on calculations.

REFERENCES

Aghion, P. and P. Howitt (1992). "A Model of Growth through Creative Destruction". *Econometrica*, **60**, 323–351.

Aghion, P. and P. Howitt (1998). *Endogenous Growth Theory*. Cambridge, MA: MIT Press.

Bhidé, A.H. (2000). *The Origins and Evolution New Businesses*. Oxford: Oxford University Press.

Brockhaus, R.H. (1980). "Risk Taking Propensity of Entrepreneurs". *Academy of Management Journal*, **23**, 509–520.

Busenitz, L.W. (1999). "Entrepreneurial Risk and Strategic Decision Making". *Journal of Applied Behavioral Science*, **35**, 325–340.

Cozzi, G. and P.E. Giordani (2011). "Ambiguity Attitude, R&D Investments and Economic Growth". *Journal of Evolutionary Economics*, **21**, 303–319.

Ellsberg, D. (1961). "Risk, Ambiguity and the Savage Axioms". *Quarterly Journal of Economics*, **75**, 643–669.

Freeman, C. and L. Soete (1997). *The Economics of Industrial Innovation* (third edition). Cambridge, MA: MIT Press.

Ghirardato, P., F. Maccheroni and M. Marinacci (2004). "Differentiating Ambiguity and Ambiguity Attitude". *Journal of Economic Theory*, **118**, 133–173.

Gilboa, I. and D. Schmeidler (1989). "Maxmin Expected Utility with Non-Unique Prior". *Journal of Mathematical Economics*, **18**, 141–153.

Giordani, P.E., K.H. Schlag and S. Zwart (2010). "Decision Makers Facing Uncertainty: Theory vs. Evidence". *Journal of Economic Psychology*, **31**, 659–675.

Grossman, G.M. and E. Helpman (1991a). "Quality Ladders in the Theory of Growth". *Review of Economic Studies*, **58**, 43–61.

Grossman, G.M. and E. Helpman (1991b). *Innovation and Growth in the Global Economy*. Cambridge, MA: MIT Press.

Hansemark, O.C. (2003). "Need for Achievement, Locus of Control and the Prediction of Business Start-ups: A Longitudinal Study". *Journal of Economic Psychology*, **24**, 301–319.

Hofstede, G.H. (2001). *Culture's Consequences: Comparing Values, Behaviors, Institutions and Organizations across Nations*. Thousand Oaks, CA: Sage.

Hurwicz, L. (1951). "Optimality Criteria for Decision-Making under Ignorance". Cowles Commission discussion paper No. 370.

Hvide, H.K. and G. Panos (2013). "Risk Tolerance and Entrepreneurship". CEPR discussion paper No. 9339.

Kihlstrom, R.E. and J.-J. Laffont (1979). "A General Equilibrium Entrepreneurial Theory of Firm Formation Based on Risk Aversion". *Journal of Political Economy*, **87**, 719–748.

Knight, F. (1921). *Risk, Uncertainty and Profit*. Boston, MA: Houghton Mifflin.

Lucas, R.E. (1978). "On the Size Distribution of Business Firms". *Bell Journal of Economics*, **9**, 508–523.

Rigotti, L., M. Ryan and R. Vaithianathan (2008). "Tolerance of Ambiguity and Entrepreneurial Innovation". Mimeo.

Roland, G. (2005). "Understanding Institutional Change: Fast-Moving and Slow-Moving Institutions". University of California at Berkeley, Mimeo.

Romer, P.M. (1990). "Endogenous Technological Change". *Journal of Political Economy*, **98**, S71–S102.

Rosenberg, N. (1996). "Uncertainty and Technological Change", in R. Landau et al. (eds). *The Mosaic of Economic Growth*. Stanford: Stanford University Press.

Shane, S., E.A. Locke and C.J. Collins (2003). "Entrepreneurial Motivation". *Human Resource Management Review*, **13**, 257–279.

Scherer, F.M. and D. Harhoff (2000). "Technology Policy for a World of Skew-Distributed Outcomes". *Research Policy*, **29**, 559–566.

Schmeidler, D. (1989). "Subjective Probability and Expected Utility without Additivity". *Econometrica*, **57**, 571–587.

Schumpeter, J.A. (1934). *The Theory of Economic Development*. Cambridge, MA: Harvard University Press.

Schumpeter, J.A. (1939). *Business Cycles: A Theoretical, Historical and Statistical Analysis of the Capitalist Process*. New York: McGraw-Hill.

Warneryd, K.E. (1988). "The Psychology of Innovative Entrepreneurship," in W.F. van Raaij et al. (eds). *Handbook of Economic Psychology*. Dordrecht: Kluwer Academic.

Wu, B. and A.M. Knott (2006). "Entrepreneurial Risk and Market Entry". *Management Science*, **52**, 1315–1330.

14. Venture capital contracts and the institutional theory: differences between public and private Spanish venture capital firms*

Mª Camino Ramón-Llorens and Ginés Hernández-Cánovas

1. INTRODUCTION

A large body of literature on financial contracts examines the importance of different terms included in venture capital (VC) contracts aiming to control the opportunism problems that surround the VC–entrepreneur relationship. In this context, institutional theory proposes that organizations and their strategies are influenced by the institutional settings in which they operate, and are shaped by the institutional legacies which reflect the culture, history and polity of the particular country or region (Doh and Guay, 2006). Therefore, we propose that VC contracting within a country should be quite homogeneous because all firms are subject to the same institutional environment. However, we expect that some field organizations might be more standardized than others as a result of institutional pressures within the field.

The evidence provided by Jog et al. (1991) in Canada and Isaksson (2004) in Sweden shows that VC contracts are quite homogeneous in their inclusion of covenants. However, several studies show that VC contracts are complex and non-standardized (Barney et al., 1994; Gompers and Lerner, 1996; Bengtsson and Sensoy, 2009). These opposite results leave the door open for new empirical contributions that, using samples of VC companies in other environments, shed light on this issue.

By analysing a survey dataset of 41 Spanish venture capital firms (VCFs), this study intends to fill a gap by examining the contractual arrangements that Spanish VC companies use in their relationship with the portfolio companies. Our results show that covenants in VC contracts are standardized, the most common being those that require the entrepreneur to provide economic and financial information to venture capitalists in order to control the investment once it has been made. However, between public and private VCFs there is some heterogeneity in the design of contracts due to coercive pressure exerted by the government on public entities, resulting in the private sector being the stronger in the application of standard terms.

Our chapter yields two specific contributions. First, it is one of the first empirical contributions analysing financial contracts of VCFs in Spain. Existing studies on VC contracts use samples of firms from different countries – the US, Belgium, Sweden, the UK, Finland, Canada, Germany and China, among others. Second, we investigate whether the existing differences in the use of covenants in financial contracts depend on the public or private origin of the resources, because we expect some organizations' field might be more standardized than others as a result of institutional pressures within the field. If financial contracts are dependent on the nature of the VCF, it means that the same business proposal might receive different treatment depending on the VCF that the entrepreneur approaches.

The chapter proceeds as follows: Section 2 discusses previous research; Section 3 presents the data and method; Section 4 presents the results; and Section 5 concludes.

2.   INSTITUTIONAL THEORY

According to Bruton et al. (2005), venture capitalists are subject to different institutional forces which can influence their behaviour. These forces are studied by Institutional Theory, which considers the processes by which social and cultural pressures become established as rules for social behaviour, making organizations homogeneous over time. DiMaggio and Powell (1983) call this tendency toward homogeneity "isomorphism", which occurs when organizations seek cultural and political legitimacy. They delineate three forces driving institutionalization:

1.   Coercive isomorphism is an exogenous force arising from political pressures and the need for legitimacy.
2.   Normative isomorphism is an endogenous force that stems from the influence of professionalization and the role of education.
3.   Mimetic isomorphism is an endogenous force resulting from circumstances of uncertainty.

The coercive dimension of Institutional Theory refers to exogenous pressures exerted on one organization by another in which the first one is dependent (DiMaggio and Powell, 1983; Scott, 1995). This regulatory dimension of Institutional Theory is mainly driven by the provisions of government legislation, as well as by industrial agreements and standards that control the behavior of firms (North, 1990; Bruton et al. 2010).

In the VC context, government action or state intervention plays an important role in the development of institutional legitimacy by exerting pressure through their control of funding or by the exercise of their power to regulate (Frumkin and Gelaskiewicz, 2004; Cornelius, 2005). Public venture capitalists as perceived by policy makers have goals similar to their own (Cornelius, 2005), such as the promotion of a region's economic growth or small-firm growth rather than obtaining high profitability (Jeng and Wells, 2000; Cumming and MacIntosh, 2006; Brander et al., 2009; Munari and Toschi, 2010). As a consequence, coercive isomorphism should be stronger in the organizational field of public VC firms, resulting in differences in the use of covenants between public and private VC firms.

Empirical evidence regarding the development of Institutional Theory as an instrument to understand financial contracts in the VC industry is scarce. Suchman (1995) examines 108 financial contracts from two important VC funds in California's Silicon Valley during the period 1975–1990. He finds that VC contracts become standardized over time due to normative isomorphism, and that standardization declines with geographical distance from Silicon Valley. Later, in Sweden, Institutional Theory supports the results of Isaksson et al. (2004), who find that some differences between public and private VCFs may result from the political pressures on public organizations. Private venture capitalists turn towards standardized covenants, whereas public ones lean towards situational elements.

Isaksson et al. (2004) show that different VC firm structures lead to different contractual terms. Institutional Theory supports their results, and they conclude that Swedish legal contracts become standardized.

Our study is set in Spain, an emerging VC market where VC investment involves not only great effort from entrepreneurs but also entails high risk for investors (Del Palacio et al., 2012).

3. DATA AND METHODOLOGY

In this section we present the data, methodology and variables used in our analyses to check whether the covenants used in financial contracts are homogeneous across the Spanish VC industry in general and across public and private VCFs in particular.

3.1 Data

We obtained the data by means of a postal survey addressed to the 70 Spanish VCFs registered by the Spanish Venture Capital and Private Equity Association (ASCRI) in June 2002.[1] The design of the questionnaires received valuable contributions provided by prestigious economists specializing in financial risk assessment, particularly related to the valuation of ventures. Before sending out the questionnaire, we contacted the 70 VCFs to check their willingness to participate in the survey and to identify the person in charge of making funding decisions. Three of the companies were reluctant to respond to the surveys, one was unreachable and six had not made VC operations in recent years. Of the remaining 60 questionnaires that were finally sent, 41 were returned up to February 2003, which corresponds to a response rate of 68.33 per cent.

3.2 Methodology

Since some organizations' field might be more standardized than others as a result of institutional pressures within the field, we perform a discriminant analysis in order to determine whether there are any differences between venture capitalists' contractual choices depending on the origin of the resources. The discriminant analysis is conducted because it is a technique that allows for the identification of variables that best discriminate between two or more groups in order to identify whether certain groups of VCs act in a similar way.

To carry out the discriminant analysis we use the variables that construct our hypothesis as the dependent variables, i.e. firm structure (public or private capital). For the independent variables we use the 25 covenants. We perform the analysis by the stepwise inclusion method in order to minimize Wilks's lambda in each step.

3.2.1 Independent variables
Using a five-point Likert scale (1 = little important; 5 = very important) the questionnaire collects information concerning the most important covenants included in VC contracts identified by previous empirical literature.

Based on previous research, we have classified the contractual covenants into four dimensions, which allow us to better study and understand the venture capitalists' behaviour in designing the financial contracts:

1. covenants in the pre-investment relationship;
2. covenants in the post-investment relationship management;

3. covenants on specific events in the post-investment period; and
4. exit covenants.

In total, 37 VCFs out of the 41 valid questionnaires gave their scores in all the variables.

3.2.2   Dependent variables

We classify the VC firms in our sample as public or private according to their own assessment given in the survey: 30 (73.17 per cent) of the firms are private and the remaining 11 (26.83 per cent) are public.

4.   RESULTS

4.1.   Description of Covenants

For each VCF we reclassify the independent variables on a new scale consisting of three levels. Variables that take on the values 1 and 2 have been classified as seldom used; those covenants that score 3 are classified as sometimes used; and variables that take on the values 4 and 5 are classified as almost always used.

Next, each term is classified as rare, situational or standard. When a term is seldom used by over 80 per cent of the respondents, it is called rare. When a term is almost always used by over 80 per cent of the respondents, it is called standard.[2] Finally, covenants that cannot be classified as either standard or rare are called situational (Table 14.1).

In our sample, 36 per cent of the covenants used by the VCs are classified as standard, whereas 64 per cent are situational ones used to deal with specific contexts. No covenants are rare. These results suggest the existence of some heterogeneity in the design of contracts through the inclusion of so-called "situational covenants".

4.2   Differentiating Strategies

Although the above analyses confirm that VC contracts are mostly standardized, they also show the existence of some degree of heterogeneity. Therefore, in this section we want to assess the origin of those differences in the design of the contracts.

We use a discriminant analysis in order to determine whether there are any differences between venture capitalists' contractual choices depending on their public or private fund structure. We carry out the analysis using the firm's structure as dependent variable. As independent variables we use

Table 14.1   Analysis of rare, situational and standard covenants

	Rare	Situational	Standard
Pre-investment agreements			
Control for reliability of the information provided in the business plan (due diligence)		x	
Post-investment relationship management			
Limitations on contracting external advisors		x	
Right of VCs to serve on board of directors (BoD)			x
Veto rights of VCs on:			
New issue of shares			x
Executive salary		x	
Important decisions			x
Financial limitations			
Limitation on important expenses are established		x	
Limitation on external indebtedness of the company		x	
Limitation on loan, transfer or advance in loan to administrators		x	
Loyalty clause			
Non-compete clause		x	
Managers cannot spread own technology		x	
Informational requirements			
Periodic presentation of accounting states			x
Periodic economic and financial reports			x
Yearly audits			x
Presentation of the next budget			x
Information on substantial matters that may affect any aspect of the business			x
Veto rights of the VCs in particular agreements			x
Standstill agreement		x	
Specific events in post-investment period			
VC has the power to force changes in BoD		x	
VCF can intervene if objectives are not achieved		x	
Provides compensation for breach of contract		x	
Anti-dilution ratchet		x	
Timeline is fixed for the firm to complain about errors or omissions		x	
Exit			
Timing of exit		x	
Length of contract		x	

the 25 covenants included in the survey. The analysis is performed by the stepwise inclusion method in order to minimize Wilks's lambda in each step, resulting in 100 per cent of correctly classified observations.

Table 14.2 shows the 11 contractual covenants (45.83 per cent) that differ significantly between the two groups. Among public VCFs, 4 covenants are rare, 6 are situational and only 1 is standard, whereas in private VCF there are no rare covenants, 7 situational and 4 standard. The main differences between the two groups are: the right of VCs to serve on the board of directors; the firm's obligation to provide information about substantial matters that may affect any aspect of the business; and the power of the VCs to force changes to the board of directors, which are situational for public VCFs and standard for private ones. The non-competition clause is rare for public firms and standard for private ones. Moreover, the penalties for breach of contract or the timeline for the firm to complain about errors or omissions are rare for public VCFs and situational for private ones.

As we propose, and according to Isaksson et al. (2004), because of coercive isomorphic pressures there is no standardization between the covenants included in financial contracts by public and private VCFs. The difference between them is that the private sector is stronger in the application of standardized covenants.

5.   DISCUSSION AND CONCLUSION

This chapter provides new evidence on VC contracts based on a sample of 41 Spanish VCFs. On the basis of Institutional Theory we investigate whether Spanish VC contracts are standardized.

In line with the study of Isaksson et al. (2004) in Sweden, this analysis reveals that the Spanish contractual arrangements are standardized, with the most commonly reached being those that require the entrepreneur to report information to the venture capitalists in the post-investment relationship. However, some differences in the design of contracts between public and private VC firms appear due to a lower degree of isomorphism within the group of public companies. This is the result of the coercive pressures exerted by the government on them, making their behaviour heterogeneous not only in relation to the industry but also within the field.

Our results contribute to shed light on the financial contracts used by venture capitalists, a field of research that has so far received little discussion in the Spanish literature. Furthermore, this chapter has clear benefits for policy makers, firms and venture capitalists. A better understanding of covenants included in VC contracts can help firms understand the particular terms and constraints of VCs before providing capital. Venture

Table 14.2   Analysis of rare, situational and standard covenants for public and private VCFs

	Public			Private		
	Rare	Situational	Standard	Rare	Situational	Standard
Pre-investment agreements						
Control for the reliability of the information provided in the business plan (due diligence)		x			x	
Post-investment relationship management						
Right of VCs to serve on BoD		x				x
Limitation on loan, transfer or advance in loan to administrators		x			x	
Non-competition clause	x					x
Managers cannot spread their own technology		x			x	
Information about substantial matters which may affect any aspect of the business		x				x
Presentation of the next budget			x			x
VC has the power to force changes in BoD	x				x	
Provides compensation for breach of contract	x				x	
Timeline is fixed for the VCF to complain about errors or omissions	x				x	
Exit						
Length of contract		x			x	

capitalists can use the information from this study to better understand the contractual arrangements used in their fields. And policy makers will acknowledge the effect that their pressure has on the design of VC contracts and, therefore, on industry efficiency when providing funds to firms.

There is, however, one note of caution with regard to our results. Qualitative information about VC firms is difficult to obtain and often has to come from survey data, as in our sample. We recognize that survey data might create potential biases and possible measurement problems (Zacharakis and Meyer, 1998). However, we consider that our sample has large enough coverage of the VC industry (68.33 per cent) that valid conclusions can be drawn, albeit cautiously.

Further studies could expand the scope of research to include new variables which may affect the VC contract from an institutional perspective, such as the location of the firm or the gender of the venture capitalists.

NOTES

*   The authors acknowledge financial support from the Fundación Séneca (Project 15403/PHCS/10) and the Ministerio de Ciencia e Innovación (Project ECO2011−29080).
1.   Asociación Española de Entidades de Capital Riesgo.
2.   The 80 per cent cut-off is selected following the scheme proposed by Isaksson et al. (2004).

REFERENCES

Barney J.B., Busenitz, L., Fiet, J. and D. Moesel, 1994. The relationship between venture capitalists and managers in new firms: determinants of contractual covenants, *Managerial Finance* **20** (1), 19–30.

Bengtsson, O. and B.A. Sensoy, 2009. Changing the nexus: the evolution and renegotiation of venture capital contracts. Working Paper, Fisher College of Business.

Brander, J., Egan, E. and T. Hellmann, 2009. Government sponsored versus private venture capital: Canadian evidence, in Lerner, J. and Shoar, A. (eds) *International Differences in Entrepreneurship*, Chicago: University of Chicago Press.

Bruton, G.D., Ahlstrom, D. and L. Han-Lin, 2010. Institutional theory and entrepreneurship: where are we now and where do we need to move in the future? *Entrepreneurship: Theory and Practice* **34**, 421–440.

Bruton, G.D., Fried, V.H. and S. Manigart, 2005. Institutional influences on the worldwide expansion of venture capital, *Entrepreneurship: Theory and Practice* **29** (6), 737–760.

Cornelius, B., 2005. The institutionalisation of venture capital, *Technovation* **25** (6), 599–608.

Cumming, D.J. and J. MacIntosh, 2006. Crowding out private equity: Canadian evidence, *Journal of Business Venturing* **21**, 569–609.

Del Palacio, I., Zhang, X.T. and F. Sole, 2012. The capital gap for small technology companies: public venture capital to the rescue? *Small Business Economics* **38** (3), 283–301.

DiMaggio, P.J. and W.W. Powell, 1983. The iron cage revisited: institutional isomorphism and collective rationality in organizational fields, *American Sociological Review* **48** (2), 147–160.

Doh, J.P. and T.R. Guay, 2006. Corporate social responsibility, public policy, and NGO activism in Europe and the United States: an institutional-stakeholder perspective, *Journal of Management Studies* **43** (1), 47–73.

Frumkin, P. and J. Gelaskiewicz, 2004. Institutional isomorphism and public sector organizations, *Journal of Public Administration Research and Theory* **14** (3), 283–307.

Gompers, P. and J. Lerner, 1996. The use of covenants: an empirical analysis of venture partnership agreements, *Journal of Law and Economics* **39** (2), 463–498.

Isaksson, A., Cornelius, B., Landström, H. and S. Junghagen, 2004. Institutional theory and contracting in venture capital: the Swedish experience, *Venture Capital* **6** (1), 47–71.

Jeng, L.A. and P.C. Wells, 2000. The determinants of venture capital funding: evidence across countries, *Journal of Corporate Finance* **6**, 241–289.

Jog, V., Lawson, W., and A. Riding, 1991. The venture capitalist/entrepreneur interface: expectations, conflicts and contracts, *Journal of Small Business and Entrepreneurship* **8** (2), 5–20.

Munari, F. and L. Toschi, 2010. Assessing the impact of public venture capital programmes in the United Kingdom: do regional characteristics matter? European Financial Management Symposium.

North, D.C., 1990. *Institutions, Institutional Change and Economic Performance*, New York: Cambridge University Press.

Scott, W.R., 1995. *Institutions and Organizations*, Thousand Oaks, CA: Sage.

Suchman, M.C., 1995. Localism and globalism in institutional analysis: the emergence of contractual norms in venture finance, in Scott, W. and Christensen, S. (eds), *The Institutional Construction of Organizations*, Thousand Oaks, CA: Sage.

Zacharakis A. and G. Meyer, 1998. A lack of insight: do venture capitalists really understand their own decision process? *Journal of Business Venturing* **13**, 57–76.

15. Exploring SMEs' strategic response to the financial and economic crisis: empirical evidence from Catalonia

Eleni Papaoikonomou, Xiaoni Li and Pere Segarra

1. INTRODUCTION

According to economists, the recession that started in 2007 in the United States and soon expanded to other developed economies is the worst since the Great Depression of the 1930s. This context poses a great challenge for firms that need to adequately adapt to the changing environment through the adoption of strategic measures. Nevertheless, little is known about the processes that determine the adoption of certain strategic decisions instead of others, even though much research has focused on identification of corporate strategic responses in times of uncertainty. Towards this more general aim, we have established the following objectives:

- To examine how firms perceive and respond to the current crisis. We consider it important to keep in mind that decisions in firms are taken by people, so their perceptions with regard to the magnitude and severity of the crisis may affect their decision making.
- To develop a typology that differentiates between firms that perceive different degrees of severity of the crisis and adopt different strategies to respond to seemingly similar threats. To do that we carry out a cluster analysis.

There might be different factors affecting individuals' perceptions of the crisis, such as psyche and personality traits (Miller and Ireland, 2005). Nevertheless, the scope of this study is not to understand how individuals' perceptions are formed, but whether their perceptions regarding the crisis and the magnitude of its impact on their firm lead to the adoption of certain strategic behaviors. This chapter is based on a survey of the decision makers of Catalan small- and medium-sized enterprises (SMEs) carried out in 2011.

We place special emphasis on SMEs because they are considered the backbone of all economies and play a key role in economic recovery and future growth (Koellinger and Thurik, 2012). In Europe, they represent 99 percent of all businesses and count for two-thirds of private sector jobs (European Commission, 2010). Similarly, SMEs also account for 99 percent of businesses in Spain and Catalonia according to the Spanish National Statistics Institute. Furthermore, much research has traditionally focused on strategy formulation in large manufacturing firms, ignoring SMEs (Liberman-Yaconi et al., 2010; Johnson et al., 2003; Barker and Barr, 2002).

Given the importance of SMEs for global, European and national economies, it is timely to examine the strategic response of SMEs in the current context of crisis. To do that, we have been guided by Hofer's framework of turnaround strategies, and have incorporated other strategies such as internationalization, product differentiation, niche marketing and so on.

The chapter is organized as follows. The next section provides insights regarding the theoretical background of strategic responses in times of environmental uncertainty and the development of the role of perceptions within the context of SMEs. The third section describes the methodology employed. Subsequently, findings of the analysis are presented. Policy implications are drawn and discussed in the last section.

2.　HOW DO FIRMS RESPOND IN TIMES OF CRISIS?

Much research has been carried out in this field. In his seminal study, Hofer (1980) examines 12 cases of financially distressed businesses; identifies main types of turnaround situations and turnaround strategies for firms under difficulties; and suggests a framework to match specific strategies with specific situations. According to Hofer, there are two types of turnaround, strategic and operating, and three approaches to cope with an economic recession: asset reduction, cost reduction and revenue generation.

According to Hofer, each of these strategies reflects a different degree of severity of the operating situation. More specifically, cost reduction is employed by firms that operate above their break-even point and need to increase their profitability, but asset reduction is a last resort solution for firms that operate far below the break-even point. Revenue enhancement would be a type of strategy found in between the other two.

In a later study, Hambrick and Schecter (1983) sampled exclusively mature industrial business units, and found that a large number of businesses employed cost and/or asset reduction, but not revenue generation. Recessions present many small businesses with a major dilemma: to cut costs so as to survive in the short run at the risk of reducing their capacity to adapt adequately; or to maintain greater capacity to generate opportunities for long-run growth and value creation. In general, retrenchment strategies are a rather common practice to cope with declining financial performance. Studies of small enterprises demonstrate the importance during recessions of both a cost-cutting approach (Michael and Robbins, 1998; DeDee and Vorbies, 1998; Robbins and Pearce, 1993; Churchill and Lewis, 1984) and a revenue-generation approach (Latham, 2009; Shama, 1993). According to Michael and Robbins, firms tend to shed cost and asset factors that can be easily repurchased and have low specificity for the firm, such as hourly workers instead of executives, advertising instead of marketing channels and raw materials in inventories instead of machinery and equipment. Nevertheless, Latham (2009) found that small software companies tended to adopt revenue-generating strategies, such as targeting new customer segments, rather than reducing costs. Pretorius (2008) offers a matrix of strategies according to the firms' resources and the causality of the distress. Regarding the present crisis, a more recent study by Duquesnois et al. (2010) focusing on French wine producers indicates the adoption of revenue-generation strategies like differentiation and niche marketing to increase turnover.

3.   DO PERCEPTIONS MATTER?

There is an ongoing debate as to whether SMEs can better take advantage of arising opportunities or are the hardest hit by the crisis (Latham, 2009). Influenced by the 'Carnegie School' tradition, we consider that strategy formulation and decision making depend on the subjective realities of bounded rationality of the decision makers of the firms (Cyert and March, 1963). For instance, Schwenk (1984) argues that decision makers perform a number of tasks related to strategy formulation, such as goal setting, problem identification and alternatives generation. Thus, these tasks that define the firm's strategic direction largely depend on decision makers' perceptions and opinions. Also, much research has been conducted on how demographic characteristics of decision makers in large firms – such as career experience or educational level (Herrmann and Datta, 2005) – affect decision makers' worldviews and, so, the decisions they make. In general, strategic decision making in small firms resembles more bounded-rational and intuitive patterns than rational patterns (Liberman-Yaconi et al., 2010).

In line with these studies, we embrace the assumption that firms are run by individuals and that strategic decision making is bound to the subjective worldviews and perceptions that these individuals form. It is important to take into account the perceptual subjectivity of decision makers since, as Bratton et al. (2007, p. 212) state, "the perception processes mean that individuals usually interpret other people and situations differently and so routinely hold different views of reality, which in turn strongly influence their attitudes and actions." Smart and Vertinsky (1984) found that the adoption of a certain strategy depends on executives' perceptions of the context and future impact of that strategic change on the firm. Also, firms tend not to respond unless they identify stimuli that have an impact on them (Barker and Barr, 2002). Furthermore, Latham (2009, p.197) explains that in his study, managers of larger firms felt "handcuffed by their size" and strongly perceived the damaging effect of the recession that led them to formulate respective strategies. On that basis, Latham proposes that future research should address the relationship between managers' attitudes and strategy formulation to external threats to the firm.

4.   CATALONIAN SMEs IN TIMES OF CRISIS

We collected data through a survey. Initially, the questionnaire was administered online through emails to the company managers. However, due to the relatively low response rate, we followed up with structured face-to-face interviews based on the same questionnaire. In total, 96 valid responses were collected. The time span for the collection of data was between February and August 2011. We selected this timeframe because the financial and economic crisis already started in 2007 and the recessionary effects were evident and 'felt' in that period. Also, it was expected that a large number of firms would have already taken some type of measure to deal with the crisis. So, respondents could base their answers both on strategic measures already adopted since the beginning of the crisis and by considering the situation at the time of the survey.

Catalonia was selected as broader context of study because it has suffered a severe economic slowdown (Li et al., 2011) during the present crisis, presenting a higher rate of unemployment in the European Union (EU) zone according to Eurostat data.

In terms of firm size, we mainly use the criterion *number of employees* and limit our sample to firms employing one to 250 people, in line with the EU criterion of classification for SMEs. The sector composition and employment size of the sample are displayed in Table 15.1.

To elaborate the questionnaire, we divided the questions into three

Table 15.1   Sector composition and employment size of sample

Sector composition	Number of companies	Percentage of companies
Construction	8	8.3
Agriculture	6	6.3
Manufacturing	31	32.3
Service	42	43.8
Others	9	9.4
Total	96	100.0
Employment size		
Micro (<10 employees)	27	28.1
Small (10–49 employees)	52	54.2
Medium (50–250 employees)	17	17.7
Total	96	100.0

major sections. The first section focused on demographics of the business and the decision maker (such as sector, number of employees, total annual revenues, types of financing used by the business, business experience of the decision maker, etc). The second section focused on the managers' perceptions regarding the recessionary effects of the crisis on the economy as a whole and on their firm. It is important to mention that the questions in this section were developed on the basis of a literature review conducted and the findings of a previous qualitative study carried out by our research team during 2010 with regard to the perceptions of 205 Catalan businessmen of the economic crisis (see Papaoikonomou et al., 2012). In this study, 16 types of difficulty emerged, such as lack of access to credit and lack of qualified personnel. The third section included questions on the strategic response of the SMEs. The turnaround strategies framework by Hofer (1980) served as a guide to elaborate the questions in this section.

In terms of analysis, we carried out a non-hierarchical typological analysis identifying the existing clusters of SMEs sample according to the degree of difficulty perceived in the crisis to examine whether different perceptions with regard to the crisis led to the adoption of different types of strategic decision.

5.   RESULTS: PERCEPTIONS, DIFFICULTIES AND STRATEGIES

The analysis was carried out using K-means clustering, a non-hierarchical method which has been shown to be quite robust (MacQueen, 1967; Hair et al., 1998; Punj and Stewart, 1983). In this way, we can identify firms that adopt different behaviors according to their perceptions of the crisis, and also relate the results obtained according to the strategic responses applied. There are no rules of thumb about the sample size necessary for cluster analysis (Dolnicar, 2003), although some authors recommend a large sample size when many clustering variables are used (Mooi and Sarstedt, 2011).

Applying K-means analysis, we detected three optimal groups of clusters regarding the perception of degree of difficulty in the context of the current crisis for our sample.

We saw that 37 percent of the total sample (Cluster 3, n = 36) understand that the current context presents many difficulties for their survival and growth; 20 percent (Cluster 2) perceive a lower degree of difficulties; and the rest (Cluster 1) perceive a medium degree of difficulty. Across clusters, a consistent finding is a noteworthy decrease in sales and gross profits and the increasing delinquent accounts of clients. In general, most firms are positioned in the distress and crisis categories of Pretorius's (2008) matrix, even though we do not have data on their resource scarcity or abundance.

We also asked whether firms faced the same difficulties encountered before the start of the crisis in 2007. The purpose was to understand whether for the participants there are structural factors whose emergence is not related to the crisis per se, but their negative impact was accentuated during the crisis. All groups identified a lack of qualified personnel, high employee costs and the emergence of new competitors as problems existing before the crisis.

Our objective was also to understand the type of actions they adopted to deal with the crisis. For that purpose, we adopted Hofer's framework, including different actions related to cost reduction, asset reduction and revenue generation. Regarding revenue generation, we were interested in strategies that aim at short- and long-term revenue such as investment in R&D. In total, 32 different actions to deal with the crisis were included in the questionnaire: 12 related to cost reduction; six to asset reduction; and 14 to short-term and long-term revenue generation. Firms that did not adopt any action given in the survey could also indicate other action taken, or that no action was adopted at all. We made the following useful observations.

Cost Reduction

Some 63.5 percent of firms in our sample reduced energy and phone expenses (n = 61), 61.5 percent carried out cost reduction by firing employees (n = 59) and 59.4 percent took other measures such as reducing advertising (n = 57); 80.6 percent (29 out of 36) of the firms in Cluster 3 (high perception of crisis) claimed to deal with the crisis by cutting their energy and phone bill, as opposed to 58.5 percent and 42.1 percent of Clusters 1 and 2 respectively. Also, more firms in Cluster 3 (72.2 percent) took the decision to fire employees as a means to survive the crisis. In contrast, in Cluster 2 – the cluster with the lowest degree of perception with regard to the severity of the crisis – only 36.8 percent decided to lay off employees as a result of the crisis. From these findings, we may infer that the more negative the perceptions regarding the difficulties of the crisis, the more firms tend to adopt measures to cut their costs and deal with it.

Asset Reduction

With regard to actions adopted for asset reduction, 71.9 percent of firms (n = 69) have taken no action at all and 15.6 percent (n = 15) prefer to sell fixed assets. In general, the firms prefer other types of strategy such as reducing costs instead of selling assets, which could seriously compromise their production capacity. However, it is interesting to note that only firms in Cluster 3 chose to eliminate non-profitable products and units as a way of creating a healthier business portfolio. Regarding the sale of fixed assets, 21.1 percent of firms in Cluster 2 decided to sell machines, equipment and other fixed assets, compared to 19.4 percent of firms in Cluster 3 and 9.8 percent in Cluster 1.

Revenue Generation

Our analysis found that revenue-generation strategies are more common than asset-reduction strategies, but less popular than cost-reduction strategies. According to our findings, 66.7 percent of all firms in the sample decided to reduce the prices of their products to adapt to the new market situation. The percentage is higher in Clusters 1 and 3, indicating that the perceived severity of the crisis translates into lower cost offering to attract more consumers. Also, almost 39 percent of firms in Cluster 3 adopted niche marketing and focused on specific, more profitable segments in the market.

Furthermore, it is interesting to note that firms in Cluster 1 and 3 engaged more in revenue-generation strategies such as training employees, diversification into other sectors and investing in R&D when compared to firms in Cluster 2. Instead, a large percentage of firms in Cluster 2 considered other types of revenue generation as more plausible solutions, such as further promotion of existing products and adaptation of product offering (68.4 and 42.1 percent respectively).

Table 15.2   The most commonly adopted measures in the sample

Action	Percentage of total sample carrying out the action	Percentage within Cluster 1	Percentage within Cluster 2	Percentage within Cluster 3
Reducing product prices	66.7	68.3	57.9	69.4
Reducing energy and phone bill	63.5	58.5	42.1	80.6
Reducing personnel	61.5	63.4	36.8	72.2
Reducing advertising costs	59.4	68.3	26.3	66.7
Reducing administrative costs	55.2	61	26.3	63.9
Promoting existing products	54.2	46.3	68.4	55.6
Reducing salary bonuses	49.0	51.2	31.6	55.6
Buying fixed assets	39.6	51.2	26.3	33.3
Reducing costs in other promotion efforts	37.5	41.5	26.3	38.9
Readapting products	36.5	68.3	57.9	69.4

Table 15.2 identifies the most commonly adopted measures. We can observe that the majority of firms tend to adopt measures to cut down on different types of costs instead of adopting strategies for short- or long-term revenue generation. Table 15.2 also compares the percentages of firms adopting these measures within each of the identified clusters.

6.   DISCUSSION AND IMPLICATIONS

The results of this study have led to the identification of three clusters according to the perceived severity and magnitude of the impact of the global financial crisis. We notice that most firms link the crisis and the uncertainty that it provokes to lack of liquidity, decrease in sales and limited access to credit. Other difficulties such as finding qualified personnel, employee costs and the emergence of new competitors may hinder firms' survival, but they existed pre-crisis. The crisis has simply highlighted their impact on the firm.

The study also revealed that firms in these three clusters demonstrate different patterns of behavior. In general, firms of Cluster 2 with lowest sensitivity to the difficulties of the crisis demonstrate a more passive pattern of behavior. Exceptions aside, they adopt fewer measures in all three categories: cost reduction, asset reduction and revenue generation. Firms in Cluster 1 and 3 that perceive more strongly the negative impact of the current crisis seem to deal with it through the adoption of various strategies that, even though focusing more on reducing costs, also involve strategy formulation (diversification to other sectors, low prices, niche marketing). Indeed, according to Naidoo (2010), market-oriented firms are more likely to survive the current economic crisis if they sustain a competitive advantage against their rivals by focusing on a narrowly defined segment. Previous studies link firm behavior in turnaround situations with more objective variables, like resource scarcity (Pretorius, 2008), but we think that the inherent subjectivity in decision making should be also considered.

The great majority of firms in Cluster 3 clearly show that they try to become more efficient through cutting down on costs that are considered unnecessary, such as administrative costs, energy and phone bills and advertising. Also, it seems that the more negatively perceived the impact of the crisis, the more firms tend to lay off employees to cut down on costs. The majority of firms in Cluster 1 (63.4 percent) and 3 (72.2 percent) chose to fire employees, and did not easily divest fixed assets. This shows that fixed assets are considered vital for the continuance of the firms, while firing employees is seen as an easier way to reduce costs. This could also be related to the perceived lack of qualified personnel; employees with low specificity for the firm and relatively easily replaceable are the first to be laid off (Michael and Robbins 1998). At the same time, only 2.8 percent of firms in Cluster 3 mention that they hire personnel to improve their production capacity.

These are interesting findings, especially because unemployment in Spain reached 24.4 percent in March 2012, the highest rate in 18 years according to Eurostat figures. Therefore, we believe that the way decision makers in firms perceive the crisis affects the measures adopted and the strategy formulation to deal with the crisis. For instance, 69.4 percent of firms in Cluster 3 reduced their prices to adapt to a new market situation where consumers crave for low-cost offerings. Also, a high percentage of firms in Cluster 3 chose to reduce personnel to become more cost effective. This, though, has social implications that need to be taken into account by policy makers. Furthermore, only 12.5 percent of firms in our whole sample considered investing in R&D. Even though the figure is higher for Cluster 3 (19.4 percent), this indicates that most of the sample firms focus on cost cutting to survive and cope with the crisis, instead of innovation and growth.

In general, the most widely used response to the current crisis is to reduce costs, especially those related to salaries and administration. This resembles business models with a high labor base rather than knowledge base. The results reveal more short-term cost-reduction measures and the necessity for more proactive strategies. Moreover, it raises questions regarding the possible "legitimization" of massive layoffs under the banner of economic crisis (Baccaro, 2010).

The results of this study may be useful for both policy makers and SMEs. Policy makers need to take into account the psychological component of the crisis and understand that not all firms perceive the current economic crisis in a similar way; neither will they react in the same way. While cost cutting may be desirable to a certain extent so that the efficiency of the firm increases, it should be accompanied by incentives for firms to retain or hire employees and invest more in innovation and R&D. In the long run, cost-cutting strategies may compromise the firms' competitiveness and market position. Government policies can be designed to meet the needs of specific contextual conditions, considering the role of perceptions and encouraging innovation so as to improve the competitiveness and survival of SMEs facing distress. Also, public authorities should transmit information regarding the corresponding level of risk of the crisis to create awareness in the most passive group of firms (Cluster 2) and encourage more active patterns of behavior.

REFERENCES

Baccaro, L. (2010) "Does the global financial crisis mark a turning point for labour?," *Socio-Economic Review*, Vol. 10, pp. 341–348.

Barker, V.; Barr, P. (2002) "Linking top management attributions to strategic reorientation in declining firms attempting turnarounds," *Journal of Business Research*, Vol. 55, No. 12, pp. 963–979.

Bratton, J.; Callinan, M.; Forshaw, C.; Sawchuk, P. (2007) *Work and Organizational Behaviour: Understanding the Workplace*, 2nd edn, Basingstoke: Palgrave Macmillan.

Cyert, R.M.; March, J.G. (1963) *A Behavioral Theory of the Firm*, Englewood Cliffs, NJ: Prentice Hall.

DeDee, J.K.; Vorbies, D.W. (1998) "Retrenchment activities of small firms during economic downturn: an empirical investigation," *Journal of Small Business Management*, Vol. 36, No. 3, pp. 46–61.

Dolnicar, S. (2003) "Using cluster analysis for market segmentation: typical misconceptions, established methodological weaknesses and some recommendations for improvement," *Australasian Journal of Market Research*, Vol. 11, No. 2, pp. 5–12.

Duquesnois, F.; Gurău,C.; Le Roy, F. (2010) "Wine producers' strategic response to a crisis situation," *International Journal of Wine Business Research*, Vol. 22, No. 3, pp. 251–268.

European Commission (2010) "SMEs and the environment in the European Union," DG Enterprise and Industry report. Accessed March 27, 2014. http://ec.europa.eu/enterprise/policies/sme/business-environment/files/main_report_en.pdf.

Hair, J.F.; Anderson, R.E.; Tatham, R.T.; Black, W.C. (1998) *Multivariate Data Analysis*, 5th edn, Upper Saddle River, NJ: Prentice Hall.

Hambrick, D.C.; Schecter, S.M. (1983) "Turnaround strategies for mature industrial-product business units," *Academy of Management Journal*, Vol. 26, No. 2, pp. 231–248.

Hofer, C. (1980) "Turnaround strategies," *Journal of Business Strategy*, Vol. 1, No. 1, pp. 19–31.

Johnson, G.; Melin, L.; Whittington, R. (2003) "Micro-strategy and strategising," *Journal of Management Studies*, Vol. 40, No. 1, pp. 3–22.

Koellinger, P.D.; Thurik, A.R. (2012) "Entrepreneurship and the business cycle," *Review of Economics and Statistics*, Vol. 94, No. 4, pp. 1143–1156.

Latham, S. (2009) "Contrasting strategic response to economic recession in start-up versus established software firms," *Journal of Small Business Management*, Vol. 47, No. 2, pp. 180–201.

Li, X.; Segarra, P.; Papaoikonomou, E. (2011) "SMEs' responses to the financial and economic crisis and policy implications: an analysis of agricultural and furniture sectors in Catalonia, Spain," *Policy Studies*, Vol. 32, No. 4, pp. 61–71.

Liberman-Yaconi, L.; Hooper, T.; Hutchings, K. (2010) "Toward a model of understanding strategic decision-making in micro-firms: exploring the Australian information technology sector," *Journal of Small Business Management*, Vol. 48, No. 1, pp. 70–95.

MacQueen, J.B. (1967) "Some methods for classification and analysis of multivariate observations," *Proceedings of the 5th Berkeley Symposium on Mathematical Statistics and Probability*, pp. 281–297.

Michael, S.C.; Robbins, K.D. (1998) "Retrenchment among small manufacturing firms during recession," *Journal of Small Business Management*, Vol. 36, No. 3, pp. 35–45.

Miller, C.C.; Ireland, R.D. (2005) "Intuition in strategic decision making: friend or foe in the fastpaced 21st century?," *Academy of Management Executive*, Vol. 19, No. 1, pp. 19–30.

Mooi, E.A.; Sarstedt, M. (2011) *A Concise Guide to Market Research: The Process, Data, and Methods Using IBM SPSS Statistics*, Berlin: Springer.

Naidoo, V. (2010) "Firm survival through a crisis: the influence of market orientation, marketing innovation and business strategy," *Industrial Marketing Management*, Vol. 39, No. 3, pp. 1311–1320.

Papaoikonomou, E; Li, X.; Segarra, P. (2012) "Entrepreneurship in the context of crisis: identifying barriers and proposing strategies," *International Advances in Economic Research*, Vol. 18, No. 1, pp. 111–119.

Pretorius, M. (2008) "When Porter's generic strategies are not enough: complementary strategies for turnaround situations," *Journal of Business Strategy*, Vol. 29, No. 6, pp. 19–28.

Punj, G.N.; Stewart, D.W. (1983) "An interaction framework of consumer decision processes," *Journal of Consumer Research*, Vol. 10, pp. 181–196.

Robbins, K.D.; Pearce, J.A. (1993) "Entrepreneurial retrenchment among small manufacturing firms," *Journal of Business Venturing*, Vol. 8, No. 4, pp. 301–318.

Schwenk, C.R. (1984) "Cognitive simplification processes in strategic decision-making," *Strategic Management Journal*, Vol. 5, No. 2, pp. 111–128.

Shama, A. (1993) "Marketing strategies during recession: a comparison of small and large firms," *Journal of Small Business Management*, Vol. 31, No. 3, pp. 62–72.

Smart, C.; Vertinsky, I. (1984) "Strategy and the environment: a case study of corporate responses to crises," *Strategic Management Journal*, Vol. 5, pp. 199–213.

16. Does the financial crisis make SMEs reluctant to ask for finance in Luxembourg?*

Serge Allegrezza, Leila Ben Aoun-Peltier, Anne Dubrocard and Solène Larue

INTRODUCTION

The European Union (EU) has become increasingly interested in small-and medium-sized enterprises (SMEs) as they are prominent in the strategy to improve European competitiveness set out in Lisbon (2000 and 2005). In this context, the 2007–2009 financial crisis has drawn attention to the difficulties faced by SMEs in accessing external finance. Access to finance refers to the possibility that firms can access financial services, including credit, deposit, payment, insurance and other risk-management services (Demirgüç-Kunt et al., 2008). The euro area banks have tightened up conditions to accessing finance for nonfinancial businesses from mid-2007 to end 2009. This is problematic as access to finance is often crucial to the survival and growth of small firms and start-ups. In Luxembourg, the share of SMEs is large: they represent 99 percent of firms, about 64 percent of value added and 69 percent of total employment.

SMEs are considered a driving force of innovation and employment, and thus they are an important factor in fostering general economic performance (Carree and Thurik, 2008; Van Praag and Versloot, 2007). Despite their important role in fostering economic growth, SMEs often face financing difficulties. In this context, the purpose of this chapter is to analyze the determinants of seeking finance (in general and depending on the type of funds) and to highlight the difficulties met by Luxembourgish firms throughout the financial crisis. Those determinants can be firm size, age (as mentioned by Bougheas et al., 2006) but also past behavior (whether the firm has already asked for funding).

The chapter is organized as follows: the next section describes the Eurostat "Access to Finance for SMEs" (ATF) survey for Luxembourg and gives some relevant facts on Luxembourgish SMEs. Two following sections then provide the empirical method adopted in the study and the results. The last section concludes.

THE ACCESS TO FINANCE SURVEY: SOME EVIDENCE FOR LUXEMBOURG

The ATF survey has two main aims: 1) to uncover whether SMEs face barriers concerning the availability of finance and how these may have changed between 2007 and 2010; 2) to gather information on the firms' need for finance in the coming years. Moreover, collected data should help identify the sources from which enterprises wish to obtain finance. The final goal is to sustain policy efforts to support and incentivize firms' growth.

To be part of the sample, firms should not be subsidiaries of other businesses (regardless of whether the latter are registered in the same member state or are foreign owned). Thus, the subpopulation used in the survey consists of SMEs that have no parent company.[1] This identifies a group of firms particularly vulnerable to funding problems in times of crisis. According to Harrison and McMillan (2003), subsidiaries of foreign companies have fewer constraints to external financing than domestic firms.

In Luxembourg, 1,181 firms responded to the survey out of 1,396 selected to cover the field of investigation. Hence, the survey is almost exhaustive.[2] Nearly 48 percent of observed independent SMEs have never requested external finance, whereas 31.8 percent of firms requested finance in both 2007 and 2010. Firms that requested finance in 2010 are more numerous than in 2007 (44.3 percent versus 39.5 percent), notably in manufacturing (5.5 percent) and trade (6.72 percent). The number of loans remained stable between 2007 and 2010 (19 percent),[3] while requests for other types of funding rose: equity from 10 percent in 2007 to 12 percent in 2010[4] and other sources of finance from 21 to 27 percent (Larue et al., 2011).[5]

EMPIRICAL APPROACH

First, we investigate the determinants of seeking finance, whatever the type of funding considered (loan, equity or other sources) with a probit model. Second, we use the trivariate probit model to analyze seeking finance by type.

This section considers variables that should play an active role in seeking finance. Descriptive statistics of all variables used in the regression are shown in Table 16.1. The signs appearing in brackets within the following text indicate the expected direction of the partial effect. That is, a positive sign (+) indicates that the variable is likely to increase the probability of observing the positive outcome considered ($y = 1$). Seeking finance is influenced by past decisions, firms' individual characteristics, perceived changes in business environment and foreseen constraints on firm growth.

Regarding past decisions, we checked whether seeking finance in 2007 affected finance seeking in 2010. Such behaviors are modeled as dichotomous variables, where the base category is not seeking finance in 2007. Past decision effects on finance seeking may depend on why firms engage in seeking finance (for example, learning costs).

For the specification of seeking finance, we included firm characteristics such as turnover (in log, no particular effect expected), number of employees (in classes, no particular effect expected) and age of the firm (−). These characteristics can be considered as control variables.

In addition to its own characteristics, the firm's decision may be influenced by several types of factor, including: past behavior in funding applications; observed degradation of its financial situation; and anticipated developments of these elements for the period 2010–2013.

Therefore, we include negative perceptions of changes in business environment (in comparison to "no change" or "positive change"), as firms were asked to give a judgment on such changes between 2007 and 2010. Perceptions have been collected regarding the evolution of three types of environment. First, the evolution of fund characteristics and conditions to obtain financing are explored. A perceived rise in the cost of seeking and obtaining finance should result in decreased demand for funding (−), but it could also result in increasing the probability of asking for funding when conditions for obtaining financing can be seen as a barrier that only the applicant has experienced (+).

Second, firms were asked whether their own situation is better, worse or unchanged, notably concerning their ratio of debt to turnover. Here the sign could vary among sectors: a worse situation could encourage waiting and seeing and not asking for finance, or result in higher probability of seeking finance since needs are becoming more urgent. Finally, regarding market conditions, difficulties could increase competition and pressure to invest despite demand for the firm's products and services not increasing. Competition pressure should increase the probability of seeking funding (+) since falls in demand and poor willingness of banks to provide finance should diminish it (−). So, impact and main perceptions could vary from one sector to another.

Finally, we added some dummy variables to capture the constraints that could limit firms' growth in the future. We expect all these potential

Table 16.1 Descriptive statistics

		Observation	Mean	(std dev.)
Dependent variables				
Seeking finance in 2010	(dummy)	1,181	0.443	(0.49693)
Seeking loans in 2010	(dummy)	1,181	0.191	(0.39297)
Seeking equity in 2010	(dummy)	1,181	0.118	(0.32310)
Seeking other sources in 2010	(dummy)	1,181	0.271	(0.44448)
Seeking finance				
Seeking finance in 2007	(dummy)	1,181	0.395	(0.48897)
Firm's characteristics				
Turnover (2009)	(ln)	1,179	1.099	(0.99100)
Number of employees (2009)	(dummy)			
[10;19]		1,181	0.500	(0.50021)
[20;49]		1,181	0.375	(0.48436)
[50; 99]		1,181	0.086	(0.27977)
[100; max]		1,181	0.038	(0.19153)
Age	(years)	1,181	24.096	(17.86670)
Negative changes perceived between 2007 and 2010				
Financial situation of business	(dummy)	1,181	0.312	(0.46368)
Cost (interest and other) of obtaining finance	(dummy)	1,181	0.141	(0.34771)
Debt/turnover ratio	(dummy)	1,181	0.201	(0.40067)
Burden or effort of obtaining finance	(dummy)	1,181	0.068	(0.25140)
Willingness of banks to provide finance	(dummy)	1,181	0.199	(0.39941)
Relationships with industry competitors	(dummy)	1,181	0.228	(0.41957)

Table 16.1 (continued)

		Observation	Mean	(std dev.)
Prices of raw materials (oil, etc.)	(dummy)	1,181	0.656	(0.47516)
Demand for your products and services	(dummy)	1,181	0.438	(0.16850)
Constraints on future growth				
General economic outlook	(dummy)	1,181	0.760	(0.42755)
Limited demand in the local market	(dummy)	1,181	0.512	(0.50006)
Limited demand in foreign markets	(dummy)	1,181	0.136	(0.34328)
Necessary investment in equipment	(dummy)	1,181	0.118	(0.32239)
Not enough finance	(dummy)	1,181	0.059	(0.23623)
New entrants in the market	(dummy)	1,181	0.321	(0.46703)
Industry breakdown				
Manufacturing	(dummy)	1,181	0.092	(0.28956)
Construction	(dummy)	1,181	0.343	(0.47489)
Trade	(dummy)	1,181	0.240	(0.42704)
Transportation	(dummy)	1,181	0.065	(0.24698)
Accommodation and food services	(dummy)	1,181	0.104	(0.30558)
Other services	(dummy)	1,181	0.156	(0.36282)

Source: Authors' calculations from ATF survey 2010.

constraints to increase the probability of seeking finance. Dummy variables were also used to capture the industry breakdown income of the firms in comparison with other service sectors.

DETERMINANTS OF SEEKING FINANCE IN 2010

Influence of Previous Funding Applications

First, we note from Table 16.2 that the probability of a firm seeking finance in 2010 increases if it sought finance in the past. Past behavior seems to be the most important significant determinant, overall and for each industry. Funding application appears as a recurring action for some businesses which regularly seek external funding. The conclusion remains true when considering the type of funding requested.

Impact of Degradation Observed between 2007 and 2010

The likelihood of a business seeking funding in 2010 increases under the influence of other factors, particularly when the firm perceived negative effects of the crisis on its financial situation, its market prices or conditions of access to financing.

The surveyed firms were asked to describe the trends they have observed through their financial situation – costs of obtaining financing (interest, etc.), ratio of debt to revenue, other financing conditions (e.g. maturity, bank covenant), procedures or efforts to obtain financing, willingness of the finance company to provide financing, relations with competitors in the same industry, prices of intermediate products (raw materials, oil, etc.) – and through the applications addressing them.

Among the changes observed, five were likely to have a significant impact on seeking funding in 2010. When considering firms in the service industry, a decline in demand addressing them negatively influences their propensity to seek funding. This effect disappears in the overall sample and request types when funds are distinguished.

Two perceptions negatively influenced the probability of seeking funding in 2010: a deteriorating financial situation (for manufacturing businesses) or an increase in raw material prices (whatever the industry). When categorized by type of funding the propensity to apply for a loan or equity is negatively affected by deterioration of the financial situation, whereas an increase in raw material prices influences in the same way the propensity to ask for a loan.

Firms that perceived an increase in their ratio of debt to turnover during

Table 16.2 Determinants of seeking finance, 2010

	PROBIT (mfx)			TRIPROBIT (coefficient)		
	All	Manufacturing	Services	Loans	Equity	Other
	(1)	(2)	(3)	(4)	(5)	(6)
Seeking finance						
Seeking finance in 2007	0.601***	0.656***	0.589***	0.790***	0.979***	1.313***
	(0.026)	(0.039)	(0.044)	(0.095)	(0.117)	(0.092)
Firm's characteristics						
Turnover (2009) (*ln*)	0.007	−0.037	0.025	−0.071	0.164**	0.044
	(0.019)	(0.037)	(0.019)	(0.074)	(0.083)	(0.070)
Number of employees (2009) {*Reference class [10; 19]*}						
[20; 49]	0.028	0.039	0.042	0.154	−0.145	−0.074
	(0.032)	(0.056)	(0.037)	(0.119)	(0.138)	(0.114)
[50; 99]	0.041	0.186	−0.017	0.191	−0.562**	0.005
	(0.056)	(0.123)	(0.048)	(0.197)	(0.239)	(0.183)
[100; max]	−0.019	0.081	0.012	0.239	−0.192	−0.460
	(0.074)	(0.159)	(0.091)	(0.294)	(0.323)	(0.291)
Age	−0.001	−0.003*	0.000	−0.001	0.000	−0.003
	(0.001)	(0.002)	(0.001)	(0.003)	(0.003)	(0.003)
Negative changes perceived between 2007 and 2010						
Financial situation of business	−0.042	−0.115***	0.029	−0.250**	−0.293*	0.059
	(0.029)	(0.043)	(0.040)	(0.126)	(0.152)	(0.119)
Cost of obtaining finance (interest and other)	0.028	0.081	−0.011	0.117	0.132	−0.107
	(0.041)	(0.071)	(0.042)	(0.138)	(0.161)	(0.138)
Debt/turnover ratio	0.110**	0.267***	0.020	0.270**	0.506***	0.279**
	(0.046)	(0.084)	(0.042)	(0.127)	(0.149)	(0.126)

Burden or effort of obtaining finance	0.143 **	0.084	0.155**	0.243	0.365 **
	(0.060)	(0.083)	(0.077)	(0.156)	(0.158)
Willingness of banks to provide finance	0.004	−0.009	0.022	0.194	−0.051
	(0.041)	(0.062)	(0.049)	(0.149)	(0.148)
Relationships with industry competitors	0.012	0.041	−0.017	0.196	−0.009
	(0.033)	(0.057)	(0.034)	(0.121)	(0.118)
Price of raw materials (oil, etc.)	−0.072 **	−0.104**	−0.048*	−0.248 **	−0.045
	(0.029)	(0.048)	(0.028)	(0.109)	(0.105)
Demand for your products and services	−0.012	0.074	−0.049*	−0.110	−0.108
	(0.031)	(0.063)	(0.029)	(0.125)	(0.121)
Constraints on future growth					
General economic outlook	0.037	0.084*	0.007	0.061	0.083
	(0.031)	(0.051)	(0.034)	(0.114)	(0.110)
Limited demand in local market	0.078 **	−0.017	0.135***	0.105	0.107
	(0.031)	(0.040)	(0.043)	(0.097)	(0.095)
Limited demand in foreign markets	0.021	v0.003	0.026	0.186	0.044
	(0.039)	(0.061)	(0.044)	(0.135)	(0.134)
Necessary investment in equipment	0.070	0.199**	−0.021	0.288 **	0.189
	(0.046)	(0.085)	(0.039)	(0.135)	(0.138)
Not enough finance	0.171 **	0.055	0.275**	0.363 **	0.406 **
	(0.075)	(0.101)	(0.108)	(0.178)	(0.178)
New entrants in the market	−0.059 **	−0.017	−0.060**	−0.246 **	−0.115
	(0.025)	(0.042)	(0.027)	(0.105)	(0.100)
Industry breakdown *(reference class manufacturing)*					
Construction	−0.026	−0.041		−0.120	−0.013
	(0.044)	(0.049)		(0.165)	(0.164)
Trade	−0.024			0.034	−0.297
	(0.048)			(0.183)	(0.184)

211

Table 16.2 (continued)

	PROBIT (mfx)			TRIPROBIT (coefficient)		
	All (1)	Manufacturing (2)	Services (3)	Loans (4)	Equity (5)	Other (6)
Transportation	-0.016		0.034	-0.056	0.145	-0.038
	(0.061)		(0.056)	(0.220)	(0.252)	(0.220)
Accommodation and food services	-0.052		0.022	0.051	0.219	-0.512 **
	(0.053)		(0.049)	(0.207)	(0.239)	(0.222)
Other services	-0.055		-0.011	-0.521 **	0.016	0.058
	(0.049)		(0.037)	(0.205)	(0.223)	(0.186)
Constant				-1.217 ***	-1.879 ***	-1.280 ***
				(0.216)	(0.262)	(0.214)
$rho21$					0.231 ***	(0.078)
$rho31$					-0.240 ***	(0.071)
$rho32$					-0.251 ***	(0.077)
N	1,129	493	636		1,129	
LogL	-528.882 ***	-219.485 ***	-287.269 ***		-1310.254 ***	
Pseudo R-squared (%)	31.79	35.59	33.74			
Predictive value (%)	80.34	81.95	80.03			

L. ratio test of rho21 = rho31 = rho32 = 0:
chi2(3) = 27.6324 Prob > chi2 = 0.0000

Notes: mfx are calculated at 0 for discrete variables, 20 for age and mean for other continuous variables.
Standard errors in brackets.
*** p<0.01; ** p<0.05; * p<0.10.

the period 2007–2010 also had a slightly higher probability of seeking funding in 2010: the impact is stronger for manufacturing businesses, and remains positive and significant when distinguishing each type of financing. In conclusion, the degradation of this ratio is not a constraint for new research on funding.

Surprisingly, an increase in administrative difficulties (imposing greater efforts to obtain finance) has a significant impact on the probability of applying for funding, but not in manufacturing. This type of result (which is a priori counter-intuitive) is in fact quite general when the firm perceives some barriers or constraints to one activity or another: those businesses that are expanding feel the associated limits more strongly. However, this effect is only significant for other types of funding and is still not significant when seeking a loan or equity.

Consequences of Anticipated Developments

Firms were asked not only about perceived changes during 2007–2010 but also about their expectations of future problems, by identifying factors that could curb their growth in the coming years (2011–2013) from a list of proposals. Those factors reflect anticipated developments by firms, and are assumed to influence their current efforts to obtain funding. To sum up, growth prospects should condition firms' investment decisions, which, in turn, influence decisions on research into external funding. Factors that may limit future growth according to our sample are: the general economic outlook; limited demand in the local market; limited demand in foreign markets; difficulties investing in equipment; lack of funding; and, finally, new entrants in the market.

Thus, and quite logically, firms that anticipate growth may be constrained by limited demand in the local market or lack of funding and were more likely to apply for funding in 2010. In contrast, those that expected new entrants in their market were less likely to seek funding in 2010. These last two effects are significant only for services.

Concerning manufacturing, factors limiting growth are not all the same. In fact, propensity to seek funding in 2010 was stronger if those firms anticipated that new investments in equipment would be needed. In addition, each type of application for funding is determined by different factors. Anticipation of constraints on growth, whatever their nature, has no significant impact on research for equity. Loan applications are more common for businesses that anticipate the need for new equipment and that funding will become scarce (the latter is also significant for other sources of funding). Loan applications are less frequent when firms anticipate constraints due to new entrants in the market.

CONCLUSION

The purpose of this chapter is to investigate the determinants of seeking finance. Moreover, it aims at highlighting the difficulties encountered by Luxembourgish independent SMEs throughout the global financial crisis. To examine these facts, we use micro data from the Eurostat survey for Luxembourg on access to finance. We set some working assumptions to distinguish between lag effects, impact of individual characteristics and own perceptions (changes during the last three years and impact of growth constraints met by firms). A firm that seeks external funding may do so for several reasons, such as cash flow problems or investment policy.

Finally, in the representative sample of Luxembourgish firms that were most vulnerable in the economic context in 2007–2010, it appears that they were not seriously affected, particularly by rationing their sources of external funding. Nevertheless, the situation can change very quickly, and it should be followed with appropriate tools (e.g. a barometer).

In the long-term perspective that fits this study of structural determinants, it should be borne in mind that the investigation cannot observe the investment decisions of the company, but simply the decision to seek funding. Despite these important limits, the contribution of this survey and the different models presented are significant. First, the models emphasize the force of habit in seeking funding. Thus, firms that seek external funding are inclined to do it regularly. Second, the survey shows that when a business chooses to seek external financing, it mostly receives it (88 percent). Models cannot determine whether this result is due to a kind of self-rationing (with constraint integration). However, models clearly show that perception of the potentially negative effects of the crisis increases the likelihood of using external funding to invest. Businesses that are more aware of the risks of a crisis feel more strongly the need to consolidate and expand in order to stay in the market.

NOTES

*   Thanks are due to the members of the research team EPR2 at STATEC for their helpful comments and suggestions.
1. A complete description of our target population is available at: http://epp.eurostat.ec.europa.eu/statistics_explained/index.php/Access_to_finance_statistics.
2. The main characteristics of our sample and some information on its representativeness are provided in Larue et al. (2011). For a comparison with European results, see: http://epp.eurostat.ec.europa.eu/statistics_explained/index.php/Access_to_finance_statistics.
3. Loan finance refers to debt that you have to pay back. Bank overdraft/credit lines, preferred debt, leasing, subsidized loans or subordinated loans are excluded.
4. Equity finance refers to money or other assets given against part ownership of shares.

5. Other sources of finance may include leasing, factoring, bank overdraft, subsidized loans, trade credits, export finance facilities or mezzanine financing.

REFERENCES

Bougheas, S., Mizen, P., and Yalcin, C. (2006). Access to external finance: theory and evidence on the impact of firm-specific characteristics. *Journal of Banking and Finance*, **30**, 199–227.

Carree, M. A., and Thurik, A. R. (2008). The lag structure of the impact of business ownership on economic performance in OECD countries. *Small Business Economics*, **30**(1), 101–110.

Demirgüç-Kunt, A., Beck, T., and Honohan, P. (2008). *Finance for All? Policies and Pitfalls in Expanding Access*. Washington, D.C.: World Bank.

Harrison, A., and McMillan, M. (2003). Does direct foreign investment affect domestic credit constraints? *Journal of International Economics*, **61**(1), 73–100.

Larue, S., Dubrocard, A., and Zangerlé, G. (2011). L'accès au financement des PME autonomes en 2010. *Bulletin du STATEC*, **58**(3), 1–26.

Van Praag, C. M., and Versloot, P. H. (2007). What is the value of entrepreneurship? A review of recent research. *Small Business Economics*, **29**(4), 351–382.

PART V

Entrepreneurship, social dimensions and outcomes

17. Self-employment and independent professionals: labour market transitions and myths of entrepreneurship*

Dieter Bögenhold, Jarna Heinonen and Elisa Akola

1. CURRENT MYTHS OF ENTREPRENEURSHIP

In contrast to stereotypical assumptions, the phenomenon of entrepreneurship may look totally different when it is studied as a phenomenon embedded in the labour markets and specific occupational contexts, applications and sectors (see Welter 2011). Some types of small businesses and independent professionals belong to a category which does not fit with an image of entrepreneurship (Hytti 2005; Blackburn and Kovalainen 2008). They do not show ambition for growth and they are sometimes very close to low-income ranges, occasionally to poverty (Kautonen et al. 2010).

Our study discusses the overlapping areas of entrepreneurship, self-employment and liberal professions. Academic discussion on liberal professions has a tradition which goes back several decades. Since that time, liberal professions have been an integral part of the trend towards tertiarisation. In some respects, they can be regarded as something 'between' entrepreneurship and traditional waged work. Within this context, our study discussing the myths of entrepreneurship has two aims: firstly, the argumentation is focused on the reasoning of liberal professions as part of the category of self-employment. Secondly, the study refers to findings of a unique empirical study conducted in Finland: a survey (n = 733) including freelance journalists, translators/interpreters and artists at the blurred boundaries between waged work and entrepreneurship provides insights into their career patterns, work and different socioeconomic matters, and sheds light on many questions related to entrepreneurship and particularly its myths. Findings reveal that the life and work situation of liberal professions cannot be interpreted in simple black and white schemes, such as 'close to poverty' and pushed by missing employment chances into the sector of waged work on the one hand versus working without hierarchies and being independent and self-realised on the other.

2. ENTREPRENEURSHIP, SELF-EMPLOYMENT AND INDEPENDENT PROFESSIONS

Since the idiom 'entrepreneurship' covers wide-ranging issues – such as those relating to small- and medium-sized enterprises (SMEs), innovative ventures, business start-ups, socioeconomic perspectives, and market behavior, among others – there is no precise and commonly shared source from which universal discussion of entrepreneurship can be drawn (Davidsson 2003; Welter 2011).

Recent liberal professions exist at the interface of processes of academisation and tertiarisation. As more of these professions are involved in general trends of dynamics, especially within self-employment, one also has to start distinguishing within this category, where winners and losers (Støren and Arnesen 2011; Allen and van der Velden 2011) appear at the same time. First of all, new occupations and job profiles are emerging; these are in turn associated with the emergence of a multiplicity of new self-employed occupations and job profiles. The significance of the growth in professional services for the future of self-employed activity is revealed by a glance at the trend in those occupations, which belong primarily to the segments of business services and education, health and culture. Principle changes in society provide a basic ground for new areas of independent liberal professions as well as for new firms in the service sector, especially when the so-called creative industries (Flew 2012) also become a domain of professional expertise and when trends of globalisation and company strategies of outsourcing interact (Bharat 2012).

Interpreting new markets as a complex result of occupational changes at a macro level and social mobility within the life-course of individual agents gives an idea of how changes serve as sources of newness.

3. DATA AND METHODS

The empirical part of this study attempts to draw a picture of the division of self-employment and professions. Specific mobility channels between dependent and non-dependent work will be investigated, in particular for the case of some professionals with a university degree in Finland. The focus is on specific professionals – freelance journalists, translators/

interpreters and artists – who, due to a lack of a traditional career structure, may actively seek or are forced to take freelance work and work in a self-employed capacity (see Fraser and Gold 2001).

3.1 Data

The surveys were sent to the members of three professional associations: the Freelance Journalists' Association (SFJ), the Finnish Association of Translators and Interpreters, and the Artists' Association of Finland. These professions have not been widely studied from the perspective of self-employment/entrepreneurship. The data is unique as, given the changing nature of the labour market, the selected professions are positioned at the blurred boundaries, where waged work and self-employment co-exist and constitute an individual's livelihood.

The sampling frame was comprised of 2,036 self-employed professionals and the data collection generated 733 responses (response rate 36 per cent): 89 per cent of all self-employed professionals worked alone – only 3 per cent had employees and 7 per cent had other owners involved with their business. The role of the data is to illustrate our discussion on the professions and their mobility at the blurred boundaries.

3.2 Measures

Profession was measured with a three-category variable based on the professional association of the respective respondent. *Desirability of self-employment* was measured by combining two different variables: how long the respondents had considered self-employment before starting their activities and how they had prepared for self-employment. We categorised the desirability of self-employment into three groups. The group 'high' includes respondents who had considered self-employment for a long time (from several months to several years) and built their earlier career in and/ or trained for the profession in order to be self-employed. The group 'low' contains those respondents who had not really considered self-employment and who had not prepared systematically for it.

Entrepreneurial behavior was measured with four original items concerning the self-assessed perception of creativity and risk-taking. *Customer focus* was assessed with two original items related to number of assignments and role of customer needs. *Satisfaction with the way of working* was measured with four original items describing self-fulfillment and suitability of life situation for self-employment.[1]

3.3 Analyses

Cross-tabulations and analyses of variance (ANOVA) were utilised to examine the differences across the professions. In the results section only statistically significant differences among professions are reported in the tables. If the chi square tests were statistically significant, post hoc tests were conducted to find differences among the three professions. If not indicated otherwise, the differences between all professions were statistically significant. Statistical significances between some of the professions are indicated in the tables with a symbol (a, b or c), where a = the difference in relation to freelance journalists, b = the difference in relation to translators/interpreters and c = the difference in relation to artists.

4. FREELANCERS AND ARTISTS: HETEROGENEOUS WORKING LIVES WITHIN NECESSITY, CHALLENGES AND SATISFACTION

In the following we will take a closer look at different routes to self-employment, formation of livelihood, organisation and content of work, as well as satisfaction with self-employment at the boundaries of waged work and entrepreneurship. The differences between professions are demonstrated by the exemplary data on freelance journalists, translators/interpreters and artists.

4.1 Routes to Self-Employment

There are two different socioeconomic paths to self-employment. On the one hand, an individual may become self-employed for reasons of self-fulfilment and self-realisation, indicating that self-employment is a desirable option among other possible options (i.e., waged work). On the other hand, self-employment may be the only available option to participate in working life and exercise a particular profession due to a poor labour market situation (Bögenhold 2004; Bates and Servon 2000). Our empirical data comes from professions in relation to which the labour market situation is either poor or inadequate (Akola et al. 2007). However, as shown in Table 17.1, there are differences between professions with regard to desire and preparation for self-employment.

Artists stand out as a particular group: almost 80 per cent had prepared and trained to work as an artist, which evidently implies working in a self-employed capacity. Most of the translators/interpreters and freelance journalists belonged to the group in the middle, indicating that the idea of

Table 17.1   Desire and preparation for self-employment, and prior labour situation

	Freelance journalists	Translators/ interpreters	Artists	Total
Desire and preparation for self-employment (p < 0.001)	% (n)	% (n)	% (n)	% (n)
High	19.4	18.9	77.9	34.1
Middle	51.9	55.0	18.4	44.8
Low	28.7	26.1	3.7	21.2
Total	*100.0 (160)* [c]	*100.0 (238)* [c]	*100.0 (136)* [a, b]	*100.0 (534)*
Labour market situation before self-employment (p < 0.001)	% (n)	% (n)	% (n)	% (n)
Waged work (permanent, temporary, occasional)	65.0	58.6	24.7	52.2
Unemployed	8.6	9.3	3.4	7.6
Economically inactive (students, different kinds of leave)	26.4	32.1	71.9	40.2
Total	*100.0 (220)* [c]	*100.0 (321)* [c]	*100.0 (178)* [a, b]	*100.0 (719)*
Unemployed during the past 5 years (p < 0.001)	% (n)	% (n)	% (n)	% (n)
Yes	13.0	15.9	35.4	19.8
No	87.0	84.1	64.6	80.2
Total	*100.0 (215)* [c]	*100.0 (321)* [c]	*100.0 (175)* [a, b]	*100.0 (711)*
How well have the salaried positions corresponded to your education? (p < 0.001)	% (n)	% (n)	% (n)	% (n)
Well	66.8	54.5	37.3	54.1
Partly	24.8	30.1	45.3	32.2
Not much	8.4	15.4	17.4	13.7
Total	*100.0 (202)*	*100.0 (286)*	*100.0 (161)*	*100.0 (649)*

Note: a = difference in relation to freelance journalists; b = difference in relation to translators/interpreters; c = difference in relation to artists.

being self-employed is not totally strange but that they had not actively prepared themselves for self-employment.

Similarly, Gold and Fraser (2002) found in their study that freelance translators 'just grew' into a freelance career and self-employment without any real planning. The status of the work was simply a means to an end, although there was perhaps some initial compulsion rather than a conscious choice to become self-employed. However, later they wanted to remain self-employed and not move back into employment.

Table 17.1 demonstrates the prior labour market situation of the studied professions: 65 per cent of the freelance journalists and 59 per cent of the translators/interpreters worked in waged work prior to self-employment. About 72 per cent of the artists were economically inactive prior to self-employment, as most of them entered self-employment immediately after their studies. Unemployment was not an important route to self-employment. In all of the studied professions less than one-tenth were unemployed prior to self-employment, but during the past five years 13 per cent of the freelance journalists, 16 per cent of the translators/interpreters and about 35 per cent of the artists had faced unemployment. These figures clearly demonstrate the differences in the labour markets and salaried job opportunities among the studied professions.

4.2 Formation of Livelihood

Several studies have highlighted the dramatic loss of income an individual may face when moving from employment to self-employment (e.g., Blanchflower and Shadfort 2007; Shane 2008), indicating the precarious nature of entrepreneurship (Carter 2011). On the other hand, contradictory evidence also exists suggesting that the living standards of entrepreneurs exceed those of employees (Cagetti and De Nardi 2006; Carter 2011). In the study of Fraser and Gold (2001) they found that typical earnings of freelance translators were comparable to average earnings for similar groups nationally. In addition, although the translators had other sources of income (such as copy-editing and teaching, or even non-language activities) they mostly chose to pursue other activities rather than be forced to do so because of the low income derived from translations. Table 17.2 presents annual income figures among the studied professional groups.

Of the studied professions, the freelance journalists were better off than the others. About half of the respondents had an annual income of €30,000 or more from self-employment, and only 8 per cent earned less than €10,000, whereas the situation was much worse among the artists: 75 per cent earned less than €10,000 a year and only 6 per cent earned more

Table 17.2   Annual income from self-employment and waged work

	Freelance journalists	Translators/ interpreters	Artists	Total
	% (n)	% (n)	% (n)	% (n)
Income from self-employment, € (p < 0.001)				
0–9,999	7.7	23.5	75.4	31.8
10,000–29,999	42.1	41.0	18.3	35.6
More than 30,000	50.2	35.5	6.3	32.6
Total	*100.0 (209)*	*100.0 (310)*	*100.0 (175)*	*100.0 (694)*
Perception of current income from self-employment (p < 0.001)				
Good	32.3	34.3	17.7	29.4
Satisfactory	44.1	39.9	33.3	39.5
Poor	23.6	25.9	48.9	31.1
Total	*100.0 (220)[c]*	*100.0 (321)[c]*	*100.0 (186)[a,b]*	*100.0 (727)*
Annual variation of income from self-employment (p < 0.001)				
A lot	27.4	30.5	69.2	39.5
A bit	53.9	51.3	24.3	45.2
Not much	18.7	18.2	6.5	15.4
Total	*100.0 (219)[c]*	*100.0 (318)[c]*	*100.0 (185)[a,b]*	*100.0 (722)*
Development of income during self-employment (p < 0.001)				
Improved	59.5	62.8	60.4	61.2
Remained about the same	17.3	22.4	18.1	19.7
Weakened	19.1	11.0	9.3	13.1
Difficult to say as my income varies a lot annually	4.1	3.8	12.1	6.0
Total	*100.0 (220)*	*100.0 (317)*	*100.0 (182)*	*100.0 (719)*
Parallel waged work (p < 0.001)				
No	86.0	66.7	53.1	69.4
Yes, one or several	14.0	33.3	46.9	30.6
Total	*100.0 (222)*	*100.0 (294)*	*100.0 (180)*	*100.0 (696)*

Note: a = difference in relation to freelance journalists; b = difference in relation to translators/interpreters; c = difference in relation to artists.

than €30,000 from self-employment. The translators/interpreters' position was in the middle, with 35 per cent of the respondents earning more than €30,000 and 24 per cent less than €10,000. Accordingly, about one-third of the freelance journalists and translators/interpreters perceived their income from self-employment as good, whereas the share was 18 per cent among the artists, almost half of whom considered their income to be poor. Annual incomes varied a lot.

We also studied whether the respondents were engaged simultaneously with waged work in order to create a 'portfolio' of work activity for themselves, as the concept of portfolio work and career suggests (Clinton et al. 2006). Only 14 per cent of the freelance journalists, 33 per cent of translators/interpreters and 47 per cent of the artists had parallel waged employment. It seems that this merely reflects the income gained from self-employment rather than the labour market situation. In addition, it seems that translators/interpreters would have preferred employment to self-employment if vacancies had been available. The artists with a modest income from self-employment needed to supplement it with waged work, even though waged work would not necessarily serve their professional needs and desires.

4.3 Organisation and Content of Work

Freelance work usually involves tasks that are required for a limited time, and therefore 'termination' is an intrinsic property of the freelance work relationship (Storey et al. 2005). The customer base may be restricted to only one or two clients, but may also cover wide client bases providing a portfolio of work. A genuine portfolio with a range of assignments from different clients distinguishes the self-employed from the home-working wage labourer (Fraser and Gold 2001). Accordingly, although the self-employed may have autonomy and flexibility of getting organised, their independence is still quite limited due to market factors and the commercial nature of the customer relationship.

Similarly, Clinton et al. (2006) found that portfolio workers experience their working lives through processes of high levels of autonomy, uncertainty and social isolation. Financial uncertainty is acknowledged, although the uncertainty – of not knowing the future and where the next offer of work will come from – can also be perceived as a pleasant and exciting experience. It is necessary, however, to make a further distinction between uncertainty and job insecurity (Clinton et al. 2006). However, most self-employed freelance translators, for example, do not intend to grow or expand their business (Gold and Fraser 2002). Success is defined in more modest terms, such as 'getting by' – referred to as staying in the game, not necessarily as winning (Storey et al. 2005).

Additional insights drawn from our sample suggest that the great majority of freelance journalists (79 per cent) and translators/interpreters (83 per cent) worked mainly at home, whereas about half (51 per cent) of the artists worked in their own or rented premises separate from their home. Freelance journalists perceived themselves to be more customer focused than the other professional groups. Interestingly, artists put only little emphasis on customer focus, but rather conduct their work based on artistic terms. However, they perceived their work to be highly entrepreneurial, whereas the entrepreneurial work dimension of freelance journalists and translators/interpreters, particularly, scored much lower. The work of the artists includes by the way many entrepreneurial characteristics – such as unique products, innovative renewal of activities, creativity and investments – as well as separate work premises. Perhaps the modest customer focus is reflected in their small-scale operations and modest income, respectively.

4.4   Satisfaction with Self-Employment

When studying portfolio work and careers, Fenwick (2003) found two contrasting views: a mixture of liberating and exploitative elements, which are related to individuals' conflicting desires for both contingency and stability. On the one hand, self-employed portfolio workers enjoy freedom and autonomy in their work and declared, thus, high satisfaction. On the other hand, the additional stress of uncertain income and contract juggling with client relations is also acknowledged, although not emphasised. Accordingly, anxiety, risk and contingency are perceived both as exhausting and exhilarating by the individuals involved (Fenwick 2003; Clinton et al. 2006). The emphasis lies on professional or occupational identity, and self-employment may only be a means to an end – i.e., to conduct one's profession.

In our study the self-employed were highly satisfied with their way of working as self-employed freelancers or artists. Although satisfaction among the artists was lowest, even they were reasonably happy with their work. Further analyses indicate that, understandably, income level (both in absolute terms and in subjective perception) was positively associated with satisfaction.

5.   CONCLUSIONS AND IMPLICATIONS

This study discusses myths of entrepreneurship which are ongoing in academic reflections. Based on our analysis, the studied professions at the blurred boundaries of entrepreneurship and waged work are clearly

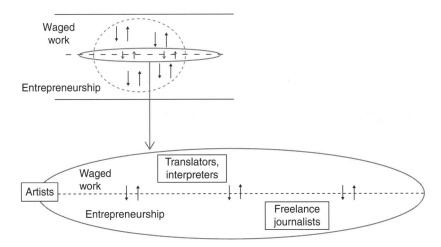

Figure 17.1   The studied professions at the blurred boundaries of entrepreneurship and waged work

different and the manifestations of entrepreneurship vary, reflecting the work itself and the labour market situation within the professions (Figure 17.1; Akola et al. 2007).

Particularly for translators/interpreters, entrepreneurship appears as a flexible way of earning a living. Self-employment involves small-scale activity with unstable income. Although the translators/interpreters are satisfied with their way of working, their work includes only a few entrepreneurial characteristics, and it seems that they would prefer waged work to self-employment if they could make a choice in the first place. For freelance journalists, entrepreneurship appears a tempting opportunity. In comparison to the translators/interpreters, their work has more entrepreneurial characteristics and the customer focus is stronger. The labour market situation is more favourable for them, and many consider self-employment as a viable option offering improved livelihood. The economic scale of self-employment is also wider in comparison to translators/interpreters. For artists, self-employment is a prerequisite or an elementary part of their activities – they simply need to work in a self-employed capacity in order to be able to create art as they have no real options in the labour market. Artists do not, however, perceive themselves as entrepreneurs, but as artists in the first instance, which is reflected in their modest customer focus and income. Otherwise their work has many entrepreneurial characteristics, including separate working premises.

The analytical approach of taking entrepreneurship as a phase in the career of a person helps contextualise the entrepreneurial decision

(Gustafsson 2006) within the work–life story and history of the individual (Cohen and Mallon 2001; Dyer 1994; Hytti 2005; Mallon and Cohen 2001). By looking at different professions at the blurred boundaries of waged work and entrepreneurship we have reasoned that certain professions can be seen as part of the category of self-employment. The term entrepreneurship is very often used in an undifferentiated way, and it therefore easily generates myths and stereotypes, which are challenged by our study.

NOTES

* The authors gratefully acknowledge the financial support of the Academy of Finland (no. 124311).
1. The statements used in the factor analysis are available upon request from the authors.

REFERENCES

Akola, E., J. Heinonen, A. Kovalainen, T. Pukkinen, and J. Österberg. 2007. *Yrittäjyyden ja palkkatyön rajapinnalla? Työn ja toimeentulon rakentuminen eri ammateissa 2000-luvun Suomessa [At the boundaries between entrepreneurship and waged work? Organising work and livelihood in different professions in the 21st century in Finland]*, Työpoliittinen tutkimus 326/2007, Työministeriö. Helsinki: Hakapaino Oy.

Allen, J., and R. van der Velden, eds. 2011. *The Flexible Professional in the Knowledge Society: New Challenges for Higher Education*. Dordrecht: Springer.

Bates, T., and L. Servon. 2000. Viewing self employment as a response to lack of suitable opportunities for wage work. *National Journal of Sociology* **12**, no. 2: 23–55.

Bharat, V. 2012. *Strategic Outsourcing: The Alchemy to Business Transformation in a Globally Converged World*. Berlin, Heidelberg: Springer.

Blackburn, R., and A. Kovalainen. 2008. Researching small firms and entrepreneurship: past, present and future. *International Journal of Management Review* **11**, no. 2, 127–148.

Blanchflower, D.G., and C. Shadforth. 2007. Entrepreneurship in the UK. *Foundations and Trends in Entrepreneurship* **3**, no. 4, 257–264.

Bögenhold, D. 2004. Entrepreneurship: multiple meanings and consequences. *International Journal of Entrepreneurship and Innovation Management* **4**, no. 1, 3–10.

Cagetti, M., and M. de Nardi. 2006. Entrepreneurship, frictions and wealth. *Journal of Political Economy* **114**, no. 5, 835–870.

Carter, S. 2011. The rewards of entrepreneurship: exploring the incomes, wealth, and economic well-being of entrepreneurial households. *Entrepreneurship Theory and Practice* **35**, no. 1, 39–55.

Clinton, M., P. Totterdell, and S. Wood. 2006. A grounded theory of portfolio working: experiencing the smallest of small businesses. *International Small Business Journal* **24**, no. 2, 179–203.

Cohen, L., and M. Mallon. 2001. My brilliant career? Using stories as a methodological tool in careers research. *International Studies of Management and Organisation* **31**, no. 3, 48–68.

Davidsson, P. 2003. The domain of entrepreneurship research: some suggestions. In *Advances in Entrepreneurship, Firm Emergence and Growth*, eds. J. Katz and D. Shepherd, vol. 6, 315–372. Oxford: Elsevier/JAI Press.

Dyer, W.G. Jr. 1994. Toward a theory of entrepreneurial careers. *Entrepreneurship Theory and Practice* **19**, no. 2, 7–21.

Fenwick, T. 2003. Flexible and individualisation in adult education work: the case of portfolio educators. *Journal of Education and Work* **16**, no. 2, 165–184.

Flew, T. 2012. *The Creative Industries: Culture and Policy*. London: Routledge.

Fraser, J., and M. Gold. 2001. Portfolio workers: autonomy and control amongst freelance translators. *Work, Employment and Society* **15**, no. 4, 679–697.

Gold M., and J.J. Fraser. 2002. Managing self-management: successful transitions to portfolio careers. *Work, Employment and Society* **16**, no. 4, 579–597.

Gustafsson, V. 2006. *Entrepreneurial Decision-Making: Individuals, Tasks and Cognitions*. Cheltenham, UK and Northampton, MA, USA: Edward Elgar Publishing.

Hytti, U. 2005. New meanings for entrepreneurs: from risk-taking heroes to safe-seeking professionals. *Journal of Organizational Change Management*, Special Issue: Change in the Feminine: Women in Change, **18**, no. 6, 594–611.

Kautonen, T., S. Down, F. Welter, P. Vainio, and J. Palmroos. 2010. Involuntary self-employment as a public policy issue: a cross-country European view. *International Journal of Entrepreneurial Behaviour and Research* **16**, no. 1–2, 112–129.

Mallon, M., and L. Cohen. 2001. Time for a change? Women's accounts of the move from organizational careers to self-employment. *British Journal of Management* **12**, no. 3, 217–230.

Shane, S. 2008. *The Illusions of Entrepreneurship*. New Haven: Yale University Press.

Storey, J., G. Salaman, and K. Platman. 2005. Living with enterprise in an enterprise economy: freelance and contract workers in the media. *Human Relations* **58**, no. 8, 1033–1058.

Støren, L.A., and C.Å. Arnesen. 2011. Winners and losers. In *The Flexible Professional in the Knowledge Society: New Challenges for Higher Education*, eds. J. Allen, and R. van der Velden, 199–240. Dordrecht: Springer.

Welter, F. 2011. Contextualizing entrepreneurship: conceptual challenges and ways forward. *Entrepreneurship Theory and Practice* **35**, no. 1, 165–184.

18. How distinct is social entrepreneurship from commercial entrepreneurship?

Alicia Rubio Bañon, Nuria Esteban-Lloret and Antonio Aragón Sánchez*

1. INTRODUCTION

Every year social entrepreneurs mingle with the CEOs of the world's largest corporations and prominent politicians at the World Economic Forum (WEF) in Davos, Switzerland. Social entrepreneurs are the stars at global events such as the Clinton Global Initiative (CGI). Finally, social entrepreneurs' ventures are the favourite investment of philanthropists, i.e., the Eli Lillys or Bill Gates of this world.

Social entrepreneurs have been the driving force behind the rapid expansion of the social sector; they identify opportunities to address an underserved social market and offer creative solutions to complex persistent social problems. Social entrepreneurship (SE) has been seen as an important mechanism for supporting economic activity in areas deemed unprofitable by the commercial sector, offering innovative solutions to complex and persistent social issues by applying traditional entrepreneurship models.

Social companies share the pursuit of revenue generation with commercial firms, but they also seek to achieve social goals such as positive social and environmental impact (Di Domenico et al., 2010), which means that social and commercial entrepreneurs have different intentions when they decide to create a business because they seek to increase social capital and enhance community cohesion (Mair and Noboa, 2006).

Although SE developed originally as a subfield within entrepreneurship, there has been almost no research on the differences or particularities between commercial entrepreneurship (CE) and SE, with no clearly defined research agenda for SE (Short et al., 2009). Moreover, SE academic research has primarily utilized case studies as a means to describe rather than analyse the phenomenon of SE (Meyskens et al., 2010).

Thus, drawing on the Global Entrepreneurship Monitor (GEM) analytical framework, this chapter offers a comparative analysis of CE and SE to discover more about the differences between the two types of entrepreneurship.

The remainder of the chapter is organized as follows. In the first section, we draw on previous literature to present a conceptual framework of SE as a step toward the development of a body of theory on SE. Next, we present an empirical study where we test our hypotheses. The chapter concludes by presenting implications for social entrepreneurial practice and research.

2.   LITERATURE BACKGROUND

This research follows a broader conceptualization of SE (Meyskens et al., 2010) as an innovative, social value creating activity that can occur within or across the non-profit, business or government sector (Austin et al., 2006). Thus, a social entrepreneur is a person actively involved in the creation of a social firm who identifies opportunities to address an underserved social market and offers creative solutions to complex persistent social problems. They seek to provide real social improvements to their communities, as well as attractive returns for their investors (Dees, 2001).

Although SE has existed for many centuries, economic research has only been around for a few decades (Kistruct and Beamish, 2010), focusing on:

- SE partnerships (Seelos and Mair, 2007);
- community-based enterprise (Peredo and Chrisman, 2006);
- social entrepreneurs' ethical concerns (Zahra et al., 2009);
- developing this framework on established theoretical frameworks (Meyskens et al., 2010; Miller and Wesley, 2010; Nicholls, 2010; Short et al., 2009);
- the legal characterization of the social enterprise (Kistruct and Beamish, 2010); and
- CE versus SE (Urban, 2008; Austin et al., 2006; Thomson et al., 2000).

Thus, as a phenomenon, SE is far from an anomaly; and, as a field of study, there is a need for large theoretical strides to catch up with the practice (Kistruct and Beamish, 2010).

Most of the models used define entrepreneurship as the result of a combination of individual, organizational or environmental factors that influence how and why entrepreneurship occurs.

But, in fact, entrepreneurship arises, ultimately, from the actions of particular persons. Consequently, understanding why and how these persons act as they do is crucial to comprehend the entire process (Baron, 2004) and determine what motivates some individuals to initiate a venture while others do not (McClelland, 1961).

Following Gartner (1985), it is possible to identify human capital and psychological individual differences. The human capital variables include knowledge, education, skills and experience, and the psychological individual differences concern differences in personality characteristics, cognitive characteristics and motivational patterns (Gelderen et al., 2005).

This so-called cognitive approach points out the manner in which an individual's process information is central (Gelderen et al., 2005) and provides valuable tools for the field of entrepreneurship, contributing to understanding three key aspects of the entrepreneurial process (Baron, 2004):

1. Why do some people but not others choose to become entrepreneurs?
2. Why do some people but not others recognize opportunities for new products or services that can be profitably exploited?
3. Why are some entrepreneurs so much more successful than others?

Also Reynolds et al. (2005) proposed a model, which is the basis of the GEM research programme, that integrates different blocks of variables related to the influence of the creation of businesses in a particular territory and differentiates between two types of factor: those that affect and modify the framework in which already established businesses compete; and those that affect the level of opportunities and the capabilities of the new entrepreneurs.

On the basis of the cognitive approach and GEM's analytical framework, we propose that some of the key elements that are critical for CE provide the bases for developing a framework for SE: alertness to opportunities, entrepreneurial self-efficacy and fear of failure.

2.1   Alertness to Opportunities

Opportunity identification – a favourable set of circumstances for starting a new venture – is one of the most distinctive types of entrepreneurial behaviour (Shane and Venkataraman, 2000; Gaglio and Katz, 2001). In fact, entrepreneurs' decisions often stem from their belief that they have identified an opportunity no one else has yet recognized, and so can benefit from being the first to enter the marketplace (Baron, 2004).

In order to analyse the opportunity identification process among entrepreneurs, we need to address the essential issues of how market environments are represented in the minds of entrepreneurs, and whether these representations differ from those of other market actors in any substantial way (Shaver and Scott, 1991).

Like commercial entrepreneurs, social entrepreneurs recognize opportunities to create or innovate, but for them the social mission is explicit and central and affects how social entrepreneurs perceive and assess opportunities. The process of seeking opportunities is similar for both because it is the initiation point of the entrepreneurial process, although opportunities for social entrepreneurs are likely to be distinct from opportunities in the commercial sector and need to be examined in their own right (Austin et al., 2006). These differences are based on Doyle and Ho (2010), Meyskens et al. (2010) and Zahra et al. (2009):

1. The primary focus of returns for CE is economic, while in SE the focus is on social returns (Austin et al., 2006). They emphasize the value contribution to society (Zarha et al., 2009).
2. The context in which these opportunities surface, are recognized and are exploited is different for social and commercial entrepreneurs, so the entry barriers and the resources mobilized for both are also different.
3. The type of organization that emerges to address opportunities also differs between each type of entrepreneurship.

So, as is shown, the primary need to seek opportunities is the same for both types of entrepreneurship, and, despite the differences observed, we affirm that there is a positive relationship between the capacity of the entrepreneur to perceive opportunities and the probability of starting a new business.

Hypothesis 1: Individuals with high alertness to opportunities are more likely to be entrepreneurs, commercial or social, than those with low alertness to opportunities.

2.2   Entrepreneurial Self-Efficacy

Self-efficacy theory (Bandura, 1997) has been extensively applied in studies on entrepreneurial motivation, intentions and behaviour which include entrepreneurial self-efficacy (ESE) as an explanatory variable (Chen et al., 1998; McGee et al., 2009). ESE is rooted in a person's belief in his or her own competence, and high and low levels of self-efficacy have serious consequences for an individual's self-belief in their ability to perform in a range of situations, such as innovation and opportunity recognition in entrepreneurship (Arenius and Clercq, 2005).

Some studies have theorized that ESE influences the development of entrepreneurial intentions, and hence the probability of venture creation (Kickul et al., 2008; Boyd and Vozikis, 1994), while others have proposed a predictive model of entrepreneurial intentions in which self-efficacy plays a critical mediating role (Zhao et al., 2005). If ESE is low, an individual will not act, even if there is a perceived social approval for that action (Boyd and Vozikis, 1994). So, if ESE is high, the motivation to become an entrepreneur will increase.

The skills necessary for commercial and social ventures are similar. For both they have to know the industry; the key suppliers, customers, competitors and talent that they need to bring into their organization, and they must also be recognized by others for their reputation and capabilities. However, reputation capabilities, which usually rely on a network of contacts, make a difference between the two types of entrepreneurship because managing those relations is crucial for social entrepreneurs. Their limited access to resources makes their ability to develop a strong reputation that invokes trust among contributors one of the most important capacities for the social entrepreneur (Austin et al., 2006).

Social entrepreneurs also must be skilled at managing a wider range of relationships, and acknowledge the participation of other individuals, organizations and committees, and volunteers in entrepreneurial ventures (Doyle and Ho, 2010). They must explore partnerships and alliances in order to expand their impact and spread their methods of creating social value (Meyskens et al., 2010), and they may involve their stakeholders in the creation, management and governance of their social enterprise in order to operate a networking strategy (Di Domenico et al., 2010).

Despite these differences, we propose that the relationship between the probability of starting a new business and the perception that one has the right skills to do it is positive for both types of entrepreneurship.

Hypothesis 2: Individuals with high ESE are more likely to be entrepreneurs, commercial or social, than those with low ESE.

2.3 Fear of Failure

When a potential entrepreneur decides to start a business, risks associated with the specific business proposal must be carefully analysed. Risk-taking propensity is defined as: "the perceived probability of receiving the rewards associated with success for a proposed situation, which is required

by an individual before he will subject himself to the consequences associated with failure, the alternative situation providing less reward as well as
severe consequences than the proposed situation" (Brockhaus, 1980: 513).

Fear of failure (FF) is one of the main reasons why people do not
choose entrepreneurship as a career, because failing as an entrepreneur is
perceived to cause not only economic loss but also a sense of shame, and
possibly social exclusion (Ojasalo, 2004).

Since most individuals are risk averse, and since the perceived FF is an
important component of the risk attached to starting a new business, a
reduced perception of the likelihood of failure should increase the probability that an individual will start a new business (Arenius and Minniti,
2005; Weber and Milliman, 1997).

While most entrepreneurs operate under conditions of risk, social entrepreneurs face a specific set of challenges because they purposely locate
their activities in areas where markets function poorly (Di Domenico et al.,
2010). Even though they are closer to risk and failure, social entrepreneurs
do not let fear keep them from pursuing their visions; they take calculated
risks and manage the downsides so as to reduce the harm that will result
from failure. They understand the risk tolerances of their stakeholders and
use this knowledge to spread the risk to those who are better prepared to
accept it (Dees, 2001). These results lead us to affirm that:

*Hypothesis 3: Individuals with low FF are more likely to be entrepreneurs,
commercial or social, than those with high FF.*

3. EMPIRICAL STUDY

Our analyses were undertaken on a representative sample of the adult
population in Spain. The unit of analysis pertains to the individual level,
and we used data collected as part of the 2009 Global Entrepreneurship
Monitor (GEM) study. GEM is an ongoing multinational project created
to investigate the incidence and causes of entrepreneurship within and
between countries. We collected data through telephone interviews using
a standardized questionnaire during the spring of 2009. We used a representative sample of adults (18–64 years old), yielding a total of 28,888
individuals. In order to ensure that the respondents correctly reflect the
population from which they are drawn, GEM assigns each respondent a
weighting factor that takes into account gender and age. More information
about the GEM study and its methodology is provided in Reynolds et al.
(2005).

3.1   Variables and Analyses

To identify individuals in the process of starting a business, respondents were asked if they were alone or with others in currently trying to start a new business, differentiating between entrepreneur and non-entrepreneur. To identify individuals in the process of starting a social business we also asked if their activity had a particularly social, environmental or community objective, differentiating between social and non-social entrepreneurs.

Entrepreneur opportunity recognition was measured by asking whether they thought that good opportunities for starting a business would exist in the area where they lived. For ESE, we asked whether they believed themselves to have the knowledge, skill and experience required to start a new business. Finally, to measure the risk perceived in order to identify the level of FF, respondents were asked whether FF would prevent them from starting a business. We also included three control variables – age, gender and education level. Age was ranged between 18 and 64; gender was measured by a dummy variable; and education by a fourth-category variable.

In order to test our hypotheses, we ran three binominal logistic regression models. The difference between the models takes root in the sample of individuals used. For the first model we used the total sample of 28,888 interviewed individuals. Model II tests commercial entrepreneurs, using a sample of 28,672 individuals, excluding 216 social entrepreneurs. For model III we constructed a subsample formed of 27,630 individuals, excluding commercial entrepreneurs. We used the Wald test to test the significance of the individual regression coefficients. In order to make interpretation of the results easier, we also report the odds ratio for each of the predictor variables.

3.2   Results

As shown in Table 18.1, in model I and II all the variables considered are significant in predicting the decision to become an entrepreneur. Age is significant and negatively associated with the dependent variable in both models, suggesting that a commercial entrepreneur is usually a young person. Gender is also negatively associated with the dependent variable, suggesting that a commercial entrepreneur is usually a man. Finally, education level is also significant and negatively associated with the dependent variable, suggesting that a commercial entrepreneur is usually a person of a low education level.

On the other hand, all the perceptual variables introduced are highly significant in both models. In particular, the results show that ESE and alertness to opportunities are positively and significantly related to being

Table 18.1 Logistic regression model

Variable	Model I: entrepreneurs			Model II: commercial entrepreneurs			Model III: social entrepreneurs		
	B	Wald χ	Exp(B)	B	Wald χ²	Exp(B)	B	Wald χ²	Exp(B)
Age	−0.024***	82.394	0.976	−0.024***	80.953	0.976	−0.003	0.202	0.997
Gender	−0.285***	21.290	0.752	−0.302**	22.687	0.740	−0.186	1.489	0.831
Education level		23.377			23.139			71.084	
None	−0.810***	13.394	0.445	−0.893***	15.395	0.409	−2.076***	21.230	0.125
Some secondary	−0.773***	16.676	0.462	−0.837***	18.511	0.433	−2.640***	51.285	0.071
Secondary	−0.875***	20.133	0.417	−0.913***	20.813	0.401	−2.176***	35.001	0.113
Post-secondary	−0.663***	12.997	0.515	0.745***	15.493	0.475	1.183***	16.546	0.306
PO	0.675***	109.649	1.964	0.648***	953260	1.912	0.932***	37.110	2.539
ESE	20.499***	482.260	12.172	2.466***	460.827	11.778	1.181***	36.322	3.259
FF	−0.617***	96.044	0.540	0.650***	100.935	0.522	0.196***	1.677	0.822
				Model diagnosis					
N	28,888			28,672			27,630		
Model χ²	14.684***			18.210***			19.019**		
Block χ²									
Overall % correct predictions	94.6			94.8			99.2		
R²	0.177			0.174			0.094		

Note: ***, ** and * indicate significance at the 1 percent, 5 percent and 10 percent level, respectively

an entrepreneur. The coefficient on the variable alertness to opportunities suggests that those who perceive opportunities are almost 1.9 times more likely to be entrepreneurs than those who do not perceive these opportunities.

As already mentioned, ESE is positively and significantly related to being an entrepreneur, suggesting that those who perceive themselves as possessing the necessary skills are almost 12 times more likely to be entrepreneurs than those who do not believe themselves to have the necessary skills.

The variable FF is negatively associated with the dependent variable, suggesting that an entrepreneur is a person with low FF; it means that individuals who have high FF are only half as likely to start a new business as those who do not.

It is thus possible to define a commercial entrepreneur profile as a young man with low education level, high alertness to opportunities, high self-efficacy perception and low FF.

In model III, we have the results for the social entrepreneurs' sample. In this case, not all the variables initially considered for analysis were finally entered in the model. There is no significant relation between the dependent variable and three of the variables: age, gender and fair of failure. Education level, ESE and opportunity recognition are significantly related to being an entrepreneur, as was predicted and just like for commercial entrepreneurs. Thus, to define a social entrepreneur profile we can say that it is a person with low education level, high alertness to opportunities and high self-efficacy perception.

Regarding the stated hypotheses in this study, hypothesis 1, and hypothesis 2 can be accepted, and hypothesis 3 only partially.

4. DISCUSSION AND CONCLUSIONS

The core contribution of this research is the insight it provides into the study of SE. First, this study contributes to the social entrepreneurial literature by highlighting the differences between SE and CE using an analytical framework on how to approach the social entrepreneurial process more systematically and effectively. The results show that while commercial entrepreneurs are usually young men with high ESE, high opportunity perceptions and low FF, the probability of becoming a social entrepreneur does not depend on gender, age and FF.

The language of SE may be new, but the phenomenon is not (Dees, 2001). There have always been people who start new ventures with a social improvement proposition. But the recent boom in social entrepreneurial activities opens up some avenues of exploration for SE theory development and practice by presenting an exploratory comparative analysis of the extent to which elements applicable to business entrepreneurship, which has been more extensively studied, are transferable to SE (Austin et al., 2006).

The purpose of this chapter was to explore the extent to which elements applicable to business entrepreneurship are transferable to SE. In doing so, we examined what scholars have said about CE, and then with quantitative research we tested the commercial model in a social entrepreneurs' sample. Our findings highlighted that there are significant individual differences between commercial and social entrepreneurs.

First, our results suggest that the relationship between the likelihood of becoming a social entrepreneur does not depend on gender. While in CE the results show that men are more likely to start new ventures, in SE we did not find this result. Although women have made great strides in recent years towards closing the entrepreneurship gap, concerns persist that they are under-represented among business owners because they lack the same motivations as men when considering entrepreneurship as a career choice (Mueller and Conway Dato-on, 2008).

Second, the likelihood of being a commercial entrepreneur is highest among young individuals. This is consistent with existing empirical and theoretical literature showing that new firm creation tends to be a young man's game (Lévesque and Minniti, 2006; Arenius and Minniti, 2005; Reynolds et al., 2005). However, the results for social entrepreneurs are quite different. For them the probability of starting a new venture for addressing unmet social needs does not depend on the age of the entrepreneur.

Results show a negative relationship between a person's level of education and the likelihood of becoming a commercial or a social entrepreneur. But, for social entrepreneurs we found that individuals who have a post-secondary level of education are less likely to start a social venture compared to those who have a lower education degree, which is not observed for commercial entrepreneurs. It reflects that the key element for social entrepreneurs is not education but persistence, combined with a willingness to make adjustments as one goes along: the models they develop and the approaches they often take change as the entrepreneurs learn about what works and what does not work (Dees, 2001). They build their ventures on their life experiences that have created awareness of and information about particular areas that shape opportunity development (Doyle and Ho, 2010).

This result can be unexpected because the level of education typically influences individuals' opportunities for employment. However, the direct influence of education on entrepreneurship is a complex phenomenon (Allen et al., 2007) which has been shown to influence business creation, but only in richer countries, for entrepreneurs' postgraduate training and for high-tech start-up rates (Arenius and Minniti, 2005).

The results of the study also show that there are three individual factors that significantly distinguish commercial entrepreneurs from social entrepreneurs: (1) opportunity perception; (2) self-efficacy perception; and (3) risk perception. ESE emerges as the most important component of the decision to start a new business, as previous studies show (Arenius and Minniti, 2005; Baron, 2004), followed by opportunity perception (Kirzner, 1979). The positive impact of these variables is easily reconciled with the previous theory of entrepreneurship according to which confidence in one's skills and alertness to unexploited opportunities are necessary conditions for entrepreneurial action (Arenius and Minniti, 2005; Kirzner, 1979).

Regarding risk perception, we found marked differences between commercial and social entrepreneurs. In line with previous studies (Weber and Milliman, 1997; Arenius and Minniti, 2005), results suggest that a commercial entrepreneur is a person with low perception of risk. However, we do not have any evidence of the relation between FF and the decision to become a social entrepreneur. So, in this case, risk perception does not reduce the probability of starting a social venture. This result can be explained by a theory often used as a theoretical foundation for commitment and trust in relationship marketing: social exchange theory. This view points out that relational exchange participants can be expected to derive complex, personal, non-economic satisfaction (Dwyer et al., 1987). In CE, transactions are typically considered as an exchange of money for a product or service. However, in SE not all the benefits are economic in nature. In the case of non-profit organizations (NGOs), economic rewards may include such items as tax breaks and gifts, and social rewards include emotional satisfaction, spiritual value and the sharing of humanitarian ideals.

Most of the important benefits involved in social exchange do not have any material value on which an exact price can be put at all, as exemplified by social approval and respect (Blau, 1964). That is, social rewards are often valued more than economic rewards. When an entrepreneur decides to start a business and analyses the risk associated with the venture, the perceived probability of receiving rewards associated with success and the consequences associated with failure vary if they are planning to start a commercial or a social venture. Commercial ventures are subject to market discipline; if they do not create value they tend to be out of business. However, for social entrepreneurs the social mission is explicit and central: they are also subject to market forces, but markets do not work as well for social entrepreneurs and social value is usually difficult to measure. As a result, it is much harder to determine whether a social entrepreneur is creating sufficient social value to justify the resources used in creating that value (Dees, 2001). So social entrepreneurs have no relation to fear; they know they are creating social value, public goods and harms, and benefits for people who cannot afford to pay, which means that the variables 'fear of failure' and 'economic returns' are not as important as they are for commercial entrepreneurs. They are persistent; they do not give up when an obstacle is encountered (Dees, 2001).

Highly related to risk tolerance is the type of business being created. The results may be influenced by the fact that 64.5 per cent of social entrepreneurs belong to the services sector. This sector has minor risk levels derived from the minor investments necessary for starting and maintaining the business.

The results have potentially important implications. On the one hand, this study of the nature of SE contributes to the growing literature that is questioning the differences between SE and CE. On the other hand, these findings have potentially important implications for public policy. The results reinforce the importance of SE, which should be at the centre of many policy questions. As Dees said (2001), we need social entrepreneurs to help us find new avenues if we want social improvement.

For researchers, a multitude of rich avenues merit further exploration. This comparative analysis reveals commonalities between social and commercial entrepreneurs, but we also highlight some important differences regarding mission, capabilities, resources and performance measures, among others. For a deeper study of the social entrepreneur's individual approach it is necessary to introduce new variables in the model. Persistence, social relations, creativity and leadership are important variables that could be considered.

It is our hope that this study furthers the understanding of social entrepreneurship, and stimulates and enables further scholarly exploration of the exceptional issues surrounding social entrepreneurship.

NOTE

*   The authors would like to thank the Cátedra de Responsabilidad Social Corporativa of the University of Murcia and the Fundación Cajamurcia for their generous support.

REFERENCES

Allen, I.E.; Elam, A; Langowitz, N.; Dean, M. (2007): *Report on Women and Entrepreneurship*. Boston: Center for Women's Leadership, Babson College.
Arenius, P.; Clercq, D. (2005): On opportunity recognition. *Small Business Economics*, n°24, pp. 249–265.
Arenius, P.; Minniti, M. (2005): Perceptual variables and nascent entrepreneurship. *Small Business Economics*, n°24, pp. 233–247.
Austin, J.E.; Stevenson, H.H.; Wei-Skillern, J. (2006): Social and commercial

entrepreneurship: same, different, or both? *Entrepreneurship Theory and Practice*, vol. 30, n°1, pp. 1–22.

Bandura, A. (1997): *Self-Efficacy: The Exercise of Control*. New York: Freeman.

Baron, R.A. (2004): The cognitive perspective: a valuable tool for answering entrepreneurship's basic "why" questions. *Journal of Business Venturing*, n°19, pp. 221–239.

Blau, P.M. (1964): *Exchange and Power in Social Life*. New York: Wiley.

Boyd, N.G.; Vozikis, G.S. (1994): The influence of self-efficacy on the development of entrepreneurial intentions and actions. *Entrepreneurship Theory and Practice*, summer, vol. 18, n°4, pp. 63–77.

Brockhaus, R.H. (1980): Risk taking propensity of entrepreneurs. *Academy of Management Journal*, vol. 23, n°2, pp. 509–520.

Chen, C.C.; Greene P.G.; Crick, A. (1998): Does entrepreneurial self-efficacy distinguish entrepreneurs from managers? *Journal of Business Venturing*, n°13, pp. 295–316.

Dees, J.G. (2001): The meaning of social entrepreneurship. Available at www.case atduke.org/documents/dees_sedef.pdf. Accessed 7 August 2010.

Di Domenico, M.L.; Haugh, H.; Tracey, P. (2010): Social bricolage: theorizing social value creation in social enterprises. *Entrepreneurship Theory and Practice*, vol. 34, n°4, pp. 681–703.

Doyle, P.; Ho, M. (2010): How opportunities develop in social entrepreneurship. *Entrepreneurship Theory and Practice*, vol. 34, n°4, pp. 635–659.

Dwyer, F.R.; Schurr, P.H.; Sejo, O. (1987): Developing buyer–seller relationships. *Journal of Marketing*, vol. 51, n°2, pp. 11–27.

Gaglio, C.; Katz, J.A. (2001): The psychological basis of opportunity identification: entrepreneurial alertness. *Small Business Economics*, vol. 16, n°1, pp. 95–111.

Gartner, W.B. (1985): A conceptual framework for describing the phenomenon of new venture creation. *Academy of Management Review*, vol. 10, pp. 696–706.

Gelderen, N.; Thurik, R.; Bosma, N. (2005): Success and risk factors in the pre-startup phase. *Small Business Economics*, n°24, pp. 365–380.

Lévesque, M.; Minniti, M. (2006): The effect of aging on entrepreneurial behavior. *Journal of Business Venturing*, n°21, pp. 177–194.

Kickul, J.; Wilson, F.; Marlino, D.; Barbosa S.D. (2008): Are misalignments of perceptions and self-efficacy causing gender gaps in entrepreneurial intentions among our nation's teens? *Journal of Small Business and Enterprise Development*, n°15, pp. 321–335.

Kirzner, I.M. (1979): *Perception, Opportunity, and Profit*. Chicago: University of Chicago Press.

Kistruct, G.M.; Beamish, P.W. (2010): The interplay of form, structure, and embeddedness in social intrapreneurship. *Entrepreneurship Theory and Practice*, vol. 34, n°4, pp. 735–761.

Mair, J.; Noboa, E. (2006). Social entrepreneurship: how intentions to create a social venture are formed. In J. Mair, J. Robinson, and K.N. Hockerts (eds), *Social Entrepreneurship* (pp. 121–135). Basingstoke: Palgrave Macmillan.

McClelland, D.C. (1961): *The Achieving Society*. Princeton, NJ: Van Nostrand.

McGee, J.E.; Peterson, M.; Mueller, S.L.; Sequeira, J.M. (2009): Entrepreneurial self-efficacy: refining the measure. *Entrepreneurship Theory and Practice*, vol. 33, n°4, pp. 965–988.

Meyskens, M.; Robb-Post, C.; Stamp, J.A.; Carsrud, A.L.; Reynolds, P.D. (2010): Social ventures from a resource-based perspective: an exploratory study assessing global Ashoka Fellows. *Entrepreneurship Theory and Practice*, vol. 34, n°4, pp. 661–680.

Miller, T.L.; Wesley, C.L. (2010): Assessing mission and resources for social change: an organizational identity perspective on social venture capitalists' decision criteria. *Entrepreneurship Theory and Practice*, vol. 34, n°4, pp. 705–733.

Mueller, S.; Conway Dato-on, M. (2008): Gender-role orientation as a determinant of entrepreneurial self-efficacy. *Journal of Developmental Entrepreneurship*, vol. 13, n°1, pp. 3–20.

Nicholls, A. (2010): The legitimacy of social entrepreneurship: reflexive isomorphism in a pre-paradigmatic field. *Entrepreneurship Theory and Practice*, vol. 34, n°4, pp. 611–633.

Ojasalo, J. (2004): Attractiveness and image of entrepreneurship: an empirical study. *International Journal of Entrepreneurship*, vol. 8, n°4, pp. 73–92.

Peredo, A.M.; Chrisman, J.J. (2006): Toward a theory of community-based enterprise. *Academy of Management Review*, vol. 31, n°2, pp. 309–328.

Reynolds, P.D.; Bosma, N.; Autio, E.; Hunt, S.; De Bono, N.; Servais, I.; López-García, P.; Chin, N. (2005): Global entrepreneurship monitor: data collection design and implementation 1998–2003. *Small Business Economic*, vol. 24, n°3, pp. 443–456.

Seelos, C.; Mair, J. (2007): Profitable business models and market creation in the context of deep poverty: a strategic view. *Academy of Management Perspectives*, vol. 21, n°4, pp. 49–63.

Shane, S.; Venkataraman, S. (2000): The promise of entrepreneurship as a field of research. *Academy of Management Review*, vol. 25, n°3, pp. 217–226.

Shaver, K.G.; Scott, L.R. (1991): Person, process, choice: the psychology of new venture creation. *Entrepreneurship Theory and Practice*, vol. 16, n°3, pp. 23–45.

Short, J.; Moss, T.W.; Lumpkin, G.T. (2009): Research in social entrepreneurship: past contributions and future opportunities. *Strategic Entrepreneurship Journal*, vol. 3, pp. 161–194.

Urban, B. (2008): Social entrepreneurship in South Africa: delineating the construct with associated skills. *International Journal of Entrepreneurial Behaviour and Research*, vol. 14, n°5, pp. 346–364.

Weber, E.U.; Milliman, R.A. (1997): Perceived risk attitudes: relating risk perception to risky choice. *Management Science*, vol. 43, n°2, pp. 123–144.

Zahra, S.A.; Gedajlovic, E.; Neubaum, D.O.; Shulman, J.M. (2009); A typology of social entrepreneurs: motives, search processes and ethical challenges. *Journal of Business Venturing*, vol. 24, pp. 519–532.

Zhao, H.; Seibert, S.E.; Hills, G.E. (2005): The mediating role of self-efficacy in the development of entrepreneurial intentions. *Journal of Applied Psychology*, vol. 90, n°6, pp. 1265–1272.

19. Self-employed people and pension: is old age poverty the inevitable dark side of an entrepreneurial society?

Uwe Fachinger and Anna Frankus

INTRODUCTION

One of the characteristics of the structural development of occupation and labour markets over the last decades is the increase in self-employment. Analyses show that, on the one hand, this can be seen as an indication of successful economic policy, a demonstration of the flexibility of labour markets, and an increase in overall wealth. On the other hand, these developments also may reflect the poor economic situation of households. For example, many people became solo self-employed out of the need to earn a living. The latter case may pose serious economic and social problems for an entrepreneurial society if a social risk – such as illness, accident, unemployment (i.e., a lack of orders or contracts) – occurs over a longer period of time. In contrast to dependent employees, a large portion of self-employed people are not mandatorily covered by social security systems. Therefore, with development into an entrepreneurial society, there could be a danger of an overall growth in poverty risk.

This will be exemplified for old age pensions, as this is quantitatively the largest part of a social security system. The central aims of old age pension systems are avoidance of poverty and maintenance of living standards and quality of life in old age. In most countries, old age security is designed as a three-pillar system composed of statutory, occupational, and private pension schemes. No matter how an old age pension system is constructed, self-employed people must rely heavily on private insurance to maintain their living standard after retirement, as they are either not covered by the statutory pension systems or the system only ensures a subsistence level. Obviously, these people also are not covered by occupational pension schemes.

In this context, we study the ability and willingness of people or households with earnings mainly from independent work to save money, and examine their specific kinds of old age provision. To analyse these aspects, one must go into more detail as individual decisions occur against a background of existing systems and their specific regulations. These problems are exemplified by the situation in Germany, based on the Microcensus of the Federal Statistical Office of Germany with data for the period 1989–2009.

The result is, *cum grano salis*, that on average, for households with a solo self-employed head, the ability to save is largely insufficient. The analysis also indicates that, for a larger portion of solo self-employed people, the willingness to save is rather low. As a result, with development into an entrepreneurial society, the group of seniors without old age provision would grow, and, in the end, poverty among seniors would become a serious social problem.

BACKGROUND

The central aims of old age pension systems are the avoidance of poverty and the maintenance of living standards or quality of life in old age. To reach these goals, in most countries old age security is designed as a three-pillar system composed of statutory, occupational, and private pension schemes for employees (European Commission 2010; OECD 2011); but, for most self-employed people, such systems do not exist. On the contrary, self-employed people depend to a high degree on private provisions as:

- statutory pension systems only ensure a subsistence level; and
- self-employed people are not covered by occupational pension schemes.

Taken as a whole, these people are generally free to arrange their old age provision according to their individual preferences, and therefore are able to choose an optimal form of cover. The forms of risk insurance against longevity that may be chosen by self-employed people could be very different. The differences in old age provision depend, for example, on the type of self-employment (e.g., freelancer, craftsperson, or free profession) or the company size. In general, there are three forms of old age provision on which the self-employed are able to base their pensions:

- The firm can be transferred to others, persists, and must pay regular income to the retiree. This only works as long as the firm exists and makes a constant profit until the death of the retiree.

- The firm or business property can be sold and the capital received can be annuitized (converted into a stream of regular income until death).
- The self-employed must save money for old age as long as they are active, and choose forms of insurance that guarantee income replacement during retirement until death.

Regardless of which type of cover is chosen, the success of all efforts to acquire provision that can guarantee an adequate standard of living until death is determined by two aspects:

- the willingness to save; and
- the ability to save.

The following provides a closer look at people's (households') ability and willingness to save out of income that mainly stems from self-employment. This means that only a certain group of self-employed people are considered as self-employment is multifaceted and includes, in addition to so-called successful entrepreneurs, people who are regular employees but also self-employed part time.[1]

ABILITY AND WILLINGNESS TO SAVE

First, the *ability to save* requires an appropriate income. Low income will not enable people to save adequately because of unavoidable expenditures needed to maintain a subsistence level. Low income means low contributions to any form of old age provision, and inevitably leads to low pension entitlements. The ability to save, however, depends not only on the amount of earned income but also on the specific needs of the individual and the household. Therefore, the situation of the individual and the household in regard to expenditure should be considered together to judge the ability to save accordingly. The amount of expenditures depends, inter alia, on the number and age of household members and on the number of people in the household who have special needs.

The *willingness to save* requires awareness of the need for old age provision. Hence knowledge of the financial consequences of (in)adequate insurance is relevant. In principle, to choose adequate insurance individuals must know how much money they need to handle occurrences of risk. Furthermore, willingness to save depends on knowledge of how to save. So-called financial literacy, in combination with knowledge of the social security system of the specific country, is relevant. As can be seen for old age pensions in Germany, more than 4,000 products of government-subsidized retirement accounts are available. It is not at all easy to decide which one will best fit individual needs. In addition, self-employed people have to know whether or not it is mandatory that they be insured by the statutory pension scheme, as this is not always the case. This may be illustrated by a recent example. For freelance teachers, membership of the German statutory pension insurance scheme (GRV) has always been compulsory, but this was not generally known. Many such teachers ignored their obligation to pay and got into arrears with their payments. During the paradigm change of the social security system in Germany, the GRV became aware of this situation, which caused people to remargin the outstanding contributions for the last four years, which amounted to nearly one year's gross annual income.

Another aspect that influences the assessment is myopia (short-sightedness) or positive time preference. Myopia leads to the underestimation of future needs, especially in cases in which the time span between saving and dissaving is large (e.g., insurance for long-term care or old age provision).

A further aspect that must be considered in relation to risk prevention in connection with willingness to save is trust. Especially with a large accumulation period, individuals must trust the security of their financial preparations. If trust is low, as often occurs in the wake of a financial crisis, willingness to save also may be low.

In addition to individual circumstances, social risk management must bear in mind the situation of the other household members and to what extent they are insured, if at all. For spouses, the question is whether there are derived entitlements to benefits without contributions. In Germany, surviving spouses and children are eligible for GRV pension benefits. Such entitlement may reduce the willingness of self-employed people to save if their spouses are insured by the GRV. This means that, for the assessment of the willingness to save, the whole household situation relative to social risk management must be taken into account.

In summary, ability and willingness to save are relevant to an individual's social risk management. However, if the ability to save is low, especially in case of low income, even a high degree of willingness to save will not lead to enough accumulated wealth and will not prevent self-employed people from low entitlements to old age provision.

To answer questions about the consequences of promoting self-employment relative to old age provision of self-employed people, empirical analyses are necessary. Therefore, an analysis of the income situation of the self-employed will yield an impression of the ability to arrange adequate social risk management for old age pensions.

EMPIRICAL EXAMINATION

Description of the Data Set

The following section provides a description of the data in which the focus lies on information about ability and willingness to save. The analysis is based upon German Microcensus data from the Statistical Office Germany (Statistisches Bundesamt 2012). The Microcensus is a representative survey that covers 1 per cent of the total population. The Microcensus is a household panel with detailed information about household composition and employment of household members. The survey offers information "in a detailed subject related and regional breakdown on the population structure, the economic and social situation of the population, families, consensual unions and households, on employment, job search, education/ training and continuing education/training, the housing situation and health" (Körner and Puch 2011, p. 26). The data were recorded using the Computer-Aided Personal Interviewing (CAPI) method.

In addition to the main set of questions, the 2009 Microcensus collected information on the structure of old age provision of the population (Statistisches Bundesamt and GESIS 2011). The information consists of:

- Pension scheme – mandatory insured. Question: "Have you had compulsory insurance within the statutory old age pension system during the last week?"[2]
- Pension scheme – not mandatory but voluntarily insured (in reference week): "Have you been voluntarily insured within the statutory old age pension system during the last week?"[3]
- Private life or pension insurance as old age provision – total sum insured: "Do you have private life insurance as an old age provision? If yes, please quote the insurance sum."[4]
- Form of the supplementary occupational pension: "Do you have an occupational old age provision in addition to the statutory old age pension? If yes, please specify the type of provision."[5]

For the analysis only, the scientific use files could be used, which give slightly different results from the official statistics (Schimpl-Neimanns and Herwig 2011). However, as the analysis focused on the basic structure and not on individual information, the differences between the two data sets did not seriously bias the results.

There are some problems concerning the collection of the data that are more serious: Most of the data were self-reported. The statistics rely on respondents for (subjective) evaluations of their own income conditions

(Statistisches Bundesamt 2006). This is a major problem for information about income. However, the income information is used in many analyses with the caveat that it is not very credible but provides some indication about the distribution. Note that the self-reported classified information in the Microcensus about income level and distribution deviates considerably with respect to income distribution in other surveys (Münnich 2000, p. 689). Therefore, the results of the empirical analysis based on income information of the Microcensus should be interpreted with great caution. However, no satisfactory information concerning the incomes of self-employed people is available elsewhere.

All in all, although the Microcensus does not provide a reliable survey of the income situation of private households, its data at least offer some insight into the income situation of self-employed people. Therefore, the Microcensus is used as a more differentiated sample of income in self-employment in the absence of more specific information for Germany.

Another problem is the unawareness of the self-employed of their specific social security insurance. As analyses have shown, some self-employed people do not give credible information about their old age provision (Dräther et al. 2001; Fachinger et al. 2004). The reasons for this situation could be manifold. For example, some of the self-employed do not care about their insurance, leaving those aspects to their tax advisers; others may have misleading information. However, there are indications that most of the information appears to be trustworthy. As in the case of income, there is no other representative database for information about the social risk management of self-employed people.

Another aspect merits mention. The Microcensus is a cross-sectional survey. Therefore, the information about old age provision only reflects the situation at one point in time. However, one can assume that most self-employed people will have had previous experience as employees. This means that some of the self-employed in 2009 will have entitlements as members of occupational and statutory pension schemes.

RESULTS

The starting point for the description of the *ability to save* is the income of the self-employed from specific occupations. To give an impression of the heterogeneity of self-employed people, they are divided into subgroups by status and gender. Figure 19.1 shows the division of monthly net incomes of self-employed people with and without employees.

The data show considerable diversity in income distribution of self-employed people. The situation of the solo self-employed may be described

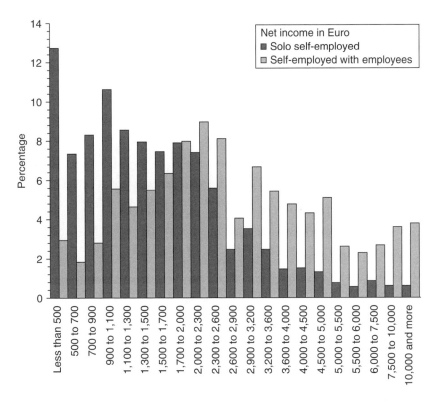

Source: Authors' calculations based on the scientific use file of the Microcensus of the Federal Statistical Office Germany.

Figure 19.1   *Net income of self-employed people, from self-assessment, Germany 2009*

as precarious and poverty stricken, as 39 per cent of them have a net monthly income of less than 1,100 EUR; further, 31.9 per cent earn between 1,100 and 2,000 EUR. On the other hand, nearly 24.4 per cent of self-employed people with employees have a monthly net income of more than 4,000 EUR, and 10.1 per cent have incomes greater than 6,000 EUR. However, the solo self-employed especially appear to have rather low incomes in 2009.

A closer look differentiates the category of solo self-employed people by gender. This is done to find some indication of income discrimination between women and men. The differences in income of males and females are not as significant as they are between solo self-employed and self-employed with employees. However, 56 per cent of women have a

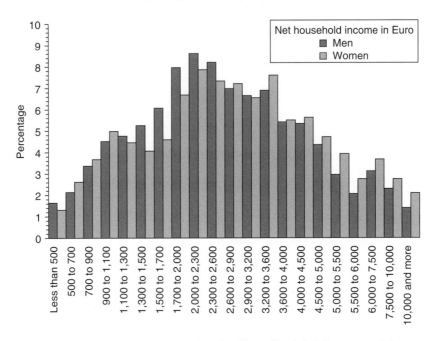

Source: Authors' calculations based on the scientific use file of the Microcensus of the
Federal Statistical Office Germany.

*Figure 19.2   Gender-specific household income of solo self-employed
people, from self-assessment, Germany 2009*

monthly income of less than 1,100 EUR, whereas 28 per cent of men have
an income below 1,100 EUR.

Income from self-employment is only one source of household income.
To get a better understanding of the ability to save, the total household
income has to be considered.[6] The analysis is conducted for the solo
self-employed, as this group seems to have a very low ability to save from
earned income. Figure 19.2 shows the distribution for female- and male-
headed households. The distribution is nearly the same.

To get a better feeling for the distribution, a comparison with other
income measures may be useful. In 2009, the average net household income
for all households was 2,873 EUR (Statistisches Bundesamt 2011, p. 548).
Taking into account that the German government report on poverty and
wealth defined poverty as having a household income of less than 60 per
cent of the average household income – which is approximately 1,700
EUR (Bundesregierung 2009, pp. 40–41) – it consigns about 27 per cent of
all households that rely on solo self-employment to the poverty category.

Table 19.1   Solo self-employed old age provision (%), 2009

	Men	Women	All
Pension scheme: statutory insurance			
Yes	16.5	17.6	16.9
No	83.5	82.4	83.1
Pension scheme: voluntary insurance			
Yes	19.5	17.4	18.7
No	56.6	60.1	57.9
Private life or pension insurance(s)	32.6	29.5	31.5

Source: Authors' calculations based on the scientific use file of the Microcensus of the Federal Statistical Office Germany.

Our descriptions underline positions already found in previous debates on inequality and heterogeneity within self-employment (Merz 2006; Merz and Zwick 2003; for the UK, see Parker 1999). However, 27.8 per cent of male-headed households and 25.7 per cent of female-headed households have a monthly income of less than 1,700 EUR, and therefore must be classified as precarious or poor. It should be clear that the ability to save is rather restricted for those households.

Therefore, the question is whether, how and what kind of old age provision solo self-employed people deploy. This also can be interpreted as an indication of the *willingness to save* as those insurances are voluntary.

The Microcensus gives some general information about the old age provision of self-employed people. Table 19.1 lists the percentages of insurances. As can be seen, only a minority of solo self-employed people are members of the statutory pension scheme. Furthermore, not even one-third of them have a private life or pension insurance. Therefore, overall, the old age provision of this group is rather low.

Even for those who are insured through the pension scheme, however, the risk of old age poverty exists, as the contributions and entitlements are income related. Therefore, low income means low contributions and low entitlements. Unfortunately, the size of the entitlements is unknown. However, information about the total sum insured is revealed. Authors' calculations based on the Microcensus show that the majority of solo self-employed people with private insurance have cover of 25,000 EUR or more. Of the people who have private insurance, 25.4 per cent of men and 15.2 per cent of women even have insurance with a total sum of more than 100,000 EUR. Nevertheless, one-third of solo self-employed women have a total sum insured of 25,000 EUR or less.

Note that this is based on a snapshot at one point in time only. It is unclear whether solo self-employed people will be able to maintain the payments for the insurance over their whole working life. If a social risk occurs (e.g., long periods of illness or a phase of declining orders), the ability to save will decrease, thereby causing people to defer payments or even to end the contract.

Another relevant question is the extent of private life or pension insurance(s) of solo self-employed people in addition to the statutory or voluntary insurance in the pension scheme to avoid poverty in old age. Even among the lower classes (up to 10,000 EUR total sum insured), nearly half of solo self-employed people who are statutorily or voluntarily insured in the statutory pension system have additional private insurance. This leaves an even larger part of the solo self-employed without any old age provision. Overall, 44 per cent of men and 46 per cent of women are not insured through the pension scheme and possess no private insurance.

CONCLUSION

The analysis of self-employed people and pension shed some light on the current situation. The so-called successful labour market policy in Germany during the last decades has led to an increasing number of self-employed people, and also to an increasing number of people who are not covered by any insurance against the financial consequences of the occurrence of social risks, especially regarding old age provision. The development into an entrepreneurial society may pose new challenges and threats for economic policy as the promotion of self-employment has not been accompanied by supporting measures that protect against material losses as a result of the occurrence of social risks.

The analysis of the Microcensus indicates that, in 2009, more than 1 million solo self-employed people were without any old age provision in Germany. The reasons for this are manifold, but there is at least some evidence for low ability and low willingness to save.

A consolidated view of the results indicates that low ability or willingness to save manifests in low old age provision. Combining those findings with the changing structure of the labour market, especially the development of solo self-employment, it can be stated that the danger of self-employed people having inadequate old age provision increases. However, the maintenance of one's standard of living in old age is only one aspect of social risk management; other social risks, such as illness, accident, unemployment (lack of orders or contracts) or long-term care should also be considered. Against the background of the development into an entrepreneurial society, much further research is needed to obtain a more complete picture of self-employed people's cover against material losses caused by social risks.

NOTES

1. The term "self-employment" is not fully defined in the literature (see Bögenhold and Fachinger 2012; Bögenhold 2004; Audretsch 2007).
2. Original question: "Waren Sie in der vergangenen Woche in einer gesetzlichen Rentenversicherung (BfA oder LVA, neu: Deutsche Rentenversicherung Bund oder Deutsche Rentenversicherung Knappschaft-Bahn-See) pflichtversichert?".
3. Original question: "Waren Sie in der vergangenen Woche in einer gesetzlichen Rentenversicherung freiwillig versichert?".
4. Original question: "Haben Sie private Lebensversicherung/-en (auch private Rentenversi cherung/-en) zur Altersvorsorge? Falls 'Ja', geben Sie bitte die Gesamtversicherungssumme an".
5. Original question: "Haben Sie neben der gesetzlichen Altersversorgung eine zusätzliche betriebliche Altersversorgung (z.B. bAV, VBL)? Falls 'Ja', geben Sie bitte die Art der betrieblichen Altersversorgung an".
6. In general, household size should be recognized in evaluations of the income situation (Faik 1995; Shorrocks 2004; Ebert and Moyes 2003). In the Microcensus, the data on income are interval scaled; therefore, no multiplication of the income with equivalence numbers to obtain equivalence-scaled income was done.

REFERENCES

Audretsch, D.B. (2007), *The Entrepreneurial Society*, Oxford University Press, Oxford.

Bögenhold, D. (2004), 'Entrepreneurship: Multiple Meanings and Consequences', *International Journal Entrepreneurship and Innovation Management*, **4**(1), 3–10.

Bögenhold, D., and U. Fachinger (2012), 'How Diverse Is Entrepreneurship? Observations on the Social Heterogeneity of Self-Employment in Germany', in J. Bonnet, M. Dejardin and A. Madrid-Guijarro (eds), *The Shift to the Entrepreneurial Society: A Built Economy in Education, Sustainability and Regulation* (pp. 227–41), Edward Elgar Publishing, Cheltenham, UK and Northampton, MA, USA.

Bundesregierung (2009), Unterrichtung durch die Bundesregierung. Lebenslagen in Deutschland – Dritter Armuts- und Reichtumsbericht.

Dräther, H., U. Fachinger, and A. Oelschläger (2001), Selbständige und Ihre Altersvorsorge: Möglichkeiten der Analyse Anhand der Mikrozensen und Erste Ergebnisse, *ZeS–Arbeitspapier*, 1/01, Zentrum für Sozialpolitik, Bremen.

Ebert, U., and P. Moyes (2003), 'Equivalence Scales Reconsidered', *Econometrica*, **71**(1), 319–43.

European Commission (2010), *MISSOC: Mutual Information System on Social Protection in the Member States, the European Economic Area and Switzerland*, Publications Office of the European Union, Luxembourg.

Fachinger, U., A. Oelschläger, and W. Schmähl (2004), *Die Alterssicherung von Selbständigen: Bestandsaufnahme und Reformoptionen*, Lit-Verlag, Münster.

Faik, J. (1995), *Äquivalenzskalen. Theoretische Erörterung, Empirische Ermittlung UND Verteilungsbezogene Anwendung für die Bundesrepublik Deutschland*, Duncker & Humblot, Berlin.

Körner, T., and K. Puch (2011), *Coherence of German Labour Market Statistics*, Federal Statistical Office of Germany, Wiesbaden.

Merz, J. (2006), 'Polarisierung der Einkommen von Selbständigen? Zur Dynamik der Einkommensverteilung und der Hohen Einkommen von Selbstständigen und Abhängig Beschäftigten', Munich Personal RePEc Archive (MPRA) paper, 5743.

Merz, J., and M. Zwick (2003), Hohe Einkommen: Eine Verteilungsanalyse für Freie Berufe, Unternehmer und Abhängig Beschäftigte, Munich Personal RePEc Archive (MPRA) paper, 5980.

Münnich, M. (2000), 'Einkommens- und Geldvermögensverteilung Privater Haushalte in Deutschland, Teil 1: Ergebnisse der Einkommens- und Verbrauchsstichprobe 1998', *Wirtschaft und Statistik*, **9**, 679–91.

OECD (2011), *Pensions at a Glance, 2011: Retirement-Income Systems in OECD and G20 Countries*, Organisation for Economic Co-operation and Development, Paris.

Parker, S.C. (1999), 'The Inequality of Employment and Self-Employment Incomes: A Decomposition Analysis for the U.K.', *Review of Income and Wealth*, **45**(2), 263–74.

Schimpl-Neimanns, B., and A. Herwig (2011), 'Mikrozensus Scientific Use File 2009: Dokumentation und Datenaufbereitung', Technical Reports, 2011/11, GESIS – Leibniz-Institut für Sozialwissenschaften, Mannheim.

Shorrocks, A. (2004), 'Inequality and Welfare Evaluations of Heterogeneous Income Distributions', *Journal of Economic Inequality*, **2**, 193–218.

Statistisches Bundesamt (2006), *Mikrozensus. Bevölkerung und Erwerbstätigkeit. Stand und Entwicklung der Erwerbstätigkeit. Band 1: Allgemeine und Methodische Erläuterungen, 2005*, Statistisches Bundesamt, Wiesbaden.

Statistisches Bundesamt (2011), *Statistisches Jahrbuch 2011. Für die Bundesrepublik Deutschland mit 'Internationalen Übersichten'*, Statistisches Bundesamt, Wiesbaden.

Statistisches Bundesamt (2012), *Mikrozensus. Bevölkerung und Erwerbstätigkeit. Stand und Entwicklung der Erwerbstätigkeit. Deutschland, 2010*, Statistisches Bundesamt, Wiesbaden.

Statistisches Bundesamt, and GESIS (2011), *Datenhandbuch zum Mikrozensus. Scientific Use File 2009*, Datensatzbeschreibung Statistisches Bundesamt/ GESIS – Leibniz-Institut für Sozialwissenschaften, Bonn/Mannheim.

Index